D0122174

It's All Relative

Wade Rouse

It's All Relative

TWO FAMILIES,

THREE DOGS,

34 HOLIDAYS,

~ *and* ~

50 BOXES OF WINE . . .

A Memoir

CROWN PUBLISHERS ~ NEW YORK

Published in the United States by Crown Publishers,
an imprint of the Crown Publishing Group,
a division of Random House, Inc., New York.
www.crownpublishing.com

CROWN and the Crown colophon are registered trademarks
of Random House, Inc.

Library of Congress Cataloging-in-Publication Data
Rouse, Wade.
   It's all relative : two families, three dogs, 34 holidays,
and 50 boxes of wine...a memoir / Wade Rouse.—1st ed.
      p. cm.
   1. Family life—Fiction.   2. Humorous stories.   I. Title.
   PZ7.R76218 2010
   [Fic]—dc22   2010010952

ISBN 978-0-307-71871-6

PRINTED IN THE UNITED STATES OF AMERICA

Jacket design by Kyle Kolker
Jacket photography © Radius/SuperStock

10 9 8 7 6 5 4 3 2 1

First Edition

For my mother

My holidays will never be the same

For my father

I'm still with you, buddy

For my man

You still make me believe in . . . Santa, the Easter Bunny, God, love, family, myself, but, mostly, us

For my fans

You make me wake up every morning, with a pounding heart, ready and excited to write. You make my dream come true.

CONTENTS

Readers need to know that names (besides mine, Gary's, and those of a few of our family and friends) and identifying characteristics have been changed, and, in some instances, characters were composited, locations and details recast, and time compressed. As with most family tales, I'm sure some have grown over the years, considering many were passed on to me through the generations by my parents (my mother told me many tales about my father, and vice versa), grandparents, aunts, uncles, cousins, and family friends over endless boxes of wine and slices of pie. And despite the fact that some of these holiday tales may have morphed, or become "lore" over the years, all evolved out of the Rouse House. And continue to do so today.

To spend a holiday with family, especially mine, I once told Gary, is a lot like self-catheterization: It's an experience that may cause extreme pain, something you may not always wish to revisit, but one that you'll never forget.

I relay these stories, truly, because I love my family, and because laughter, stories, and boxes of wine are what bonded us. And will forever.

Jingle Balls

When I was very young, Santa Claus used to make an appearance at my house every *few* years.

One year he would rumble through our front door, in full belly laugh and beard, carrying a sack stuffed with presents.

And then—with very little fanfare and in the days before we could order an Amber Alert—he would simply go missing.

When I got old enough, I began to understand this wasn't the way the real Santa operated. I mean, I saw the cartoon Christmas specials. Santa was supposed to come *every* year. He wasn't a solar eclipse.

So I finally gathered the nerve to ask my father one Christmas why Santa didn't come to our house more often, fearing, perhaps, that our Ozarks home was too isolated for his reindeer to find, or, worse, that I had been naughty instead of nice.

Instead I remember my father looking directly at me—as he dribbled some blood-colored wine out of a box—and saying, "Santa's preoccupied right now. Nixon needs a little extra help."

And then all the adults sitting in front of the fireplace laughed and said, "Ain't that the fuckin' truth."

I was still a tiny boy who lived in the middle of nowhere, a boy who had a fondness for ascots and Robby Benson. I still believed I might receive an Easy-Bake oven or Barbie instead of a Daisy BB gun and fishing lures. I still believed my parents might move to New York City on a whim, and I would become a Rockette.

Mostly, however, I just needed something—anything—in which to believe so I could survive another year in the Ozarks.

And if it was the fact that Santa would visit me when he wasn't busy helping the president, then so be it: I would instead laser my attention on the Easter Bunny.

Finally one Christmas, after a few no-show years, Santa came rushing through our door carrying a sack of toys and a case of Hamm's.

"Santa?" I asked.

"Damn, my jingle balls are hot!" Santa exclaimed, rather than the "Ho! Ho! Ho!" I was expecting. And then he yanked down his beard to chug a beer and lifted the low-hanging pillow I thought was his bowlful of jelly to air out his chestnuts and said, "I could be winning some big money right now playing craps instead of doing this gig. I can't believe I didn't win the company bonus this year. Damn that Joe Reynolds!"

The realization that the fat man in the red suit was actually my great-uncle came to me with shocking clarity, like Moses from the mountain.

And then my great-aunt—obviously a touch tipsy and turned on by the unexpected peek at Santa's bag of goodies—proceeded to ask Kriss Kringle when he was going to fill her stocking.

"It's getting itchy, Santa," she said, slurring slightly.

My ears were quickly covered by adult palms, but the damage had already been done.

My holidays had been obliterated forever.

That precious Christmas memory and now-famous morsel of family lore, however, led me to a number of profound conclusions:

- There was no Santa.
- The reason behind my aunt's itchy stocking was *not* that it was made of polyester.

- Joe Reynolds was bound to have a good year after a string of bad ones.
- Nixon indeed needed all the help he could get.
- And no family holiday—no holiday, period—is ever as perfect as we dream it will be.

I should know.

My family always had the best of intentions with our holiday celebrations—be it Valentine's, Easter, Fourth of July, Halloween, Thanksgiving, or New Year's—but it was the follow-through that was disastrous. We were like the Ricardo-Mertzes.

What mother would dress her son as a Ubangi tribesman—sending him out in blackface, with a 'fro, giant lip, and pillowcase—for Halloween *in the Ozarks*? Mine.

What father would bury his children's Easter eggs because—as an engineer and former military man—the fun was in the "hunt"? Mine.

What partner would dress as Oscar—his head wrapped in gold lamé—just to prove his love of the Academy Awards and of me? Mine.

Who in their right mind would dress as a leprechaun on St. Patty's Day just to get free drinks? Okay, that was me, but the point is this: Looking back today, that Santa epiphany may have been the best Christmas gift that could have ever been given to me. For I received the gift of clarity; I received the gift that kept on giving.

The Jingle Balls incident made me understand that holidays were not—and did not have to be—perfect in order to be beautiful. It made me realize that all families are dysfunctional, especially during the holidays, and that while most celebrations are well-intended, they are also usually diarrhea-inducing.

But above all else I understood that my family loved me. Why else would my great-aunt and -uncle forgo the slots and free whiskey in Las Vegas just to spend it dressed as Mr. and Mrs. Kringle with me in the Ozarks?

I was deeply loved.

And scarred.

Which is a pretty good trade-off in my holiday book.

Growing up in rural America, my family often didn't have much more than each other. We weren't poor, exactly, but we were far from well-off. What we were was a new-age family: My parents were the first generation to graduate from college, the first to work their whole lives with their minds and not their hands.

My mother's parents worked as a laborer and a seamstress, and they toiled in mines and fields and factories. They spent their lives hunting for food to keep the family fed. And yet their Christmas tree—in photo albums and in my childhood memories—was suffocated by gifts. There was always one great present—a bike, a game, a toy—underneath the tree, but many of the ones I received were made by my grandparents themselves.

My grandfather worked leather, creating hand-tooled boots and belts, wallets and purses. My grandmother sewed me ascots and vests, pants and shirts.

I despised those handmade gifts as a kid: the hand-tooled belt that featured my nickname, "Wee-Pooh," on the back; the change purse, with a scrawling "W," that held my milk money; the little ascot with threaded embellishment at the end. They were an endless source of embarrassment. When I opened gifts as a kid, I would often flinch as if there were a rattlesnake hidden inside.

I knew the horror they contained.

And yet, ironically, the gifts I remember—and the few that I kept—were those my grandparents made for me: That little change purse still holds my toll change; those quilts made from suit scraps and feed sacks continue to warm me.

My grandma used to tell me: "I may not be able to give you

material things, but I can always let you know how much you are loved. And that will make you a very rich man."

And yet after my grandparents died, I forgot the lessons I was taught and became obsessed with the materialism of the holidays, believing I was loved, or showing love, only if I purchased or received the greatest, latest, and most expensive trend. I believed a Christmas was not Christmas without a seven-hundred-dollar Burberry peacoat; that Thanksgiving was not Thanksgiving if a turkey was not presented on a Williams-Sonoma platter; that a birthday was not a birthday without being showered in gifts.

The presents were the reason for the season.

I was not alone, it seems.

Americans continuously try to fool themselves and everyone else into believing that their lives, families, and holidays are as golden as a Martha Stewart turkey by throwing cash at them. We send Xeroxed Christmas letters filled with blasphemous lies and spend weeks attempting to secure that one perfect gift, all the while knowing, deep down, it is just a ruse: While we love our families dearly and deeply, that doesn't mean money will transform them into different people or make our holidays perfect.

Even in a down economy, we remain a country obsessed with painting our holidays green: Be it birthdays or Halloween or Valentine's, we lavish gifts and food and attention on one another for a select few hours on a select few days, and then pretty much ignore each other the rest of the year.

According to the National Retail Federation, Americans recently spent a whopping $457.4 billion on Christmas gifts. That's approximately $1,052 for every American.

The National Retail Federation figures that Americans recently spent $13.7 billion to prove their love to their loved ones on Valentine's, an average of over one hundred dollars per consumer on anything sweet or heart-shaped.

Americans spend $1.9 billion on Easter candy every year, second only to the $2 billion we spend on Halloween.

And, according to the Consumer Expenditure Survey, American households collectively spend more than $420 million a year on fireworks.

At least if we can't buy love, or give it a cavity, it seems, we can blow the crap out of it.

Why?

Because we are, too often, a people scared. We crawl through life doubly defined by a fear of expressing our emotions and by a gnawing lack of self-esteem: We have trouble saying "I love you!" because we feel it's both wrong and not good enough. What we possess, what we do, what we have, who we wear and know mask our insecurities, make us seem worthwhile and loved, when really we are all united by one basic fact: We are someone's child, someone's brother or sister, someone's parent, part of someone's family. In truth, we are one big family. What we need is love and acceptance.

This dawned on me in my thirties, when I met my partner, Gary, and we began to alternate our holidays with our families. Like any newly married couple, we gleefully but silently welcomed each other into our families' madhouses, neither of us revealing the dark secrets that awaited until it was too late to escape. Perhaps we were scared the other might run. Perhaps we were scared our families weren't "good enough."

What I learned was that, yes, our families were nuts, but, more important, that I was unconditionally loved and accepted. I belonged to something greater than myself.

What I learned, after our first dual Thanksgiving, was that holidays are typically how we introduce and bring those we love into our families.

It is tradition.

It is sadism.

My mother was the Erma Bombeck of our family, the female Mark Twain of the Rouse House. In the years when our family no longer worried about money, my mom returned to her roots and reinstated the traditions of my grandparents while also initiating a new tradition of her own.

In addition to a Banana Republic shirt or Kenneth Cole gift card, my mom would gift me and Gary with something she had created: a hand-painted ornament for our own tree, or a birdhouse wrapped in bittersweet she had foraged from her woods.

And she also celebrated each holiday with a story, a tale about our family.

"These are the gifts you will keep, the ones you will remember," she told us, "because they are the ones that mean the most."

And damned if I didn't shrink that shirt or grow tired of a shoe style, but I always kept her little presents, remembered her stories.

Each year at Christmas, Gary and I still hang those treasured ornaments from my mom (and his), pulling their delicate, round bodies from individual boxes, and we retell the story of how each came to be, or the four-hour family tale my mom had told the year she gave us that ornament.

I share these holiday tales with you because I believe that nothing defines the love, dysfunction, and evolution of American families more than its holidays: Each family not only comes together as one a few times a year—despite typically cavernous distances in geography, personality, and opinion—but each family also celebrates every holiday in its own unique way. But it is the simple fact that we gather, that we come together a few times a year despite these differences, that is magical, memorable, life-changing, and life-affirming.

This is what calls us home.

Holidays are—like Campbell's soup—life condensed.

They are a time capsule.

They are when we notice the aging of our mother's face in the reflection off the tree lights, how much our nieces and nephews have grown when a birthday is celebrated, and how much we miss those we have lost when the Thanksgiving table is arranged with one less place setting.

Yes, my family was, and still is, largely nuts.

But I remember to this day how much I was loved. And that will always carry me through the holidays.

My family's stories—no matter how unique, bizarre, beautiful— are my gift.

And I am pleased to pass them, like a fruitcake, along to you. May these tales help you remember what is truly important as you celebrate with family, no matter the holiday. And, most important, may these stories make you laugh when you want to cry, or cry when you want to laugh.

So happy hellidays, from my family to yours.

And may your jingle balls never be itchy!

JANUARY

"The only way to spend New Year's Eve is either quietly with friends or in a brothel. Otherwise when the evening ends and people pair off, someone is bound to be left in tears."

—W. H. AUDEN

Witchy Woman

I believed, for a good many years, that my mother was a witch because she levitated my bed on a New Year's Eve in the early 1970s after my parents had returned from a fancy party.

Before they left, I remember my mother sashaying from her bathroom smelling like Jean Naté. She had never looked more enchanting. She was wearing a plunging black blouse and shimmering pendant, black palazzo pants with legs so wide they ballooned whenever she walked, and very high cork platforms, all of which gave her the look of a sexy Endora.

My grandma had come over to babysit me and my brother, Todd, and—like any good grandmother—she had given us anything we wanted, including lethal doses of sugar. I had ingested, at least, two or three Nehi grape sodas, a quart of vanilla ice cream with chocolate syrup, a dozen or so chocolate-chip cookies, and a quarter of a homemade cherry-chip cake with sour-cream icing that my grandma had made.

I was more wired than a trapeze artist that New Year's, and could not sleep when my grandma tried to put me to bed. More than anything, though, I just wanted to see my mom when she arrived home from her party.

Glamorous nights were a rarity in our tiny Ozarks town, which made me sad for my mother, whom I believed had an otherworldly beauty. Maybe because she was a nurse who wore white uniforms all day, my mother tended to embrace a more sophisticated, darker look during her off-hours. She wore her black hair cropped short and her makeup thick, lips bright red and eyes catlike. She loved to dress in the latest fashions, and the early-seventies style, with its flowy fabrics, seemed to suit her personality well. Even as a kid I saw the joy it brought her when she got the chance to dress up, let loose, and be a different person than a mother or nurse.

My parents had just given me a Polaroid camera that Christmas, and I had instantly fallen in love with it. Holding that Polaroid was like holding Wonder Woman's lariat: It gave me a magical power to capture the truth in those around me, a chance to make sense of a world that captivated and scared me by looking at it from a different perspective.

I had already become obsessed with recording my life—writing simple stories and poems—and now with my Polaroid I could obsessively record other people's lives, too.

I loved that camera, with its aluminum-and-faux-leather body.

I slept with that camera the week following Christmas, clutching it tightly to my body like a teddy bear.

And I used that camera on New Year's to capture the resounding dullness of my life.

So while my grandma snored on the couch, I clicked a photo of her.

And while my brother slept—drooling like a rabid dog, a huge string of saliva concreting his mouth to the pillowcase—I snapped a Polaroid.

I remember lying in bed, waiting, watching the clock in my bedroom that New Year's night as it turned from eleven fifty-nine to midnight.

I took a Polaroid of the clock, of the new year.

And then I heard laughter, uproarious and ear-shattering—the kind of out-of-body laughter that I only heard on *Hee Haw* or *Laugh-In*. I jumped out of bed in my footed pj's and ran to the living room, where my mother was blowing not one but two New Year's noisemakers, the horns extending and then bending at grotesque angles from her mouth like devil tongues, one curling straight up into her nostrils, the other diving into her bosom.

"Mom?" I asked nervously, as if I didn't know this woman.

She bent down and looked at me. Her makeup was smudged and out of focus, like some of the Polaroids I would take that didn't develop correctly, and she smelled like all the old men who came out of the local liquor store. I had never seen my mother like this.

I snapped a Polaroid.

"Mom?" I asked again. "Is that you?"

"Why aren't you in bed, sweetie?"

I knew this voice.

"I missed you!" I screamed, hugging her leg. "I want to have fun, too! I want to go to a party!"

So my mom found two birthday hats, plopped them on our heads, poured me some apple cider, and then lifted me onto her feet and we danced as she sang "Raindrops Keep Fallin' on My Head."

"Take our picture!" I yelled at my dad, handing him my Polaroid.

"Ready for bed now?" my mom asked when the song and picture were over.

"No! One more! 'Candy Man!' "

So my mother sang a little Sammy Davis Jr., and we shimmied around our tiny rental house.

I was giggling by then, spinning like a tiny top, when I looked up to see that my mom had turned the exact shade of the Wicked Witch of the West from *The Wizard of Oz*.

"Mommy?" I asked.

She was groaning now instead of singing, and she sprinted to the bathroom and slammed the door.

"Mommy? Are you okay?"

And then my mother coughed up her spleen.

She emerged from our lone bathroom a different woman, not laughing and singing but cursing and moaning.

"Champagne," she moaned. "I can't drink champagne."

"Let's dance, Mommy!" I said, trying to cheer her up.

She looked at me in a troubled sort of way, the way I look today at people who rave about the food at Applebee's or the Olive Garden.

And then I screamed like only a kid who is still jacked up on sugar and wants to play can scream.

My mother covered her ears and then rubbed her face, and when she dropped her hands she looked like a Picasso painting: Everything was distorted, a bit off.

She grabbed me by the arm and tugged me toward the bedroom, my footed pj's sliding along the wood floors.

"Stop screaming!" she begged. "Please, Wade. Stop screaming."

Which made me scream even more.

"Stop! Stop! Stop!" my mom yelled.

Now, my brother could sleep through a tornado. Had, in fact, actually slept through a tornado, and he was still glued to his pillow by that thick layer of spit.

My mom forced me into bed while I continued to rage.

Then I started to cry, uncontrollably and loudly.

My mom sat on the edge of the bed and began to cry, turning green once again.

"Wade, please be quiet."

I screamed.

"Wade," she cried, rubbing her head and her face, "if you don't be quiet this very second, I will levitate your bed."

I didn't know what "levitate" meant.

My mother stood up and waved her hands over my bed. She shut her eyes and lifted her arms toward the heavens. She began to hum.

"I will lift your bed off the ground and into the air, and rattle it until you stop," she told me in a trancelike state. "And if you don't, you will sleep suspended in midair, and you won't be able to go to the bathroom in the middle of the night because you will simply fall to the ground."

And then, with her eyes half shut, looking possessed, my mom started to chant the following:

Hmmmm, spirits, lift Wade's bed off the ground...
And when it's up, spin it around.

Well, this was about the scariest thing a six-year-old boy, who loved both his mother and Mother Earth more than anything, could imagine.

I shut my mouth, my teeth chattering, and then I shut my eyes, and I could swear my bed was lifting off the floor, and then spinning like a merry-go-round.

Hmmmm, spirits, keep Wade's bed in midair,
Until morning comes, and I release my stare.

I popped open an eye and saw my mother, as green and wickedly magical as the wicked witch, her arms outstretched, humming and chanting. She was, I now knew, levitating my bed.

So I did the only thing I could: I grabbed my Polaroid and snapped a photo.

Of my mother, the witch, her twinkling pendant releasing an evil spell.

I knew I would need proof to show the authorities what had occurred this night.

I knew I would need evidence to show my dad and brother that their wife and mother was really from Salem.

I shook my Polaroid, defiantly, in front on my mother.

"I have proof!" I screamed.

Shut your eyes, shut them NOW!
And do not look or you'll be turned to a cow!

Now, I certainly didn't want to be a cow, so I clamped my eyes shut again, and they remained that way until the next morning, when I awoke to find my mom sitting on the edge of my bed, shaking me, hugging me, apologizing, asking if I was okay, if I had slept.

"Is my bed back on the floor, Mommy?" I asked.

She hugged me and said she had to go take some aspirin.

As soon as she left, I retrieved the Polaroid picture that I had stashed under my pillow. Here was my evidence to the world.

The Polaroid was black.

So I shook it.

It was as if a picture had never been taken.

I shook it again. Harder.

Nothing.

Her powers had destroyed it!

That New Year's morning, my dad made Belgian waffles for breakfast and my brother and I blew my parents' leftover noisemakers all day long while my mother moaned through clenched teeth, shutting all the curtains in the house to keep out the bright light, just like any witch would, I knew.

Caramel Corn, Comas, Coupled

I woke with a start last New Year's Eve after my head had fallen into the giant red enamelware popcorn bowl I was holding in my lap.

Homemade caramel corn was stuck to my chin.

I jerked upright and looked over at my partner, Gary, whose head was painfully tilted sideways—like a broken jack-in-the-box. He was drooling the remnants of his ice-cream sundae.

"Get up!" I shouted, staring at the clock in our basement. "Just look at ourselves! We're pathetic."

"It's New Year's Eve," Gary said sleepily. "It's what we do on New Year's Eve. It's called relaxing."

"It's eight P.M.!" I said. "We're not relaxing. We're comatose."

It seemed shocking to me that we had managed to become our parents some time between dinner and *Wheel of Fortune*.

Of course, we'd attended our share of New Year's Eve parties over the years; we'd even tossed a few of our own.

But the hoopla, the pressure, the resolutions seemed meaningless when compared to one simple fact: Gary quit drinking on New Year's Eve.

In 1995 Gary walked out, very drunk, on a nightmarish relationship. He was sporting a new Armani jacket that his wealthy, older boyfriend had bought for him to wear to dinner at a very tony restaurant, but after being told repeatedly to "shut up and look pretty," Gary bolted from the restaurant bawling, before dramatically hailing a cab, crab-walking his way up the stairs and into his tiny apartment, and promptly puking on his new Armani.

The next day he managed to crawl his very hungover body to his first-ever AA meeting. He has been sober fifteen years, and for an emotional man who cries when he sees Suzanne Somers on QVC, I consider this an accomplishment more extraordinary than men walking on the moon.

But it is not always easy.

Since I have been in a relationship with Gary, we have not been able to celebrate New Year's Eve with a stupid wild night like most of our friends, who tend to wake up naked the following morning next to someone with recessed gums and more body hair than a Yeti.

"But he was wearing a ball cap," they always say the next day. "He looked cute at the time."

Technically, I *could* drink on New Year's, considering I am not an alcoholic, but that would make me the bad guy, like those husbands who continue to bring their eight-hundred-pound wives honey buns and two-liter jugs of Mountain Dew before the authorities are called and their spouses are airlifted out of the trailer park.

Our New Year's Eves are, therefore, purposely boring. Gary and I spend them eating and then promptly lapsing into a coma.

We no longer, out of respect for Gary's sobriety, even make resolutions.

In fact, the older we've grown, Gary and I have become more life-lessons guys than new-year's-resolution people. We truly believe that important decisions shouldn't be saved and announced one night every year, but that they should evolve naturally, no matter the day or month. Otherwise, we believe, life becomes stalled with inertia, and when resolutions are made they seem forced, false, and, as a result, doomed to be ignored or to fail.

"Life should be conquered every day," Gary believes, "not one night a year. Life is too short."

It's a great theory, I always believed, but honestly I had never really been tested. In fact, my last New Year's resolution—to watch bowl games all day without moving from the couch, changing out of my pajamas, or eating anything that didn't contain Velveeta—had exceeded my wildest expectations.

And then our phone rang.

"Happy New Year!"

It was Elise, one of our best friends from the city, who is all tornadic energy. She loves parties. I mean, she throws parties for every holiday, from Earth Day to Cinco de Mayo.

She *adores* New Year's Eve.

"I just made my New Year's resolutions!" she announced with great pride, shouting over a raucous crowd in the background. "I'm losing twenty pounds by March, doing hot yoga three times a week, and only investing my money in green companies. Oh, and I might move to Costa Rica. Just thought you'd like to know! What are you two up to?"

She caught herself before I could say a word.

"Oh, I'm sorry," she yelled. "Go back to sleep! Ciao!"

She hung up, a dial tone replacing the party raging in the background.

I looked over at Gary.

He *was* asleep again.

In fact, it looked like his head had been rubber-cemented onto his body by a three-year-old.

When did our lives become so boring and calculated?

I wanted to be respectful, but didn't we need to shake things up a bit?

Shouldn't we at least resolve to stay awake until midnight?

"Get up!" I said, shaking Gary. "We're making New Year's resolutions."

"No! No, that's a mistake," Gary said, wiping his mouth. "First of all, we don't believe in them. And second, if you utter them, you have to mean them. Otherwise it's bad luck. You might as well just go shatter a mirror in front of me."

"I just want to have some fun," I said, a bit testily.

"Fine," he remarked.

"I'll go first, then," I said, adjusting my sweats, whose mustard color made me look like I had jaundice. "Here's one: I resolve to look nicer for you when you get home at night. Instead of wearing old, comfy clothes all the time, I'll dress like I'm in *Ocean's Eleven*."

Gary eyed me suspiciously. "You don't get dressed during the day as it is. You write until noon in a ball cap and pajamas with pine trees on them, and then you change into sweats. You're very Johnny Depp in *Secret Window*."

"That changes *now*," I said.

I ran upstairs and threw on a pair of dark Banana Republic jeans, a choker, and a black Lycra top that made me feel as if I'd been encased in plastic wrap.

When I returned, I spun around like a fashion model and said, "Your turn!"

Gary scrunched his face and smoothed his hair down. It looked like he had gotten electroshock therapy. He stared into our Christmas tree, bedecked with hundreds of ornaments and lights, and then inhaled deeply, the whiff of our seven burning sugar-cookie-scented candles making his mouth water. "Okay, I resolve to spend less money on unnecessary items, like holiday ornaments and pretty candles. Your turn."

I looked at the TV. I had been watching reruns all day of *Project Runway* and *House Hunters International*.

"I vow to watch less reality TV."

I sounded less than convincing, but continued. "I'm smarter than those shows, right? So, from now on, I'll watch more Discovery and rent important documentaries."

Gary nodded enthusiastically. "And I'll read more!"

I glanced down at the stack of *Better Homes and Gardens, Coastal* and *Midwest Living*s, *People*s and *InStyle*s Gary kept by the couch.

"I'll read more *books*," he clarified, standing up and heading toward our bookshelves. "Like *Moby-Dick*. I've never read *Moby-Dick*. I mean, what a great title, right?"

He yanked the classic off the shelves, the heft making him go, "*Ooofff!*"

We both sat back down on the couch.

"Happy New Year's!" Gary and I sang to each other.

Then I flipped on the History Channel and began watching a documentary about a pale queen with a lot of hair who desperately needed a tan and a run-in with some thinning shears. Gary put on his glasses—the ones he wore to make him "look smart"—and began to read *Moby-Dick*.

His mouth was moving.

I sat awkwardly, upright, rigid, in my tight clothes, like Kelly Ripa.

"This is fascinating," I said, nodding at the television.

"So is this," Gary said, nodding at the book.

After fifteen minutes, we both started fidgeting. I pulled off my choker and spun it round and round like a lasso, wondering what this queen would have looked like if Tyra Banks had gotten hold of her and given her a makeover on *America's Next Top Model*. Gary's eyes were drawn to a picture of Reese Witherspoon in a magazine.

"I can't take it!" I said.

"Ishmael is such a stupid name!" Gary said. "And *Moby-Dick* isn't about a giant wiener at all!"

I ran upstairs and changed back into my sweats, flipped the TV to *House Hunters,* and began screaming, "Pick the second condo, you idiots! You can always gut the kitchen!"

Gary yanked open our cabinet doors—exposing the uncomfortable fact that he'd obviously invested our Roth IRA in Yankee Candles—and said, "We're getting low on sugar cookie and pumpkin spice."

I began to laugh, which incited Gary, and when we both could finally breathe again, he looked over at me and asked, very seriously, "Are you compromising your life by being with me?"

It was the last question I expected to be asked.

"Are you?" he implored. "I'm an alcoholic. You're not. I know it can't be easy, but I would never want you to compromise. I would never want that."

There are unexpected moments—like when I watch my aging mother baste a Thanksgiving turkey, or see my best friend zip up her daughter's coat and then kiss her on top of the head—that spontaneously make me want to cry. And then there are unexpected moments that redefine relationships: not knock-down, drag-out fights over money or an affair, but a quiet question that forces you to turn your life over in your head.

This was both.

I looked at Gary, which was too hard, and then up at *House Hunters*—some couple quarreling over cul-de-sacs and kitchens—and it was then the correlation became apparent: Relationships, like searching for a home together, are full of compromises, a tense tug-of-war at times. You do not always win every battle, but you understand that no home is perfect, that it's more about your gut reaction and attraction to the overall structure than the house's lack of granite countertops or its dated downstairs bathroom.

I looked back at Gary.

I knew that I had never had a serious moment of doubt that this is where I should dwell.

Gary *was* home.

I would sacrifice my life for him; sacrificing one night, truly, was nothing in the larger scheme of things.

So I grabbed my partner, pulling him toward me, and looked him in the eye, making the only resolution that would really ever matter:

"I will love you forever."

Then we both fell asleep on the couch, entangled in one another—my arm his, his leg mine, our weaknesses and addictions and foibles and strengths and courageousness each other's—finally waking around one A.M. on New Year's Day, my head back in the popcorn bowl, Gary's bobbing awkwardly.

FEBRUARY

"The only acting you ever see at the Oscars is when people act like they're not mad they lost. Nicole Kidman was smiling so wide, she should have won an Emmy at the Oscars for her great performance. I was like, 'If you'd done that in the movie, you'd have won an Oscar, girl!'"

—CHRIS ROCK

One Unfortunate Cookie

As a way to make up for what Gary believes is my lifelong sacrifice of New Year's Eve for him, we now celebrate Asian style, going out for dinner on Chinese New Year.

This tradition started quite by accident years ago, when we ordered Chinese food on Chinese New Year, something we didn't realize until the delivery person informed us of that fact.

"Free egg roll because it's Chinese New Year."

"Really?" I said. "The Chinese have New Year?"

I knew this came out wrong, and was about to correct myself and say, "Today is the Chinese New Year?" but I was cut off by the delivery person.

"No, they stay in the same year forever. Are you prejudiced?"

Now, I must explain the hard-ass, Clint Eastwood–esque tone with which this was delivered. Our Chinese food was always delivered by a rather angry, rather hairy, but very proud preop transsexual who looked like Joan Jett, talked like Fred Dryer, and carried around a set of nunchucks on her studded leather belt. Gary, thoroughly intimidated, always tipped her heavily out of fear of retribution. Gary liked to believe that our tip money might be used for gender reassignment surgery instead of a much-needed makeup consult or anger-management session.

"Ten dollars for a twenty-five-dollar order!" I'd scream. "Are you crazy?"

"It's a long drive," Gary would say kindly, like he was talking to the cops from behind the front door while a killer held a gun to his spine.

"It's six blocks!" I would say.

On this first Chinese New Year, I held half of Gary's tip back.

"Five bucks? That's it?" the tranny challenged me, fingering the nunchucks.

"That's twenty percent," I said.

"Thanks, Mr. Math. You don't think I can add 'cause I'm transgendered? What do you think the *T* stands for in GLBT? '*Terrible in math*'? Do you hate anyone who's different than you?"

"What? No. No! What are you talking about?"

"I'll see you around," the tranny said. "You'll regret this tip one day."

From then on our orders were always off, seemingly on purpose.

Call me paranoid, but there were clues.

For instance, I despise water chestnuts, always insisting when I ordered that dishes be prepared without them, but I always discovered them hidden at the bottom, or spooned heavily on top.

Sometimes our food would show up cold.

Sometimes a box would be open.

Seemingly, the order after a delivery when Gary tipped heavily would be spot-on. However, if I tipped poorly, the next order would be screwed up.

"This is blackmail!" I would tell the tranny.

But she would just smile, holding out her ill-manicured hand for a tip. "Very busy tonight," she would say. "Very busy."

Which is why Gary and I began going out for Chinese—and then out on Chinese New Year: I feared she would come to our home with a carton of moo shu and a rifle, and Gary thought it would be a fun and unique way to re-create our lost New Year's Eve.

Now, to be honest, going out to a place flush with Asians was a huge sacrifice on Gary's part, because I always had a fascination with Gay-sians: those hot, thin, Asian men with dark hair and pouty lips. I had once—during my very brief dating phase before I met Gary—hooked up with such a man, who had introduced me to the wonders of the Far East.

Our favorite Chinese restaurant, the one from which we always got delivery, was a little hole in the wall not far from our neighborhood that looked as if it had been decorated by Margaret Cho's mother. It featured brightly colored fans spinning from the ceiling and a giant aquarium in the middle of the restaurant with fish the size of manatees. Calendars with rabid-looking dragons and rats and snakes lined the walls.

Gary and I were ready to gorge on what we considered to be the best buffet in town, a virtual smorgasbord of MSG and grease: egg-drop soup, General Tso's chicken, beef and snow peas, spring rolls, and some fish thing that still had its eyes, everything glistening in oil.

To be quite honest, I mostly went to drink, in order to make up for my lack of New Year's. I'm passive-aggressive that way. Supportive but selfish, honest but manipulative.

When we were seated, I immediately ordered a flaming volcano, a fruity rum drink that you slurp out of a burning ceramic skull with a couple of Krazy Straws.

The drink is made for, I would guess, three full-bodied men to share.

I ordered one for myself, a waif at best.

Ten minutes after my volcano arrived I was halfway finished and firmly believed I was Reese Witherspoon.

Part of me thought, "How can I drink? It's disrespectful. After everything Gary has been through. This is really hard for him. It's just like New Year's Eve."

But the drunker part of me thought, "Except Gary's not Chinese. I mean, I've seen his egg roll. And wasn't the lifelong sacrifice of New Year's Eve, one of America's best holidays, hard on me?"

So I finished my volcano, and, out of spite, ordered another, much to the astonishment of our waiter, whom I coquettishly told resembled Bruce Lee.

"First of all, he's black, not Asian," Gary informed me, very loudly, after he had left, "and secondly, he weighs three hundred pounds and has a fade. He looks like Ruben Studdard. Jesus Christ! You need some food in you. Oh, and you did not star in *Election,* so stop telling him that. This was supposed to be a romantic night together."

Gary led me to the buffet.

Though it was winter, we were enjoying a mild respite, with temperatures in the fifties and sixties. Any time the weather hovered above the forties, I used it as an excuse to wear slides or flip-flops, my footwear of choice. In a perfect world, I really should have been shipwrecked with Christopher Atkins on the Blue Lagoon. I never would have gotten my period, like Brooke Shields, and I would have been wholly content to run around barefoot and tan while getting my brains boinked out.

The restaurant was buzzing with Asians out celebrating their New Year, along with the usual mix of slow-moving old people and fat college kids in sweats.

"What the hell is going on?" I asked once we got in line.

The line for the buffet, which was set up in a massive U along three different walls, was backed up in a human traffic jam. I was in that fuzzy drunk place when you are just starting to feel the effects of huge quantities of alcohol on your body and mind—that lovely moment before anger, vomiting, and alcohol poisoning set in—when the lethal dosage is innocently manifesting itself as munchies.

At the moment I was feeling the need for something greasy in my stomach, so I wound my arm free from my nursemaid and staggered a few big, unsteady steps forward in line.

"Excuse me, ma'am," I said to a dead woman propped up on a pillow in a motorized cart—the kind that has a TV tray up front to hold a dinner plate. "I need a crab rangoon, or I'm gonna pass out."

She frowned at me and revved her cart.

"Oooh, and I need some duck sauce. Can't have a rangoon without duck sauce."

I ripped the packet of duck sauce with my front teeth, smiling at her the whole time, and began to squirt a dollop in the middle of the rangoon. But in doing so, an orange rivulet spurted onto my bare toes and oozed into my leather slides.

"These cost two hundred bucks," I said to her, bending down in an immediate panic to clean them off.

In my drunken haze—I had no distance perspective—I bent over and hit the dead woman's cart. In her effort to make room for me, she put her cart in reverse, and all I heard, as I wiped clean my foot and slide, was the loud "BEEP! BEEP! BEEP!" of her motorized cart heading in reverse, and then what sounded like the *Titanic*: screams and dishes breaking.

I stood up and turned to see that I had caused a Chinese chain reaction of terror, people lying on the floor amid broken glass and cashew chicken.

"Way to go, Godzilla," Gary whispered, sidling up next to me. But then, like any great dancer, Gary said, "Follow my lead."

"Are you okay, ma'am?" Gary asked the dead woman in the cart, who was now being assisted by one of her elderly companions. "You just seem so confused. Are you okay?"

Gary said all of this very loudly and very dramatically, with faux force and sincerity, just like President Bush used to do when he talked about poor people.

"What? What?" the old woman said. "What?"

"Is everyone okay?" Gary asked. "She's very sorry."

I shoved my crab rangoon in my mouth and gulped it down.

"Consider this your payback," Gary said. "Forever. Happy Chinese New Year, honey."

I was drunk. Very drunk. And at that moment his spontaneous gesture seemed way more romantic than any midnight kiss on New Year's Eve could ever be.

Gary quickly threw some cash on the table and raced toward the exit.

But, ironically, just as we were leaving, the delivery tranny—returning to the restaurant to nab another to-go order—stopped us at the door. "I saw everything," she said, grabbing me with her ill-manicured hand. "But you can buy my silence with a *big tip*."

"I'll give you a big tip," Gary said, fingering her nunchucks. "Clean up your eyebrows. They're the window to the soul of a *real* woman."

My man, I realized, could never be bought again, be it New Year's Eve or Chinese New Year.

Which is why, this time around, Gary celebrated *our* New Year's Eve by leaving the restaurant sober, in love, and very much in control of his life.

I batted one for three.

The Gay Grifters

I knew I had met someone special the afternoon I picked Gary up to attend our first Oscar party together. I was running late and arrived to find my new boyfriend standing by the curb, his head and neck wrapped tightly in shimmering gold lamé.

He *was* Oscar.

And I was smitten.

Since this was the Gay Super Bowl, it was the equivalent of a straight man picking up Pam Anderson in a mesh Patriots half shirt.

A half hour into the party, however, I simply became irritated; the gag had gotten old fast and I was tired of leading a blind, sweaty, suffocating Gary around the party by the hand. I loved the Oscars—make that I *lived* for the Oscars—and wanted to focus not only on the red-carpet fashions but also on completing my Oscar ballot.

So I began to pawn Gary off on people, or leave him leaning against a wall or a dessert table, returning to help only when I could hear him aspirate the gold lamé that kept sneaking into his mouth and nostrils.

Fittingly, I hit Oscar gold twice that night.

The first time came when I smacked Gary, hard, on his rear, and told him to stay put by me on the couch the rest of the night so I could focus. The second time came when I hit on roughly 90 percent of my Oscar picks, even predicting the Academy Award winners in little-hyped categories like Best Animated Short, or Sound.

I walked out of the party with a Benjamin in my pocket and a trunkload of movies, popcorn, and Milk Duds.

"Do you know what I learned tonight?" I asked Gary on the way home.

"That lamé is highly chafing?" he said.

"I'm not just a film buff, I'm a savant!"

"You got the gift!" Gary said, unwinding his golden mummy bandages.

"And you got the rash!" I said, mortified by his red, welted skin.

"I got it, too," Gary said.

"You sure do."

"No," he answered. "The gift. Except mine is for pageants."

I put Gary's ability to the test watching the Miss America pageant. (Gary, by the way, prefers only to watch Miss America, and not Miss USA, because he considers Miss USA "trashy," since they allow contestants to enter who have had breast jobs and cosmetic surgery.)

I challenged Gary to pick the top ten finalists based on appearance as soon as they walked onstage for the first time.

"No problem," he said confidently. "That's pretty much how I've chosen to live my life."

The cheeseball music started and we eyed the contestants, quickly but secretly scribbling on our pads of paper. I made lists of Definites, Maybes, and Be Thankful for Your State Crown. During the commercial break, we trimmed our lists to ten and then exchanged them so we could grade each other's work.

When the top ten was announced, I hit 50 percent.

Gary batted a whopping 80 percent.

"How did you do that?" I wanted to know.

"I told you: I got the gift. I mean, how do you know Best Animated Short Film? You just do."

"I have to know some of your tricks, though," I pressed. "Tell me."

Gary got off the couch, a piece of half-eaten pizza crammed in his mouth, and snapped the curtains shut in our TV room. He then picked up the phone, listened for a dial tone, and, seemingly content, placed it back down.

"What are you doing?" I asked.

"People would kill for these," he whispered. "They're not your standard Vaseline-on-the-teeth-to-keep-your-lips-from-sticking, or masking-tape-on-the-ass-to-keep-your-suit-from-riding-up secrets, but deeper ones—Harry Potter secrets. I developed these after years of sneaking into my bedroom to watch the pageant and dreaming of being on that stage, the talent competition in full gear, a fire baton blazing over my head."

"Tell me," I said to Gary, mesmerized, as though he were going to light candles and spill goat's blood all over our wood floors.

And so, in a whisper, he did:

1. Look for "Crown-Ready Hair": The hair must be stacked, especially toward the back, and look worthy of holding a diamond-encrusted tiara.

2. The evening gown must be "sexy but ladylike," "unique but not tacky." "If she looks like a lady in the streets but a freak in the sheets, she's a lock," Gary said.

3. Blondes are always favorites, but they can't be "whore blondes." "If their hair looks all Pam Anderson, they're screwed."

4. Barbie bodies. "Big breasts, no waist, curvy hips in the swim-suit competition. They have to look like Barbie," Gary told me. "America only likes to see big girls at Curves and anorexics in the movies."

5. Always pay close attention to Miss California, Miss Texas,

Miss Florida, and Miss New York. "They're robots. They've been trained to win since they were five. And they know how to go in for the kill, like the Terminator. Just watch them smile. It will curdle your blood. They always make the top ten."

6. Look for a sleeper, the cornpone gal from the Midwest or the Southern belle. "One of each usually makes the top ten," Gary said, "and each will have a cute drawl and a strong faith in 'Lord Jesus, my Savior!'"

7. And, most important, Gary told me, very seriously, "Winning contestants always sport an opaque heel." According to Gary, some pageants have begun to allow contestants to choose either a colored, strappy heel and colored hose, or the more traditional opaque heel and hose. "Tradition, always!" Gary yelled. "It's a test. And, worst of all, colored shoes and patterned hose cut off contestants' legs on TV, and can make even the leggiest of girls look like they have stumps. Only women in opaque hose and heels will make the top ten."

"What about the final question?" I had to ask, when he had revealed his secrets.

"Doesn't matter," Gary said. "As long as they don't vomit on themselves, or curse, the prettiest ones are fine. Their whole year is scripted anyway, so what's it matter?"

And then Gary nailed the winner of Miss America, picking a Southern girl with a heavy accent, breasts the size of a semi, hair that needed its own zip code, a love of God, and a burning desire to help dying children, or, as she more aptly put it, "dy'un chill'uns."

As I downed a Mich Ultra and ate Funyuns that I had fashioned into a bracelet around my wrist, I realized: We could make tons of money off the God-given talents that we had squandered for years.

So we became gay grifters.

We started small, innocently, so we could perfect our games, unsuspectingly. We attended close friends' Oscar and Miss America parties. Each and every time we would win, walking out with enough cash to make a monthly car payment and enough candy to keep us twitching the entire winter.

After a few years, however, our friends turned angry and suspicious and began disqualifying us from winning, saying the wealth needed to be spread to others, namely the straight and undeserving, those who firmly believed that *Patch Adams* was overlooked for Best Picture.

It was then I decided to up the ante.

I decided to go all *Ocean's Eleven*.

Our first foray into the big-time gambling circuit was a mammoth Oscar party held in a Ritz-esque ballroom filled with massive projection screens and catty, pretentious gays who dressed in tuxes and acted as though their invite to the *Vanity Fair* after party had been temporarily misplaced.

Tickets to the party cost a fortune and benefited some local charity that I knew had already spent its quarterly take on vodka and Brie.

But for me the highlight of the party, the reason I ponied up, was the Oscar-ballot competition.

Gary and I walked into the ballroom that night wearing our sleekest suits and silk ties, our fingers dripping in gold and silver, diamonds and lapis. Gary had slicked his hair back à la Gordon Gekko. I was carrying a money clip. Which held roughly seven dollars.

I looked around the room.

There were hundreds of competitors.

This was high stakes.

This was George Clooney and Brad Pitt and Julia Roberts type money.

But I could take them all.

"What's wrong with you?" Gary asked as we searched for a table. "You're...dripping."

I was sweating.

I never sweated.

My mouth was dry, my face and body wet.

I felt as if I'd been struck by a rattlesnake.

"You're freaking out," Gary said.

"Get me a ballot, please," I gasped.

I hunkered down over it, and—channeling the gifts I had been granted at birth—checked off my winners with more ambivalence than confidence, using the lucky Napoleon Dynamite pen Gary had given me.

"Vote for Pedro!" the pen told me.

"Vote with your gut!" my gut told me.

I mean, I had seen every film, some twice. I had taken notes. I had prepped harder for this than for my ACT.

When I was finished, I wrote my pseudonym—as we were asked to do, for fun—at the top of my ballot and turned it over to a man who'd obviously had more face work than an antique pocket watch.

I grabbed a cosmo, took a seat, and watched the night unfold.

It was a grueling four hours. Our ballot tallies were, thankfully, updated at each commercial break, and the entrants' names and scores were projected on a big screen in every corner of the ballroom.

After a few rounds, the hanging chad began to fall away, leaving me—MissFayeDunaway—alone at the top, along with only one other competitor: Liza with a Z (but of course), a rather bothersome mosquito, who remained annoyingly close as the evening progressed.

In fact, we leapfrogged each other the rest of the night—me nailing Best Foreign Language Film, Liza snagging Best Sound Mixing. And then we were tied, and stayed tied until the final award of the night: Best Picture.

I was confident.

I knew *Brokeback Mountain* would win.

It had momentum. It had great press. Ang Lee had just won Best Director. The Oscars were the gayest event of all time. It was time for the gays to break through big-time, brokeback style.

"And the winner is . . . Crash!"

"What? Are you kidding me?" I screamed, standing up, frightening the elderly gay couple sitting next to us who looked like the Smothers Brothers. "Nothing with Sandra Bullock in it can win an Oscar!"

And then I heard a series of loud whoops and a lot of screaming.

I turned toward the projection screen.

Liza with a Z had picked *Crash.*

Liza with a Z had picked Crash?

I locked in my personal GPS on Liza, toweled off with a cocktail napkin, and headed across the room with a mission.

"Where are you going?" Gary asked. "You lost. It's okay. Please don't freak. I can win it all back in Miss Teen USA!"

"No one beats me!" I yelled. "And what kind of lunatic picks *Crash* over *Brokeback*?"

I headed toward the celebration, where I found a man in pleated Dockers and a wrinkled Ducks Unlimited sweater drinking Budweiser and high-fiving a group of unattractive men.

"Liza with a Z?" I asked.

"Who wants to know?"

"MissFayeDunaway."

I stared.

He stared.

Neither of us blinked.

It was a standoff at the Gay O.K. Corral.

"Just one question," I said. "How could you pick *Crash*?"

"*Brokeback* was just too . . . you know . . . gay, dude."

I recoiled.

And then I looked him over, closely, once again.

Dockers.

Ducks Unlimited.

Wrinkles.

Unattractive male friends.

Budweiser.

Dude.

"Oh, my God! You're . . . *straight*!"

"*Ssshhhhh!* Shut up!" he said. "You think it's easy being straight and loving the Academy Awards? I can't help that I got the gift, too."

I could've blackmailed him right then and there.

I could've started screaming and pointing, "Breeder!"

And there's a good chance he would've endured the same outcome as Sebastian in *Suddenly, Last Summer*.

And yet, even though I had been beaten at my own game, I admired the prowess and intellect of my straight nemesis. I knew what it was like to be driven by a gift granted at birth.

Mostly, however, I knew I had still come out on top.

Not only because I could talk openly about my night, without fear of retribution, but also because I knew—as a PR pro—exactly what was coming next.

Just then a photographer appeared, yelled "Smile!" and snapped Liza with a Z's picture, the flash capturing the shock, horror, and bewilderment of this straight man realizing his photo would appear all over town with a caption screaming: LIZA WITH A Z WINS GAY OSCAR CONTEST!

(Not the) Son of a Preacher Man

One of the new ministers at our little town church had a wicked penchant on Ash Wednesday of making his more infrequent parishioners resemble Al Jolson.

Unfortunately, my family was among those who attended church only on the "important holidays," like Ash Wednesday, Christmas, and Easter, the holidays when, as my dad liked to point out, "God was paying particular attention and truly taking count."

Which is why instead of tracing dainty little crosses on our foreheads, as was done on the foreheads of the church deacons and Bible-study leaders, our minister made our family look as if we had just been pulled free from a collapsed coal mine.

I wanted to believe, like any person of faith, that our minister had giant hands, or a touch of Tourette's, or simply—like an untrained singer—bad technique, but I realized, the older I got, that he simply had a vicious streak.

I remember one particular Ash Wednesday when I was in junior high and my mother returned to the pew looking as though she had just crossed Oklahoma in a covered wagon.

"Are you going to work like that?" I had asked her, the contrast of her white nurse's uniform and ashen face making her look like a photo negative.

"I can't wash it off!" she said. "That'd be blasphemous."

What was blasphemous, however—after years of watching our minister work—was his evil ash-decorating techniques. For the *truly devout,* he would always keep his left hand clean, using it to hold their holy faces steady while his right index and middle fingers swept shallowly through the ashes and then softly but deftly formed a cross on their God-fearing foreheads. He would smile proudly as they left the altar.

But with heathens like the Rouses, the minister used both hands freely, as though he were in a schoolyard fight and his mission was to blind his enemies with as much dirt as he could possibly toss.

And I swear that the man of the cloth would always smirk as my family walked back down the aisle.

What was an even bigger and dirtier slap in our faces, though, was the fact that the minister always had a perfectly formed cross on his very own forehead, almost as if he had stood for hours in front of his little mirror in the rectory next door and etched it with a well-sharpened eyebrow pencil before outlining it in mascara.

This ongoing Ash Wednesday debacle was particularly difficult for me during my overweight youth because I always went to school resembling the spawn of Fat Albert and Tootie from *The Facts of Life.*

Moreover, this seemed to create a chasm between my mom and dad.

Whereas my mom loved to attend church—she enjoyed the pomp and circumstance of dressing up, dressing her boys up, having breakfast out, the ritual and order of worship—my father never generated much interest in the notion until later in life. It was my understanding that he felt church was more for those who needed forgiveness, much like a shower was for those who were dirty. If you were somewhat clean—physically and spiritually—you were good to go.

My father also frequently had to work on Saturdays, thus leaving only Sunday mornings open to enjoy a big breakfast, work in the yard, and complete projects around the house before watching pro football. Church was another commitment—another meeting, if you will—to which he just didn't want to commit.

My dad grew up going to church every Sunday, if not more. His father was a deacon in a local church and a much beloved member of a nearby small-town community. My grandfather loved to go to church, put on his suit, and talk with the townsfolk. It was an extension of his job, and one he relished. While my father loved and respected his dad greatly, I think—as most of us do as adults—he simply enjoyed a bit of distance, to walk outside of the shadow his father had created.

My father was also an engineer with, though it was never formally diagnosed, what I would term today as ADD. He used to become distracted and irritable in church, like a petulant child.

In fact, my father and I were similar in this way, though polar opposites in our obsessions. Whereas I would become riveted by women's dresses that would flare dramatically as they sashayed down the aisle or by a beautiful bonnet (I always believed the world was an "Oh, I could write a sonnet about your Easter bonnet!" away from turning into a nonstop musical), my father was distracted by the noisiness of the church's HVAC system, or whether the trusses supporting the soaring roof and steeple were structurally sound. Whenever we would begin to fade away, forget to stand or open our hymnal, my mother would often whisper our names—"James Wade!" or "Ted! Pay attention!"—in a way that sounded like sheets drying on a clothesline in a harsh spring wind. We would snap to attention for a few minutes before I would again catch a glimpse of a pretty orchid and my father would notice a gap in a window frame.

It was after one of our Ash Wednesday tire fires, perhaps our third in a row, that my father finally seemed to realize, as the white-bread Rouses jammed into an IHOP, that his family looked just like the one on *Good Times.*

As my mom excused herself to the bathroom and my brother crammed a mile-high stack of Belgian waffles and whipped cream into his mouth, that's when I decided to test my theory.

"He's doing it on purpose," I said, wiping my face clean. " 'Cause we don't go enough."

His eyes twinkled. "That's an interesting theory," he said.

My father loved theories. He loved to test them. It's what his career in engineering was all about.

Which is why my dad announced, as we yanked the foil off our TV dinners the next week, my corn embedded in my apple brown Betty, that he had invited the preacher over for dinner the following Tuesday.

As my mother aspirated a kernel, my father winked at me.

Our preacher, a middle-aged man with hair that looked as if it had been made from modeling clay, arrived on a cold February night, carrying a Bible and a long box I know my dad hoped was wine.

"What have we here, Minister?" my dad asked, before pulling out a pillar candle we all instantly knew he had simply "borrowed" from the church.

"Just a little gift," the minister said. "A token of appreciation. I have to admit, I was just so surprised to receive this dinner invitation from...you know...the *Rouses*. I see you so... *infrequently*... Easter, Christmas, Ash Wednesday."

And it was here, when he said "Ash Wednesday," that he let out a boisterous belly laugh, a guffaw more devilish than godly.

My father smiled like the Grinch. He knew instantly my theory was right.

Game on, my dad's eyes seemed to say.

"Wanna help me get this fire started?" my father asked the preacher, laughing. "I always have trouble getting one started. I think I need an expert on fire and brimstone."

The minister chuckled heartily and slapped my dad on the back.

Now, my dad was an expert fire builder. If *Survivor* had been on back in the day, my dad would have kicked Richard Hatch's big behind. And yet he stood back as the preacher lowered himself in front of our massive stone fireplace, with a hearth big enough to serve a picnic on and a grate large enough to hold a pickup. Within minutes he had built a roaring fire, and also inhaled more smoke than Susan Blakely in *The Towering Inferno*.

"I'm so sorry!" my dad said. "I must have forgotten to open the flue."

The minister turned and coughed. He looked like Nipsey Russell.

"Could you point me to the bathroom?" he asked.

My father winked at me.

My mom, a very smart woman, already knew what was happening. "Ted!" she whispered, as she did in church. When he walked away, she turned to me. "James Wade!"

But the minister walked out with a freshly washed face, and my mom had no choice but to serve the pot roast, carrots, and potatoes she had carefully prepared.

"I'd be honored if you would say grace," my mother said to the minister.

But before he could open his mouth, my dad said, "I'll do it!"

"That would be a nice change of pace," the minister said.

"Good bread, good meat: Good God, let's eat!" my dad said.

My mother gasped and stared at my father as though Linda Blair had rotated her head and puked pea soup on the preacher.

"Does the job, doesn't it?" my father said, nudging the minister.

"Well, it all smells so wonderful," said the minister, adding something along the lines of, "I just love a slow-cooked pot roast on a cold winter's night."

As my mom served the minister, my dad followed up with, "And who can eat pot roast without ketchup?"

The poor preacher didn't stand a chance as my dad handed him an upside-down bottle. "Hit it smack-dab between the five and the seven! That's how to get the goodness out!" my dad commanded.

Smack!

Plop!

Scream!

As planned, the preacher looked as if he had been shot, as if Damien himself had exacted revenge with an iron gate.

"Excuse me, folks," he said once again, heading to the bathroom.

"Ted Rouse!" my mother whispered.

"An eye for an eye!" my father replied.

"Oh, Ted!" my mother said, strangely excited. "You do know your Bible!"

"Nobody screws with our family," my dad said.

It was all very Mario Puzo in the Ozarks: Family came first.

We attended a bitterly cold Easter sunrise service a month or so later, and our family was among the first to receive blankets from the minister. My dad wrapped his arm and the blanket around me, happy our theorem had been tested and proven, and it was then I realized I'd just had a religious experience, a higher calling, if you will, a moment in my life that bonded me to my father more than church or watching football or Three Stooges movies.

Nobody screws with our family, I thought as the sun rose over the little park.

And, though it was frigid, I felt very warm indeed.

Cupid's Stupid

Al Capone's St. Valentine's Day Massacre was significantly less brutal than the one I endured as a child in my rural elementary school, where it was tradition for kids to make their own Valentine's mailboxes and then walk around the room personally delivering cards to each classmate's new P.O. box.

This was serious business to me—one of the few creative outlets I had in the Ozarks—so my creations tended to go to the extreme, blending a childish Charles Eames with a big dollop of Edith Head, not an envied mix in my rural classroom, where boot boxes outnumbered shoe boxes on Valentine's.

Yet I would spend weeks creating bedazzled, glittery mailboxes in roaring reds and pretty pinks, some that were even strung with lights.

My great undoing, however, didn't come until late grade school, when I created a Barbie-themed mailbox, using shocking pink gauze and Barbie's body parts as my foundational decor. I had always wanted a Barbie for Christmas and had never gotten one, so I "borrowed" one from a girl in school—along with her root-beer Lip Smackers—and ended up murdering Barbie. I dressed Barbie's torso à la Cupid with little pink wings and a little pink quiver filled with little pink bows. I plucked one of her arms off her body to use as a bracket for a homemade banner that stated, MY HEART OVER-FLOWS...LIKE MY MAILBOX.

But the pièce de résistance was the mailbox flag I created out of Barbie's missing legs, positioning them sideways, like a gymnastic whore, so that one long, glamorous gam could be lifted into a vertical position to show when I had received a card, or lowered to show when my box had just been emptied.

You could even see Barbie's barren plastic goody box all the way from the chalkboard.

My masterpiece was greeted with great fanfare by the friend from whom I had borrowed Barbie. When she saw her beloved doll tortured, dismembered, and hanging from my mailbox, she screamed a scream that still reverberates in my head.

That prompted our class bully, a kid who simply and scarily used an empty Camel cigarette carton to gather his Valentine's loot, to free Barbie and then open my mailbox and announce, "What have we here?"

What he discovered was three valentines that had been given to me by a male classmate with a high-pitched giggle and penchant for dribbling in his Garanimals whenever he got nervous. The "topper" was an exquisite card—a real, adult valentine, not one of those mini, childish cards—that pictured two cupids kissing. In fact, my stalker had even gone to the effort to stencil our names above each cupid's head.

My Valentine's massacre led to a long winter of humiliation, highlighted by the daily ritual of the class bully interlocking the arms of my winter jacket with those of my stalker's on the coatrack in the back of the classroom, a silhouette that, from a distance, made it look as though we were about to embark on a long, romantic walk together through a snowy forest.

The next year I decorated my mailbox in a Speed Racer theme, but that didn't stanch the bloodletting of future Valentine's massacres.

In college I remained closeted and tragically drunk, stringing along endless girls, dragging them to Valentine's dances—them in red formals that longed to be hiked up, and me flirting with death by imbibing a punch bowl full of red Kool-Aid and Everclear.

As a result, I hid from Valentine's—from love—throughout my twenties like a turncoat Cupid in holiday Witness Protection.

And then, at thirty-one, I met Gary.

And I fell in love.

Cupid actually should have been fashioned after Gary: a winged man with a big swoop of hair and a tragic weakness for buying anything from Target that was red, dipped in chocolate, or came in the shape of a heart.

The first Valentine's after Gary had moved in with me, I walked into my house after work and found it glowing, awash in red, like it was on fire.

"I did a seasonal switch," he explained.

A "seasonal switch," I came to learn, applied not only to every season but also to every holiday. Thus a seasonal switch included an all-out home overhaul.

For example, when late September rolled around, fall took full hold, with dinnerware in bright summer colors changed out for a more autumnal palette; mums were installed, pumpkins and gourds were artfully arranged on the front porch, and cotton sheets with beach umbrellas were switched out for flannel featuring oak trees and brightly colored sugar maples.

A Valentine's switch-out came complete with heart-shaped candles, red lamp shades and heart night-lights, glasses featuring Sweethearts candy, dish towels decorated with chocolate candies, and pottery that resembled open candy boxes.

Gary baked heart-shaped cookies, dyeing the dough red with

food coloring and then icing them pink. He made red velvet cake. He wore red sweaters and turtlenecks and socks.

Basically, I was banging Cupid.

And yet I knew nada about the most romantic of all holidays.

My Capone-esque massacres of the past made me flinch whenever I thought of Valentine's, and so as I approached my very first Valentine's Day in love, I made the tragic error of turning to my married, straight fraternity brothers from college for romantic gift advice.

"Okay, dude, here's the inside scoop," one my best friends, who was recently married, explained to me over beers. "I never buy my wife chocolates, because she will eat them and then accuse me of making her fat. I never buy her perfume, because it won't be the right scent for winter, or it will conflict with her pheromones, or she'll be allergic to the floral undertones, or something stupid like that. I never buy her clothes, because I'll get her an eight, and she'll be all, 'What makes you think I wear an eight? Do you think I'm that big? Are you even attracted to me?'

"So what I always do is take her to her favorite restaurant, and I always give her a sexy gift, like panties or lingerie. In a small. And she loves it. And I love it. It's a win-win."

I left our brotherly beer bash buzzed but emboldened, not realizing that I had just been given quality advice, actually shown something great, yet something that I would completely misinterpret, which I always do, much like when I see a Coen brothers movie.

I immediately made reservations at Gary's favorite restaurant in the city, a very romantic spot in a historic brick building that served just a few nightly chef specials. I wrapped Gary's gift in shiny, expensive paper, topped it with a giant red velvet bow, and dropped it off before our dinner at the restaurant so it could be "specially delivered."

I did, however, due to Gary's love of chocolate, go against my friend's advice and buy him a two-pound milk-chocolate rabbit in a foil suit and bow tie, sporting a rather mischievous grin, which I hid under the bed as a surprise after we got home and got busy.

The evening unfolded beautifully. The restaurant was romantic, the food was fabulous, and when the waiter brought over the dessert cart, he had already positioned my gift, as instructed, in the middle of the tarts and brulées.

Gary gasped.

"You are *soooo* romantic!" he gushed. "You are...*perfect*!"

"Can I stay and watch?" the cute, gay, very young waiter asked, impressed, wondering, I'm sure, if I might have a clone.

Or, at the very least, be interested in a three-way.

I looked around the restaurant. People had stopped eating and were staring, transfixed, women nudging their husbands in that irritated manner that seemed to imply, "Thanks for the wrist corsage, you jackass. Leave it to the gays to always do it right!"

Everyone was watching, wondering what amazing gift this amazing man had purchased for his sweetheart.

A ring?

An island getaway?

A vacation home?

Suddenly I felt this overwhelming pressure—like the emergency door on a plane had suddenly been thrown open midflight over the Atlantic.

Gary furiously untied my bow.

"The box is *soooo* beautiful!" he gushed.

Gary unwrapped the tissue paper—dotted with hearts.

"It's so pretty!" he gushed.

And then he pulled out a three-pack of Hanes underwear.

Gary stared at me.

The waiter stared at me.

And then laughed, thinking it was a joke.

"Good one," the waiter said. "Keep looking, sweetie," he prompted

Gary, who began sifting through the box, gingerly at first and then furiously, like a dog in the trash. His actions said it all: There's got to be something better in here somewhere.

There wasn't.

No matter how hard he searched, Gary didn't find any bling.

"Hanes?" Gary finally gasped, fuming, very loudly. "Hanes *Her Ways*? Are you *kidding* me? You got me…*underwear*? From *Penney's*?"

He yanked a sticker off the plastic bag.

I had forgotten to remove the price tag.

"They're boxer briefs," I purred, trying to sound turned on. "In black. Your favorites. And they're very sexy."

"Hanes ARE NOT SEXY!" he began yelling.

The entire restaurant was staring, as though we were a strolling mariachi band.

"What this says to me," Gary continued, standing up, knocking his chair over, "is that you are the type of man who will buy me a vacuum for Christmas and a robe on my birthday. You are the type of man who will microwave anniversary dinners and buy used cars that smell like other people."

"And travel to Mexico in July," the waiter whispered.

"Shut up," I said.

"You are not romantic!" Gary screamed, throwing his pack of underwear into my lap. "No, I take that back! You are not even… *human*!"

And then he left.

To a smattering of applause.

And I don't know if I was more humiliated by the fact that everyone in the restaurant knew I had just bought my lover Hanes for Valentine's, or by the fact that he had summed me up perfectly.

When I got to the car, Gary was waiting. We drove home, not a single word exchanged.

When we walked in the front door, our silence was oddly amplified: Our new puppy, Marge—only a few months old—did not charge the front door as usual, barking and whining, to greet us. Instead we found her passed out on the bed, literally in a coma, tin-foil spread all around her on our candy-inspired sheets.

"Oh, my God! What's wrong?" Gary said. "She's dead!"

"No, she's breathing!" I screamed. "Are you okay, baby? Margie, wake up."

"What did she eat?" Gary said, studying what looked like dried poop all over her mouth.

Marge had eaten the two-pound chocolate bunny I had hidden for Gary.

We rushed her to the emergency room at the animal hospital, where we waited an hour to see if our baby was going to survive.

Finally, the vet emerged. "She's going to be fine. Give her two or three slices of bread tonight, more tomorrow, and then watch for uncontrollable diarrhea."

And then, as if things could not get any bleaker for me on this Valentine's, the vet went ahead and added, "Marge is a very lucky girl. Just be glad it was cheap chocolate. If she'd eaten two pounds of the good, dark stuff, she'd be dead."

On the drive home, Gary, tenderly nuzzling our moaning puppy, finally looked over at me and said: "I guess it pays to be an unromantic cheapskate every now and then."

I opened my gifts from him late that night—cologne and clothes and concert tickets—and realized that the importance of Valentine's Day—any day, mind you—was not only heightened when you were a gay man but also when you realized you were finally, blessedly, in love.

The next year on Valentine's, I did two things: I bought a pair of kiddie valentines featuring kissing cupids and sent them to what I believed were the two addresses of my childhood bully and stalker. Inside each card, I wrote: "I hope you've found love. I have."

And then I surprised Gary with a trip to Puerto Vallarta.

And he packed his Hanes.

Bead Me Up, Scotty!

"**W**ade, get your ass out here!"

I inhaled deeply, peeked out my kitchen window, and saw four of my best friends, all in their thirties, sitting in an SUV, chugging beer.

It was seven A.M.

It was a Saturday in February.

It was Mardi Gras in St. Louis.

My friend Martin, who was driving, happened to catch a glimpse of my cheekbone through the kitchen shutter and laid on the car horn.

I flew out the door so the neighbors wouldn't get pissed.

"You're... *ready*?" Martin said, somewhat in shock when I got in the car.

I was wearing funky jeans to show off my booty, a new leather coat, and a formfitting black turtleneck. Around my neck was an awe-inspiring array of high-end beads I picked up at a party store, including bejeweled alligators and mini–Mardi Gras masks, beads in blue and green and purple and yellow and silver, finished by a strand of pearlized white Barbara Bush beads that hugged my throat.

I was not out of the closet yet, but I was coming out in other ways. I had lost weight, I was dressing better. Now I just needed to tell my boys that I liked boys.

Just not today.

Mardi Gras was one of my straight-guy rituals, one of the manly-man things I did to fit in with my fraternity brothers, like Super Bowl parties and fantasy football and watching *Entourage.*

I hopped into the SUV and looked at my straight friends: They were wearing baggy Levi's, tennis shoes, ball caps, and college sweat-shirts.

"So...you're ready?" Martin asked again.

"Dang right, he's ready!" Mark yelled from the backseat.

Mark was already blindingly drunk, sipping Jack straight out of the bottle while gnawing on a bagel he had adorned with a layer of Doritos.

Mark was one of my insane college friends. Mark was *always* ready: ready to run naked and scale the goalposts after a college football game; ready to wander into strangers' parties, crap in their toilet, and not flush.

But now Mark was older. Mark was an accountant. Mark was married. Mark had kids. Mark and Mardi Gras now seemed a more unlikely combination than Stephen Hawking and *Dancing with the Stars.*

"Are we ready to see some jugs?" Mark yelled. "*Are we?*"

Mark was ready, it seemed.

He grabbed my shoulders and began poking his index fingers directly into my temple.

"And this, right here," he said, the constant poking and shaking indicating me, "is the man to do that! Who wants a shot?"

Mark the accountant turned the bottle upside down and screamed, for some reason, "Fight the power! Who's with me?"

He handed me his bottle.

In college, I was a drinker of great notoriety. A twelve-pack served as my happy hour. A case made me forget I was gay. But my mythical drinking did help our fraternity finish its first-ever keg during Greek Chug when two of our chuggers went out early after being disqualified for puking in their cups and trying to continue by chugging their own vomit.

But it had been years since I pulled sixteen hours of hard drinking.

"Drink! Drink! Drink!" Mark screamed. "Chug! Chug! Chug!"

I took a tiny sip, which immediately clashed with my recent coffee and OJ, and asked for a bagel. Mark handed me his.

It was seven fifteen A.M.

We headed downtown to St. Louis, blinded by the early-morning sunshine reflecting off the Arch, and parked in a lot miles from the parade, the roads blocked off in every direction.

Everyone emerged.

Except for Mark.

He was immobile.

"Mark?"

I nudged the accountant.

He was passed out.

Cold.

We left him in the car, just like we would have in college, with a note in his pocket explaining what had happened and a Bic-pen drawing of a dick going into his open mouth.

We hopped onto a bus filled with drunks and headed to the parade route.

The Mardi Gras parade in St. Louis was huge—second only in attendance, I believe, to New Orleans—and it took place in Soulard, the funky French district, akin to New Orleans's French Quarter, that butted downtown.

The bus bumped along Soulard's cobblestone streets, past its restored row houses, alongside its jambalaya of tiny bars and restaurants, the constant, pungent odor of hops from the nearby Anheuser-Busch brewery tingling everyone's nostrils.

We were dumped off near the parade route, and my group of drunks fought our way through hordes of other drunks, eventually making our way to the front.

People were already screaming, "Beads!"

The overriding goal of any Mardi Gras parade is to accumulate as many cheap plastic beads as possible. Acquiring beads is of the utmost importance for straight men because they can be used later—when women are severely wasted—as bartering chips.

Beads for boobs.

Which was not a fair trade whatsoever in my book, kind of like the Indians selling Manhattan for twenty-four dollars' worth of trinkets.

And yet I knew that my expensive, store-bought beads provided me with a certain cachet and early advantage over other men—kind of like when an average-looking guy drives a Bentley. People think, "Who is he? How'd he get that? He must be someone very important!"

My beads served as a diversion. They were my manly fashion facade.

Which is why the entire duration of the parade, women begged me for my beads. They flashed their chests, they tossed their hair.

But those were all things I could do—with significantly more flair and drama—so their efforts went unrewarded.

That is until I ran, quite literally, into Big Red.

While standing in the alley of a bar waiting in line for the Porta Potty after the parade had ended, someone plowed into my back like a semi with failing brakes. I turned to find a very big girl with a crimson mustache. She was chugging a hurricane, which was a highly dangerous act, along the lines of putting out a fire with gasoline.

"I was here first," she said, swinging her weight toward me, ready to rumble.

Her endless supply of hurricanes had turned the rim around her mouth red, like a kid who'd eaten too many cherry Popsicles. And then she stepped back and looked me over hungrily, ogling my crotch. "Oooh! Well, well, well...Bead me up, Scotty!"

Jesus Christ. It's not bad enough that she's a big straight girl who could throw me over her back, carry me away, and then sit on my face while she finishes off a chicken skewer, but she's also a Trekkie.

"Good one," I said as my friends popped into the alley and began to whoop and wail.

I was getting drunk, but not drunk enough for this.

"What'll it take for you to give me those alligator beads?" she slurred, licking her red-stained lips. "How 'bout you be Captain Kirk, and I'll be your Uhura?"

I would've murdered her on the spot, right then and there, and gotten away with it, too, if I had only known for sure that my case would be heard by an all-gay jury led by foreman Neil Patrick Harris and my verdict rendered by Judge Kathy Griffin.

Instead I said, "I have to pee...really badly."

"Why don't we do our business together?" she asked.

Okay, I'm wondering if it's even possible for her to squeeze her own body into the Porta Potty, pivot and hover, much less for the two of us to "do our business together." We weren't circus clowns trying to cram into a VW.

"Pee-shy," I said.

"How cute! Okay, you can go first... *if* you give me those alligator beads," she said sexily, dropping her head, her brown hair falling across her face.

And then she reached down and touched my wiener.

Which immediately inverted, like a turtle's head.

Now, I paid twenty dollars for this single pair of beads— partly because the shimmery green of the alligator's scales matched my eyes perfectly—and I was not going to give them to a three-hundred-pound woman who looked like she just got shot in the mouth.

"No deal, Spock," I said.

My buzz hit me at the wrong time.

"Excuse me! *Excuse me!*" she screamed.

And then she grabbed me by the turtleneck and shook my head back and forth, like lion mothers do to their cubs. My feet weren't dangling off the ground, but it felt like it.

I began to get alarmed, mostly because *Excuse me!* was the catchphrase of an insane girl named Toni on the awful reality show *Paradise Hotel,* where whorish singles basically got drunk and slept around in order to stay in an oceanside resort paradise. Toni, like this girl, was always ready for a throwdown after a few drinks.

"Sorry. You can go ahead of me, no biggie," I said.

"Are you calling me big?"

"No...ma'am."

Big Red started kind of screaming, slurring, like drunks do, and I could just see her throwing the remnants of her saliva-strewn hurricane all over me, so I somehow worked my way loose of her meaty palms and bolted, down another alley—through which she might not fit—and then down the street, fighting to get through the crowds.

A few blocks away, I ran directly into Uhura's opposite, a malnourished woman with sketchier teeth than a rotting jack-o'-lantern. She was sporting jeans that fit like a second skin and a mangy halter, though it was roughly forty-five degrees out. She had a cigarette positioned in an empty slot where a tooth should have been, and I immediately thought: *Good for her. She's a glass-half-full type of gal.*

"I'll show you my cooch for them gator beads!" she screamed.

In less than five minutes, I'd moved from breasts to vagina.

"Don't you wanna see my cooch?"

She might as well have asked if I wanted to kick a puppy or punch an old woman in the face.

"Not particularly."

For some odd reason my response, and not her initial question, infuriated her boyfriend, who was sporting the rather frightening fashion combo of a mullet ("Business in the front, party in the back, man!"), a sequined mask over his eyes, a bushy mustache that looked like a dirty floor mat, and a T-shirt that read: SAVE THE BEAVER!, which featured a photo of Jerry Mathers with a shotgun positioned against his head.

I found this combination highly unsettling, like seeing Michael Keaton as Batman. And then he asked: "Why don't you wanna see her coochie?"

I mean, how does one even respond to a question like that?

So I yanked out my best Colin Powell impression and said, calmly, "Because it's special. It belongs to you."

"That'll be the day!" he roared. "She likes your fuckin' beads. Why don'cha wanna barter?"

I looked around in desperation. My friends were nowhere to be found. Useless as they may have been, they at least would have been able to step in and pee on somebody.

There was no option: I wanted to live. So I unkinked my pricey gator beads from the nest around my head and presented them to her.

"Here," I said, walking away, defeated. "Enjoy."

There was a hand on my shoulder.

"Oh, no, you don't," the boyfriend said. "Fair's fair. You get to see her cooch."

An honest, admirable sort of chap, I thought.

He grabbed me close and put his arms around my shoulders and those of his girlfriend, making kind of a one-man shield, and, as she slowly unzipped her jeans, my life flashed before me. Inch by inch, zip by zip, I saw, in descending order:

A pink scar...

a faded rose tattoo...

a nest of black-brown hair…
something pink and swollen that looked like it had teeth…
and some sort of wound/cut/cyst.

"You wanna touch it?" she asked.

"No. Fair's fair. We haven't bartered for that."

I looked over and saw that her boyfriend was hard and rubbing himself vigorously, like he was trying to release a genie from his bottle. He was holding me now rather tenderly, not at all in a threatening way anymore.

My life flashed before me again, and I pictured myself being dragged into a back alley and forced to videotape a Mardi Gras threesome—being pounded by Jerry Mathers while sixteen pounds of beads slammed against my chest—after which I would contract hepatitis, if I were only so lucky.

I panicked and started running, my beads bouncing into my teeth, fighting through the crowds, until I could no longer hear the couple's hacking and heavy breathing.

I was winded, still scared, still needing to pee but desperately in need of a drink—one of those giant ten-dollar hurricanes that come served in a vase—so I headed what I thought was north, to a bar where my friends said they would be if we got split up during the day.

But as I zigged and zagged through the crowd, I became disoriented.

Geography has never been one of my strongest skill sets—along with filing and organ transplant. In fact, I thought north was up until I went to college.

As a result, I found myself off the main thoroughfare and directly in front of the infamous Drag Race, the annual gay Mardi Gras competition where drag queens race each other down the street wearing high heels.

Considering I had been in the closet longer than my dad's letterman jacket, I typically would have been too scared or ashamed to stop and watch such a spectacle. But there was a large crowd, I needed a drink, and I'd had my fill of breeders.

"Nice ass," a mustached man in crotchless leather stirrup pants said to me as I tried to get in line for the bar, which wrapped all the way around the block. "Need a beer? You'll never make it inside."

I looked at the man and then at the can that he held in front of me. The beer hadn't been opened and didn't show any signs of tampering. "Thanks," I said. "Nice pants."

"I'm up for Mr. Leather this year," he said.

He smiled proudly, like I was supposed to know the prestige this bestowed.

"Good for you!" I said. "I was once up for Snow Ball King!"

And then a very cute guy—that dreamy college-jock fantasy guy, the kind who always looks as if he just got finished playing baseball—stopped in front of me and asked what it would take to get a strand of my purple beads.

I stammered.

"Wanna play ring toss for it?" he asked, smiling seductively.

I immediately got harder than rebar.

He stood by me as the drag racers began to line up, and I stood breathless—heart racing, adjusting myself like a rapper with Tourette's—next to a hot guy who wanted to play ring toss. With me.

I slammed the leather man's beer—buzz fully restored—and watched a group of drag queens in dangerously high stilettos sprint down the streets. Some were crashing and burning, ripping their stockings, bloodying their knees; others were an amazing mix of speed and dexterity, like Miss America meets Marion Jones.

When it was over, I looked over at what was surely to become my new boyfriend, the love of my life, the man who would teach me to toss a football, hold me, and have that trail of hair running down his navel that drives me insane.

He put his hand in the center of my back. I got dizzy.

"Wade?"

He knew my name?

I turned. Standing before me was a fellow coworker and his wife.

"So, what's going on?"

I fumbled for words. I was standing outside a gay bar, with a boner, between a man who had his arm around me and a man wearing crotchless pants, watching drag queens race in high heels. You might as well have set me on fire and screamed, "Flamer!"

"What a freak show, right?" my coworker laughed. "We had to see this, too. Can you believe this goes on in our town?"

His wife rolled her eyes.

"Hey, we're headed over to Bobby's. Wanna join us?"

I analyzed my options.

My coworker was wearing an XXL college sweatshirt with a cotton turtleneck underneath that made him look like he was wearing a neck brace. And Dockers. His wife was wearing mom jeans, a hoodie, and white sneakers.

Mr. Ring Toss was wearing a skintight baseball jersey that showed every muscle in his torso and jeans so tight I could see the head of his penis. Without squinting. And I had astigmatism.

"You ready?" my coworker asked.

It was one of those defining moments in life, the ones that come completely out of the blue: a test to see if you're comfortable with yourself, if you are willing and ready to embrace the next chapter.

I wasn't.

I turned, without saying a word, and left with a man whom I not only didn't like but who obviously despised gays.

"What a freak show!" he laughed again. "I mean, you just have to see it once in your life. It's like a car wreck. It's so disgusting."

We walked past throngs of straight people—flashing tits, vomiting, having sex in the street and in the open windows of their row houses—all of whom were termed by my coworker and his wife as "hilarious," "wild," "fun."

And this Mardi Gras? Well, according to them, it was "a great time."

I found my friends at Bobby's and they handed me a hurricane, and then another, until I got so wasted that my friends told me the next day I screamed, "Ring toss!" all night until I passed out in a stranger's apartment, until total blackness seemed a better option than living another day in the dark.

MARCH

Matt LeBlanc (Joey):

...Heads or tails? Heads is ducks because ducks have heads, and tails is clowns because...

Matthew Perry (Chandler):

...What kind of scary-ass clowns went to your birthday parties?

—FRIENDS

Get Outta the Box Already!

The most bizarre rural birthday party I ever attended took place at a decaying farm that, from what I could tell, didn't have anything to farm except, perhaps, dandelions and rocks. The party centered around rides on one low-slung, dirty, rather mean Shetland pony that I firmly believe to this day was two men in a horse suit; a fat clown who forgot to bring his red nose and ended up eating two whole Shotgun Sam's pizzas all by himself; and, topping it all off, a mime whom I walked in on taking a doodie in an upstairs bathroom.

The most disturbing part of this day (and there were many) was the fact that the Shetland pony talked and the mime did not.

The Shetland pony screamed, "Goddammit, kid!" when I kicked it hard with my dingo boots while riding it around a makeshift corral; however, the pooping mime never uttered a word of embarrassment to me, like "Sorry" or "Whoops" or anything. Instead he just looked at me, in whiteface, his bodysuit—yellowed and dusty from sauntering around the dirty farm—down around his ankles. He simply started performing, attempting to free himself from an invisible box that it seemed had trapped him on the toilet.

As you can imagine, I went screaming down the stairs that birthday, telling the moms in attendance that I had just witnessed a pooping mime. But when I turned around after pleading my case, the mime was already standing behind me, his face all squinched up into a goofy expression, his left palm raised into the air like he was confused, his right hand making a "he's crazy" swirl around his temple. The moms laughed and walked away, but when I turned to face the mime again, he was wagging his finger at me. It was terrifying. And that kick-started my fear of mimes—and clowns—culminating in a tearful exit from the big top the next year when the circus came to town.

To this day, any horror movie with clowns or circus people or white face paint still gives me nightmares, sends me running from the theater.

In fact, I had been to see a therapist about this fear, which had once again reared its ugly white head when I was forced to interview a clown for a feature story I was writing on unusual careers for an alumni magazine.

I hadn't been able to sleep for weeks in dread of meeting the clown face-to-face.

I told the therapist all of this, every last detail, down to the pooping mime, while she scribbled nonstop and nodded her head and sipped some sort of tea that I firmly believe had gin as a main ingredient. Then she looked at me and said, quite calmly, "I believe that you are a coulrophobiac."

"Am I going to die?" I asked. "Or be disfigured in any way?"

"No," she said. "That means you are a person with an abnormal or exaggerated fear of clowns."

"Oh," I said.

Tell me something I don't know, I thought.

"But your questions about death and disfigurement bring up a host of other issues," she said. "Does six P.M. next Wednesday work for you?"

I ended up feigning illness with the clown, and interviewed him over the phone.

I did not have to face my fear until years later, when I was set up on a blind date with a man from Sarasota whom I was told worked in PR for Ringling. This was just a couple of weeks before my birthday, at a time when I had just come out and was officially dating for the first time in my life.

"You two have a lot in common," I was told at the time by a friend, when I still worked in public relations. "PR career, writing, entertaining, movies. It's a slam dunk."

"Isn't Ringling a circus?" I asked. "Don't they have clowns and mimes?"

"He works in PR, for God's sake, Wade," my friend said. "Consider this my birthday present to you. Lord knows you need to get lucky. I'll set it all up."

I walked into our designated meeting spot, a cute little bistro with great food, and there, waiting to greet me, was a mime.

"You must be Wade," the mime said.

I wanted to run, I really did, but my legs wouldn't work.

It's like the time I met David Sedaris and wanted to give him a copy of my book and make him hysterical with laughter, and the only thing that came out of my mouth was, "You...funny."

"I came right from work and didn't have a chance to change. I'm so sorry," he said. "Oh, and happy early birthday, I'm told."

We were seated by a waitress who seemed unfazed by the fact that a man in white face paint and a white bodysuit had just gulped down a glass of water and left a half circle of grease paint around the rim.

I, on the other, was about to stroke.

In fact, I had yet to say a word and was still staring at my mime openmouthed.

"A mime is just a person in makeup," I heard my therapist say in my head. She had told me during our sessions to recite this over and over whenever I felt overwhelmed by my fear. "He is an actor."

I tried to picture Johnny Depp as a mime but knew he was too smart to ever take such a thankless role.

"Are you okay?" the mime asked.

"You're a...mime?" I finally asked in a squeaky voice. "I thought you were in PR."

"Oh, I am. I help handle the press as the circus travels from town to town, but I also work as a mime. It's my passion!"

The mime's teeth took on a yellowish hue next to his white face paint. Worse, he had that hideous acrylic stench that surfaces only when you have to dress up for Halloween or theme parties.

I sat in silence, staring at him, cradling my butter knife, thinking the world would be a much better place with one less mime in it.

He sensed my discomfort.

"Hey, would you mind if I went and washed my face?"

He grabbed a duffel bag he had shoved away under the table, and when he was around the corner, I seriously toyed with the idea of just leaving—simply standing up, running to my car, and driving away. That is, if my legs would only work.

"A mime is just a person in makeup," I told myself, before altering the line to better suit my state of mind. "A mime is just a man... and I need to have sex with a man."

When the mime returned, sans white face paint, I was stunned. He was cute, very cute, actually, in kind of a Billy Crudup sort of way. He had shed his bodysuit and changed into tight jeans and a formfitting T-shirt. He had a great body, lean and muscled, like a gymnast's.

He's smokin', I thought irrationally, kind of like when I saw Jeffrey Dahmer on TV for the first time and my initial reaction was, "He's not bad-looking...*for a serial killer.*"

And then the waitress came over to take our order and my date did exactly what I had prayed he wouldn't: He broke into mime mode. He pantomime-rubbed his belly—"I'm so hungry!" he seemed to say—before stretching his mouth into a rubber-faced smile—the "How delicious!" part of his act, I guess.

It was finally at that moment I had the breakthrough my therapist had never been able to reach: I realized maybe I wasn't *terrified* of clowns and mimes. Maybe I just despised their act.

I don't even remember what I ordered, but it got a series of mime-like gestures of jealousy, like, "Why didn't I get that?"

For the next hour I sat quietly as he entertained the waitstaff and surrounding children, doing a painfully bad Marcel Marceau shtick.

Just get out of the box already, I wanted to scream. *There has to be a lid on it, otherwise you couldn't have gotten trapped inside it in the first place.*

And it's not windy inside the restaurant, and there is no trapdoor in the floor—I can still see your legs under the table.

And please, please, stop fake crying because that little boy wouldn't give you a bite of his chocolate cake. You're just scaring the kid, and he's going to carry lifelong scars from this day, just like I have.

At the end of lunch, the mime turned his attention back to me and said, "I'm so sorry. I didn't mean to ignore you. It's just so hard being a recognized artist."

Recognized artist?

When did a mime officially become an "artist," I wanted to know? If so, shouldn't caricaturists and rodeo clowns be included in that special group of gifted performers?

"Excuse me," I said. "I need to go to the bathroom."

Instead I walked straight to the door and left.

The last image I had of my mime as I scurried past the restaurant window was of him sitting there, his mug all squenched up in a troubled look, his hands in midair, doing the "I'm confused!" bit to a nearby group of diners. As they laughed, he transformed his rubber face into some sort of goofily asinine expression and began swirling his right forefinger around his temple in order to indicate that I was crazy.

Perhaps I am, I thought as I strolled down the street, but at least I knew I was sane enough not to have sex with a mime.

I mean, can you imagine the hand gesture that would have prompted?

The O'Rouses

The only Irishman I knew growing up was my father.

Okay, he wasn't Irish in the least. And we lived in the Ozarks.

He was "pretend Irish," as my mother called it, "which is exactly like being a little bit pregnant," she'd finish. "Either you are or you aren't."

My dad looked Irish, however, with his sandy-blond-reddish hair, his short, scrappy stature, his pale skin, and, of course, his love o' the ale.

And my dad attended the University of Missouri-Rolla, an excellent engineering school that was perhaps more famous for its St. Patrick's Day celebrations. My father was in a fraternity that helped lead the green riot on campus, and every St. Patty's Day he prided himself on wearing an old sweatshirt from his frat-boy days that featured a drunken leprechaun dancing on a four-leaf clover.

When he looked in the mirror, I'm convinced he saw Danny Kaye.

I remember emerging every year as a high schooler on St. Patrick's Day morning to a giant pinch from the green Grinch.

"Ouch!"

"Where's your green?"

"Stop it, Dad! I don't wear kelly green! No one should!"

"We're Irish!" he would say.

Now, our family was about as Irish as the O'Charley's restaurant chain. We were mutts, Ozarkians, a chromosome away from being cave dwellers or performing in minstrel shows. We were anything but Irish.

I would roll my eyes dramatically at my father, who would pinch me again, harder, out of spite, before returning to a skilletful of scrambled eggs that he had dyed with green food coloring.

Every St. Pat's Day, on cue, just as I would pour my bowl of Quisp cereal, my dad would look out the kitchen window, the strong March wind whipping our oak branches around, and say, in an awful Irish brogue, "Oh, you know, a windy day is the wrong one for thatching."

Come again?

"Looks like it might rain," he'd continue. "You know, you can take the man out of the bog but you can't take the bog out of the man."

Seriously?

"May your blessings outnumber the shamrocks that grow, and may trouble avoid you wherever you go."

That's when I would grab my books, coat, and keys, and sprint for the back door.

And then I went away to college, and my father's Irish eyes smiled upon me, and my first roommate was as stereotypically Irish as you could get: Irish name. So pale as to burn under a one-hundred-watt bulb. Solar system of red hair (in fact, a full-on 'fro in homage to Julius Erving). Funny as hell. Could drink the entire Rat Pack under the table. He was even prone to offering up phrases at the drop of a hat, such as when making a toast: "May the road rise to meet you. May the wind be always at your back. May the sun shine warm upon your face. The rains fall soft upon your fields. And until we meet again, may God hold you in the palm of his hand."

Though he would lead me into more trouble than Eve, he became one of my best friends, and my father couldn't have been prouder— more so even than if I had gone on to marry Angie Dickinson.

In graduate school I seemed to have been blessed by my father's green blood again, as another Irishman danced into my life via one of my journalism classes. He, too, was clever as hell and prone to partying. I remember my first week at Northwestern, when the professors tossed us newbie reporters onto the streets of Chicago and told us to return at the end of the day to hammer out a story on deadline on a typewriter. It was so *All the President's Men*.

I returned, feeling like a real city boy for the first time in my life, only to be called out by a professor for using the verb "get" in my lead.

"Laziest verb in our vocabulary!" he screamed. "Who wrote this?"

I raised my hand, head down, the professor continuing, "Class? Give me twenty verbs better than 'get'!"

As my new classmates fed off my carcass to prove their worth, my soon-to-be new Irish friend finally said, as the class quieted down, "*Get* off his ass and *get* a life, you pathetic suck-ups!"

He saved my life. He could've led me to the top of the building after class, told me to jump, and I would've giddily catapulted to my death.

Instead I spent months slowly killing myself, hanging out with him on Rush Street, a main center of business and nightlife, which was where he lived, interned, and also worked in a club as a bartender.

When I wasn't writing, I drank.

When I wasn't studying, I drank.

When I wasn't drinking, I was drinking.

Usually with him.

Of course, St. Patrick's Day was a huge celebration not only for my friend but also for the entire city of Chicago, which has a huge Irish population and great heritage. They toss a citywide party, complete with a huge parade and an official dyeing of the Chicago River a shade of green so iridescent, so shocking, it's like seeing Mickey Rourke in person: You're mortified but mesmerized.

Considering it was my first St. Pat's Day in Chicago, my friend offered loads of advice, all bad, culminating with this: "If you want to be in the middle of all the fun, I can get you into the festivities *if...*"

Whenever anyone says "if," I shudder.

If is the word that introduces the most nightmarish of situations:

"If you only loved me as much as I love you..."

"If you would just put this in your mouth..."

"If you would only swallow these drugs in a balloon and haul them across the border you could make ten thousand dollars..."

His *if* was: "If you would be willing to sport a leprechaun costume, you could walk with my bar in the parade and get all your drinks for free."

Now, I was roughly 240 pounds. And I was sure I'd never seen a leprechaun that big, or they'd be sent to Jenny O'Craig. Still, I was intrigued. My parents were paying mucho dinero for me to attend grad school, I was not working, and any little savings seemed like a good idea.

"If you think you could find me a costume that fit..." I mistakenly uttered.

He didn't.

Instead the bar provided a Goodwill bag of green hodgepodge, including a supersized kelly-green tux with tails, a green bowtie, a giant green top hat with a bouncy shamrock, giant shiny black pilgrim shoes with big buckles, and white tights in which to shove my pant legs.

I looked like the Hulk.

Especially when surrounded by hot bartenders, including my friend, who sported "sexy leprechaun outfits" composed of a green vest and bowtie over a bare chest, a shamrock painted on their biceps.

"Holy Rosemary Clooney!" I screamed at my friend outside his bar after taking the El downtown with a throng of drunken Chicagoans taunting me with calls of "They're magically delicious!" and "Pink hearts! Yellow moons! Fat leprechaun!"

"I look like an ass!" I said.

"You do!" my friend said. "A green ass. But you get free drinks all night!"

I called my dad for some reason, at the height of my drunkenness, to wish him happy St. Patty's Day.

"Where are you?" he yelled, so I could hear him over the din.

"In an Irish bar in downtown Chicago! I watched them dye the river!"

"Are you wearing green?"

"I'm dressed as a leprechaun! And I'm wasted!"

I thought I could hear him crying.

Then he gave me the best advice of my life. "Listen, sonny boy. An Irishman is never drunk as long as he can hold on to one blade of grass and not fall off the face of the earth."

Heaven's Waiting Room

"I haven't been on holiday in years," Gary said to me the third fall after we had moved to Michigan.

"Who are you? The princess of Monaco?" I asked. "*Holiday?*"

"It's just that winter is nearly here..."

And then Gary's voice trailed off.

We were outside raking leaves at the time, and there was already a skiff of snow dotting the woods and high points in the yard. We could see our breath. Gary was blowing on his hands, and I could see him shiver.

And this was still, officially, fall.

Winters in Michigan are a lot like John Holmes's penis: awe-inspiring but way too long, leaving you to wonder—after the initial fascination and get-to-know-you phase wears off—if you can really take the whole thing.

I knew I couldn't. I'd tried. I knew, pardon the inevitable pun, what was to come.

Which is why I was already loading up on antidepressants and sleeves of cookie dough. I had already purchased an African violet to set on my windowsill overlooking the woods, a single dot of purple to cheer the vast wasteland of whiteness, knowing it would likely do as much good as placing a Nexium on the distended, pale paunch of a serial belcher.

However, I was floored to hear my ever-optimistic partner—the one who loves to ski and make snow angels, the one who doesn't go bonkers after three straight weeks of whiteout—express his desire to retreat from winter's battle.

"Why *can't* we go on holiday?"

Gary dropped his rake and was again blowing on his hands. He was staring at me with that look that kids give their moms right before they scream like a banshee at McDonald's because they received the wrong Happy Meal toy.

I was shoveling frozen coils of dog poop, my nose dripping snot.

And then I thought, Why can't we holiday?

"Holiday" is what older gays call spring break. Except that it is an extended winter vacation. It's not a week to Disneyland or a three-day Funjet trip to Punta Cana or a college frat week in Cancún. It's fleeing the cold for a more tropical clime for a few months.

We knew lots of gays who go on holiday, fleeing St. Louis or Chicago or Michigan for Fort Lauderdale, Palm Springs, the Carolinas, Costa Rica. But we weren't the jet-set gays. And we certainly weren't retired. We had two dogs, including a new puppy, Mabel, a labradoodle-beagle mix we adopted at the shelter who was a gene short of being absolutely nuts. And we had to work in order to do the little things in life, like eat and have shelter and heat.

Still, for the very first time in our lives, Gary and I had total flexibility. We had restructured our lives in order to be unstructured. We no longer had a daily nine-to-five routine to hold us back, no corporate overseer to dispense ten days of vacation and seven holidays a year.

I could write *anywhere*. And winter was slow season from Gary's work as an innkeeper.

As I raked, I realized that I hadn't been on a real spring break since college, when I went to Daytona Beach and vomited for seven days straight, sleeping on the floor on top of a float raft lined with nacho-cheese Doritos and Domino's boxes. My fellow fraternity brothers and I had stacked empty beer cans in the window of our motel room—like a holiday display at Macy's—and when the windows were fully covered, we threw the beer cans under the twin beds until our room began to rattle every time someone snored. The highlight of that last spring-break trip, however, was being accused by one of my best friends, for reasons still unknown to me, of jacking off while eating his Baby Ruth candy bars while everyone else was passed out.

More than anything, however, I remember being a young man trapped in an old soul's body, a hideously overweight closeted college gay boy who could only hide his secret and his fears by drinking until nothing made sense. I went to strip clubs and felt boobs, or so I was told, and, thankfully, remember very little, except when I would fight off my hangover and rise early—before my friends or other college spring breakers had taken over the beach—and walk, watching the ocean, watching old couples hold hands as they walked along the beaches at Daytona.

I longed to fast-forward my life. I wanted clarity. I wanted to be with someone I loved. I no longer wanted to be young.

I had all of that now.

I looked over at Gary and said, "Let's do it!"

So Gary and I researched Southern cities and rental homes that took pets. And, after the recommendation of several older friends whom we trusted implicitly, we settled on Sarasota, specifically a narrow residential key south of Sarasota and an adorable little salmon-colored Florida-style bungalow sandwiched between the bay and the Gulf of Mexico.

We booked it for nearly two months. I'd never been on vacation longer than ten days.

But this was *holiday*, I reminded myself.

We left, two neurotic dogs and two neurotic men, all panting excitedly, for Florida at four A.M. in February during a complete Michigan whiteout, our SUV packed to its gills with luggage, dog crates, food, laptops, books, beach chairs, and more skin-care products than the downtown Chicago Sephora. The trip was supposed to take roughly twenty hours total; it took us nearly three hours, in the whiteout, to drive a hundred miles.

Slowly, the farther south we drove, the snow stopped, the highways cleared, the weather warmed, and things turned this bizarre color known as green. I stopped at nearly every Starbucks on the highway, ingesting enough caffeine to power the car, if needed, with my blood.

Exhausted after driving thirteen hours, we passed out at a Best Western in southern Georgia that accepted pets, rising early to eat grits and waffles in a sad-looking lobby overlooking the highway with a gaggle of snowbirds who had trouble opening their cartons of milk with knobby, gnarled fingers. While Gary stole boxes of cereal from the buffet, cramming them down his shorts and into his jacket so we could snack on them while we drove, I was checked out by ConnieSue, a desk clerk who was entranced by the silver-and-diamond ring Gary had designed for me for my fortieth birthday.

"Is your wife's the exact same?" asked ConnieSue, an older woman with an accent thicker than the sausage gravy on the buffet.

"No, it's different," I said. I had lived in Georgia for a brief time. I knew how to play the game.

"I notice a lot more men are wearin' their weddin' bands on their right hands. It must be the newest thang. Call me old-fashioned, but I like it on the left hand, where it belongs. Anyhoo, it's eggsquisite! My fuckin' daughter-in-law—excuse my French, young man— would never do such a thoughtful thing for my son. You must have a wonderful wife."

"I do."

"Well, she shore must be somethin' special."

"She is," I replied, just as Gary waddled up with roughly fifty dollars' worth of tiny cereals on his person.

"We are set, sugar pie!" he said to me, crunching with every step. "I gotta go unload our loot!"

I said so long to a bewildered ConnieSue, and we bloated ourselves on Sugar Pops, Frosted Flakes, and Fiber One for the last leg of our trip down the long finger of Florida.

Finally, hours later, Gary and I crossed an old swing bridge and onto a tiny key no wider than a flattened snake. It was like traveling back in time into one of those old paperback mysteries or 1960s beach movies, a world filled with palms and sultry breezes and turquoise waters on both sides of the key, a road filled with sand and coconuts and wind-blown fronds. Ancient, low-slung stucco motels drenched in turquoise and aqua and sea-foam green snuggled against the sand, places with names like Sun Tan Terraces, Palmetto Arms, Gulf Breeze, Sandy Shores, The Place to Be, and Gulf Winds. Old-timers were drinking beer and sunning on lounge chairs, their faces leathery and turned toward the sun like the bloom on a flower.

And then—Bam!—the landscape changed into an episode of MTV *Cribs*. On the left was a big home, then, on the right, a giant home, then the Taj Mahal, then the Kennedy compound, and then gated Spanish-style mansions with land stretching from bay to ocean.

We searched house numbers, wondering if perhaps we had won the lottery and would be staying in one of these mansions for a few hundred dollars a week. And suddenly, there, sitting amidst these mansions like a zit on the nose of Jessica Alba, was our little bungalow, cute as a button but dwarfed in size, grandeur, and sheer shimmery, dripping opulence by homes we were to later find out ranged in the upper millions.

"We're the Clampetts," I said to Gary, as we stepped out of our SUV into eighty-degree weather, palms dancing in the wind, a Bentley whizzing by us while Marge and Mabel relieved themselves on the crushed shells that served as a lawn.

Gary spent the first forty-eight hours of his holiday bleaching like one of the Merry Maids. Since the house was a rental, it had—obviously—been previously lived in, a mystical fact that seemed to bypass Gary until he actually walked into the house.

"People have lived here?" he said, horrified, wide-eyed, as though he had happened upon a mass murder. "And there's carpet. I thought it was tile. Carpet *hides* things."

So we immediately got back in the car and went to the grocery to buy carpet cleaner and 409 antiseptic spray and Purel and more bleach than the Mayo Clinic would use in a year. We scrubbed until the house smelled like an ICU and the skin on out hands burned.

Only when Gary is close to cartilage and bone does he stop cleaning.

And then Gary, the ultimate nester, began his *Extreme Home Make-over,* covering *Three's Company* floral couches with shell-covered king and queen sheet sets he found in an old chest, transforming the furniture into clean, beachy sofas that would turn Vern Yip's head.

Satisfied that he could finally sleep and shower without getting dysentery, Gary led me again to the store, this time for food. It was then that, finally paying attention to our surroundings, we realized we were in an updated version of *Cocoon.*

It took us roughly three hours that day to make our way through Publix, considering we were the only ones flexible enough to bend over and pick up a loaf of bread without breaking a bone, the only ones not fresh out of cataract surgery, the only ones young enough and willing to help, considering the grocery-store shelvers ran when anyone said, "Excuse me, young man...?"

Gary spent twenty minutes helping an old Jewish woman with

a heavy New York accent pick out soft cheeses, while I assisted two old men in Cincinnati Reds hats—one of whom was on oxygen—search for the cheapest vitamins.

I looked in our cart. We had been in the store an hour and had one gallon of fat-free milk, which was beginning to curdle.

"I didn't realize Sarasota was like this," I said to one old man, a regular Jonas Brother who was probably only pushing seventy-five, as I handed him three canisters of Metamucil. He was sporting a Yankees hat, shorts, dress socks, and tennis shoes. The only items he had in his cart were enough bags of bagels to plug his colon for at least a month, enough Metamucil to get his pipes clean, and enough toilet paper to be ready when the dam burst.

"You didn't know Sarasota was old? Are you joshin' me, kid?" he said, scratching his groin. "Locals call this Heaven's Waiting Room."

This couldn't be, I thought.

The first real "holiday" of our lives, and we picked the Island of Assisted Living? We could've gone to Palm Springs or Key West or Puerto Vallarta, a resort town where people wore chokers instead of emergency lifeline buzzers around their necks.

Gary and I drove around Sarasota. We are what I call "immersion tourists," and we pride ourselves on delving headfirst into any community. We discovered there were more walk-in clinics and hip-replacement specialists than Starbucks.

Gary and I have a rule of thumb: If there is not a quality coffeehouse every one hundred feet, you're either driving in rural America or visiting a place you need to get the hell out of.

"We didn't follow our coffeehouse rule," Gary yelled. "It's too hot here for coffee, and old people only like Folgers. Buying a latte seems frivolous to them. We're screwed for two months!"

Still, we decided to make the most of our holiday by dedicating ourselves to working and laying out, self-obsessed goals we knew we could attain. But our fitness center was a virtual Geritol Gym filled with men in walkers and specializing in chairbound workout classes and no- to low-impact exercise.

The Geritol Gym, however, was literally crawling with cougars, older women with tight faces, tight bodies, and their late husbands' inheritances, who were looking to pull younger prey into their lairs.

While I was doing pull-ups, I watched a woman who looked a lot like Loni Anderson's mother eye Gary's crotch as he was doing bench presses, and when he sat up, she licked her collagen-injected lips hungrily before flashing picture-perfect dentures.

"How do you get soooo... *big*?" she purred at Gary.

It was like watching a porn version of *The Golden Girls*.

"Lots of protein," Gary lisped, his hands on his hips.

The cougar tilted her head, her stiff blonde hair moving as one with it, finally realizing, instinctually, that she was hunting the wrong meat.

"You're wearing the bulge shorts," I said to Gary after I had dismounted. "You know, the ones with the pouch that make your penis look like a kielbasa."

"It's a compliment," he said. "No harm, no foul."

Just then, yet another cougar—think Ann Miller—stopped by Gary's bench, lifted her fabulously old and vein-free leg onto it, and asked for "some pointers."

"I'll give you one," I said. "He's a big 'mo."

"In Sarasota?" she answered, flabbergasted.

With no excitement to lure us, our days dwindled to nothingness and centered on taking the dogs for long walks on the beach.

We laid out for hours, tanning until we looked like that old woman in *There's Something About Mary*.

We became so bored and out of touch with any semblance of a routine or schedule that we began eating at five P.M., hitting early-bird buffets for $8.95, gorging ourselves on all-we-could-eat smorgasbords of mashed potatoes and roast beef and iceberg lettuce and Thousand Island dressing.

I spent inordinate amounts of time in the grocery, agonizing over whether the paper towels with gardening implements or the ones with dancing teacups would complement our kitchen best.

"How often do you see teacups dance?" a woman who looked like she birthed Abraham Lincoln said to me.

And I considered that sage advice.

I stopped desiring lattes from Starbucks and became quite satisfied with Folgers every morning. I stopped exercising and found myself exhausted just putting bread in the toaster. Gary and I took naps and watched *America's Funniest Home Videos*. We began snacking on Saltines and juice before bed, often choking on the dry crackers if we didn't have something with which to wash them down.

I began waking early, creepy early—when infomercials were still airing—to eat a breakfast of oatmeal, a banana, and three cups of coffee (I preferred foods that could be gummed), and then go for a walk on the beach, where I could comb the Gulf shoreline for shark's teeth.

Searching for shark's teeth among the surf and sand in the early-morning hours—as the clouds gave way to blue sky, as the mist cleared from the beach—became my obsession. Typically, after the tide would roll back out, fossilized fangs of black and brown that had fallen out of the maws of sand sharks and nurse sharks would dot the shoreline, and the search would commence, a search I equated to panning for gold. It took hours to find a small pocketful, but the hunt—me standing on the sandy shore in front of a vast ocean, the sky enveloping me, looking for bits of beasts—grounded me, made me feel whole.

I was stooped over the shore early one morning, sifting shells and sand through my fingers, when an old couple approached.

"We have an adventurer!" an elderly woman yelled over the ocean wind.

"Indeed!" said her husband.

"What do you think of this find?" she asked, holding out the necklace she had around her neck. At the end was a giant white tooth featuring a massive gum line and serrated edges.

"Great white!" she yelled. "Took me ten years to find one like this."

"Rolled right up onto her feet after a huge storm," her husband continued. "She thought it was a shell at first!"

"Thought it was a shell!" she laughed.

Ira and Dottie, I was to learn, were their names, and they would become my shark's-tooth-combing companions, my early-morning beach walkers, for the remainder of my stay.

Ira and Dottie were a husband-and-wife team along the lines of George Burns and Gracie Allen. They were quick-witted and droll, together so long they were actually one person, conjoined twins who could anticipate what the other was thinking or wanted before any thought or action had even been initiated. The husband was dapper—dressed more for a night at the theater than a morning stroll on the beach, in a polo and herringbone jacket with leather shoulder pads—while she was more Debbie Reynolds glam, long-limbed, heavily made-up, long white hair pulled into an intricately twisted bun and shimmering clasp. He would begin a sentence, which she would finish; she would begin a joke, which he would complete; they would both begin stories that never ended.

They had moved from New York in the late 1980s, where he had been a professor and she had been a dancer (how off-off-Broadway would never be determined). But **Dance!**—bold, ital, capped with an exclamation point—she could—they both said—alongside stars and ne'er-do-wells, true talents and drunks. They moved to Sarasota after visiting one summer, when prices in New York's trendy beach areas began to get too expensive and too Wall Street. "The artists could no longer afford it, and who wants to go to dinner parties with financial analysts and stockbrokers?" Dottie had asked dramatically.

"Who wants to do that?" Ira echoed.

The couple had never had children but considered New York to be their baby and Sarasota their grandchild. "Suburban neighborhoods were never for us," Ira told me. "You have to live somewhere with personality, just like you have to love someone with personality."

"You have to be surrounded by life, because death is just around the corner," Dottie said.

Both of them said this nonchalantly, as if they were ordering a cup of coffee, black, no sugar or cream. And both said this knowingly, as if they were imparting a professor's wisdom to a young student. Ironically, I found incredible optimism in this statement, though it chilled me more than the early-morning breeze.

Often on our walks, Dottie would simply take off running, her old dancer's legs churning in the sand, and run headfirst into a congregation of seagulls, hundreds of them, flocked on a narrow band of beach. The birds always moved like a choreographed unit when she ran toward them, and she would spin as they flew, twirling, her hair in the wind, her arms turning, a human helicopter about to take flight.

She would return, laughing, coughing, her hazy green eyes dancing in the reflection off the ocean.

Ira would take his wife into his arms and say, "You have the spirit of a child!" before she would unwind herself from her husband's arms and pirouette to the shoreline, where she would dance in unison with the waves, the tide her partner, back and forth, side to side, arms extended, kicking high, high, higher than the waves.

"You're amazing!" I screamed one morning over the water and wind.

"You're kind!" she exhaled, returning to grab her husband's hand. "But thank you, my dear!" She sang this line, like she sang most lines, before kicking a leg—and a whole lot of sand—straight up into the air like a human geyser.

And then we would walk. And talk. About nothing important, except life and time and hopes and dreams.

Every morning, toward the end of our walks, Ira and Dottie would open a plastic Publix grocery bag they had brought with them and start throwing bits of bread and crushed crackers at a horde of gulls.

Anything having to do with birds and possible pecking of eyes caused me to panic.

"It's okay," Dottie said. "We feed them every morning and night."

"We feed them a lot," Ira continued. "Some people have their hummingbirds or wrens, we've got our gulls."

"They're a bit aggressive," laughed Dottie, "but they are full of life. We started feeding them because"—here she danced directly into the middle of the pack, like she was moving into a war zone, the birds swarming her—"because of these two."

Sitting rather still, in the middle of this chaos, were two cartoonish-looking old sea gulls, not even bothering to move. "These two we found bound in a plastic six-pack container. We cut them loose to save them, but their wings and legs were injured."

"They're slower than their comrades, but still full of life," Ira said. "We call them Ozzie and Harriet."

"Shoo, Ozzie," said Dottie. "Shoo, Harriet."

The gulls didn't move exactly, but Ozzie took a step or two to the left, squawking loudly, screaming at the top of his lungs, for his mate to hurry up. She took one high step and then another, very deliberately, going at her own pace, even stooping carefully to eat a few grains of sand. Ozzie would squawk, followed by Harriet, and it was then I knew I had seen this act before: not only from my parents, but also standing before me.

True love, I thought, solidified by time, hardened by age.

A few mornings later, Dottie and Ira surprised me by announcing, "Oh, my God, we read your first book, *America's Boy*!"

Both laughed but said nothing more.

"Where did you get it?" I asked.

"The library."

"You should have bought it. I need the royalties."

Again they laughed, but said nothing more.

"And...?" I asked. "Don't leave me hangin'."

"I can't say we enjoyed it," Dottie said, "but I can say it was something we needed to read."

"Living in New York, we always assumed it was easy for people to be themselves, no matter who they were, what they did, who they loved," Ira said. "But your memoir made us reevaluate that."

For the next few weeks we continued to walk and talk and laugh, me always turning one final time—before I would head back to see Gary and the dogs—in order to watch this old couple walking, holding hands, an image clouded on the beach, blurred by the fine mist from the ocean, until I could see nothing more than two ghosts giggling, kissing, and then disappearing.

And then one morning they *were* gone.

After the weekend, they did not meet me for our regular walk on Monday. Or Tuesday.

I had never asked where they lived. They had never offered it. So I didn't know where to look for them.

I began to ask passersby and homeowners along the beach about the couple, only to receive very little information. Sarasota, it seemed, was a town of transients, coming and going, staying one step ahead of the snow and then one step ahead of the heat.

Finally, one day, I happened to ask an older woman who walked the beach nearly every day about the couple.

"I heard Ira had a heart attack while they were visiting friends in New York over the weekend," she said. "Dottie decided to keep him there to be closer to their friends. She said she needed the support."

I ran back to Gary and cried as if something had happened to one of our own parents.

The remainder of our time in Heaven's Waiting Room, Gary and the dogs accompanied me on my early-morning walks, me continuing to search for shark's teeth and the meaning of life—this precious little sliver of time we all have but tend to waste too carelessly in youth, like pennies, finally taking on incredible importance to me.

Those simple morning walks with Gary comforted me, contented me, filled my soul, and I began to cling to each walk, each found shark's tooth, as our holiday began to dwindle, as if I were clinging to a lifesaver in the middle of the Gulf, or, worse, desperately to middle age.

Most mornings, at some point during our walks, Marge and Mabel would break loose and bound into a seawall of gulls, and then Gary would laugh and call for them. I would reach into my pocket, retrieve some bread crumbs, and toss them to Ozzie and Harriet, and then Gary would take my hand in his and say, his words carried out over the ocean and into the vast, cloudless sky by the breeze, "I love you!"

And we would continue to walk, our bodies disappearing into the mist like ghosts.

APRIL

"What do you mean, you 'don't believe in homosexuality'? It's not like the Easter Bunny, your belief isn't necessary."

—LEA DELARIA

Helen Keller
Could Find That Egg!

My father had a rolltop desk in our family room that served as his virtual home office in the 1970s. I remember sitting in his springy swivel chair as a kid and staring at three photos that adorned his desktop: One was of him in college, wearing goggles and sporting a flattop, mixing something in a beaker; one was him at work, checking the fluid levels in a piece of monstrous equipment that manufactured windows; and one was him with our family, on Easter, my brother and I holding baskets filled with faux grass and board games but no candy or eggs.

That's because even during his off-hours, my father remained an engineer, a man driven largely by mathematical precision, his mind always working on ways to outsmart the world.

Even children.

Which is why my dad used to bury our Easter eggs as if they were plutonium.

Every Easter, no matter how hard we searched, my brother and I could never locate the eggs.

I used to listen in awe to the stories of my friends' Easter-egg hunts, where they would skip around merrily, filling their baskets with tons of candy.

My father, on the other hand, would spend hours trekking through our five acres of yard and woods, searching for the perfect spots to insert his minispade and bury our eggs.

He would finally return to the porch, my brother and I watching from behind the patio door, our breath steaming the glass, and give us an excited thumbs-up. We would blow out of the house, dashing around the yard looking in every place any typical five- and nine-year-old would consider most obvious.

Patio? No.

Front porch? Uh-uh.

Planters? Please.

Hanging baskets? Right.

Ground next to the tulips? Too easy.

Low limbs of the dogwoods, or crook of the old oak? Of course not.

Rather, our eggs were buried deep in the ground, like a mob body in Jersey, only the dull tips of the plastic eggs popping through the earth.

A bloodhound couldn't have located them.

Although I was a chubby kid who would blind another child just to get the last Peep, it simply wasn't worth the effort to get so filthy and frustrated.

Instead, I would cry.

"They're still under ten, Ted," I remember my mother saying to my dad. "Wade can't even do long division yet. And we're not a family of moles. How can you expect them to find buried eggs? You have an evil streak."

But my father was a competitive sort. We had to work hard to earn our reward. And my dad always liked to win—at any game, at any price—and he seemed to revel in the fact that logic always won over emotion.

I cry. I give up. I lose.

I keep looking. And digging. I win.

So when my brother and I finally got old enough and smart enough to map out our yard, tote our own spades, and work as a team on our Easter-egg hunts, my dad, like any good engineer, improved his methodology and began scaling our solid oaks and skinny sycamores, hiding our candy-filled eggs in tree limbs and birds' nests, places no normal child, unless they were the offspring of Spider-Man and Wonder Woman, could venture, places that no parent, unless they were drunk, would allow their children to go.

"My Lord, Ted," my mother said to my dad. "We're not a family of squirrels. How can you expect them to climb that high? You have an evil streak."

Still, I know deep down that my father never did this to be mean. I believe he did it to test himself, his engineering acuity, to see if he still had game. Perhaps, when you reach a certain age, you also do such things to show your children that you are still superior.

As an adult I asked my dad about those Easter-egg hunts, and he told me, "Weren't they a blast! You know, I just wanted to make them fun. We didn't have a lot growing up, and I wanted to create great memories, make it a *real* hunt."

"Oh, it was," I told him.

And then I made him watch *Blood Diamond*.

Looking back, I don't know why my brother and I wanted to find those eggs so desperately anyway, since there was nothing hidden inside worth eating. My Depression-era grandma often filled the eggs for us, meaning we didn't even get *real* candy, like mini chocolate bars or little marshmallow bunnies. My grandma was too frugal. Instead our eggs were filled with breath mints and nickels. It was like Easter at Guantánamo.

Sometimes my grandma would insert globs of those nasty orange slices, the ones she kept in her cut-glass candy dish that always ended up melding into something resembling a spleen. Occasionally she would stuff our eggs with leftover liqueur-filled chocolates—ones she hadn't finished from Christmas—which I would mainline before becoming belligerent and then very, very sleepy.

And, to top our Easter off, my grandma didn't even use "real" Easter eggs, the petite plastic ones that clicked snugly together and came in bright spring colors. Rather, our eggs were actually leftover L'eggs containers, which at one point housed her taupe stockings.

As a result of all this, my family wisely stopped hunting eggs while I was still fairly young and instead focused our competitive spirit on playing board games and gorging on ham.

Which is why—at the age of thirty-two—when I spent my first Easter at Gary's parents' home, it came as quite a shock to discover his mom still hid eggs.

For adults and grandchildren.

In spots even Helen Keller could locate.

In fact, Gary's family had never hidden their Easter eggs outside.

One Easter, when Gary was little, he said he remembers pulling back the dark-brown curtains in the living room of his house and watching other families in the neighborhood hunting for their eggs outside.

"What's going on?" Gary asked his mother. "What kind of people hunt for eggs outdoors?

"People who've obviously never had allergies," she told him.

For Gary's mom, a woman who loves the holidays as much as her homemade dickeys, potpourri, and Buick LeSabres, the thought of anything new, any external forces that could ruin a holiday, scared her. To wit:

It might rain.

It might be too cold.

A rabid squirrel might attack a grandchild.

A baby bird might choke on a forgotten jelly bean.

So Gary's mother always held Easter in a climate-controlled

environment, where things could be monitored. If Gary's mom had known about the Biosphere earlier, she would have built that instead of a brick ranch house.

She was the polar opposite of my father.

In fact, her main Easter rule was this: No one should find it difficult to locate his booty.

As a result, she hid the same number of eggs for each person, all containing the same amount and type of candy in exactly the same location every year.

I use the word *hid* loosely. She "hid" eggs in the center of the hallway, in the middle of the dining-room table, in the bathroom sink, in my coffee cup.

And if you had any trouble finding those, his mom even decorated an Easter tree with eggs, a sort of hybrid Christmas tree decorated by a rabid Easter Bunny. I had never seen nor heard of an Easter tree before—much less known you could buy Easter-egg ornaments with which to decorate it—until I met Gary's mother.

Perhaps, I thought, watching Gary pose excitedly behind the Easter tree as his mom snapped photos, my partner still believed this Dr. Seuss tree grew in some magical place, some land where barely enough light filtered through dark-curtained clouds to grow weak, white branches that immediately had to be potted in Styrofoam.

"Easter Bunny's been here!" his mom chirped through the door my very first Easter morning in her home, just after Gary and I had finished having sex. (I do not, by the way, condone having sex on major religious holidays. I believe it's bad luck. However, I had no choice: That was the morning I learned Gary became Jeff Stryker whenever the heating and cooling vents in his parents' house turned on, because the noise used to cover his teenage moans.)

"What do we do?" I asked Gary in a panic.

"Just giggle excitedly."

Which I did.

I sounded like one of those guys just before he gets busted on *To Catch a Predator,* the ones who walk through the front door carrying sweet tea, condoms, and a bag of McDonald's just as the decoy disappears with a basket of laundry and Chris Hansen appears in the kitchen.

Instead, his mom reciprocated, giggling like a junior-high cheerleader who just found out that the cutest guy in eighth grade would go to Sadie Hawkins with her.

"I just saw the Easter Bunny jump away but heard him wish you both a 'hoppy' Easter!" she said.

"Is she kidding?" I asked Gary.

"*Ssshhhh!* It's tradition," he said.

"Any-*bunny* want some fresh muffins?" his mom continued, her mouth in the crack of the door, mere feet from my exposed crotch. "Or would you rather have some carrots?"

"Is she on crack?" I whispered.

"You're such a crank. She's excited. You're just jaded from your Easter past."

I entered to find a Stepford Easter, in which everything was perfectly choreographed. Our Easter baskets (separate from our eggs) were filled with candy and CDs and Easter-tree ornaments and gift certificates; it was like an Oscar swag bag.

Additional "surprise" eggs were placed directly in my line of sight: "What? There's one on my breakfast plate? I never would have seen it. Thanks for the heads-up!"

It was lovely and generous, but somehow I missed Easter at home, my dad hiding eggs that would have taken me all day to unearth.

I was slicing my second piece of traditional Easter coffee cake, which contained roughly four pounds of brown sugar, when I heard the table shaking. I looked up to find that Gary had inserted into his mouth fake rabbit teeth—ones that he had made out of cardboard in elementary school decades ago—and was hopping around the table, at the urging of his family.

"It's tradition," he mouthed at me, with an enormous overbite. "I'm the Easter Bunny."

His parents were laughing and clapping.

Gary was hopping.

And then he laid an egg.

Which rabbits don't do.

It was disturbing.

It was... *just what I needed to see?*

It was at that moment that I fully came of age as an adult: I no longer cursed my occasionally dysfunctional family, and I actually missed our traditions, the ones only my family celebrated, no matter how eggs-asperating they were.

In fact, all of this made me downright *hoppy* because—as it would turn out—I had doubled my dysfunction.

"Your turn!" Gary's parents urged.

I put Gary's drool-drenched cardboard rabbit teeth into my mouth and hopped around the table.

And then I laid an egg.

Because it was tradition.

Joke's on Me

"Beggin' for blurbs," as I call it, is the author equivalent of a wedgie: You know what's coming is going to be painful, but you can't stop it.

My last "official" wedgie occurred on April Fool's Day decades ago when our rural Eddie Haskell asked, "Knock, knock? Who's there?" and before I could reply, said, "Your underwear!" before lifting me into the air by my Hanes. It's a punchline I still don't get, considering the comedy was entirely physical.

Flash forward twenty years to the publication of my first memoir. One of the initial media interviews I conducted was on April Fool's Day, a week before *America's Boy* was set to publish.

I felt ready to conquer the world.

But the DJ asked what it felt like to be compared to Augusten Burroughs and Haven Kimmel, the two memoirists mentioned in my jacket copy, as well as David Sedaris.

It was then I knew I was damned.

"Have you met them?" the Morning Zoo asked me. "Are they as hilarious in person?"

The closest I have ever come to Burroughs, Kimmel, or Sedaris is "beggin' them for blurbs."

In fact, I spent weeks crafting a pitch letter to these writers I'd never met but long admired. I perfected prose that was complimentary but not stalkerish, hilarious yet poignant.

Then I spent hours staring at the "Send" icon, wondering what these authors were doing at that very moment.

Was Burroughs between pieces of Nicorette and, if so, would he be irritated when he opened the e-mail?

Was Amy Sedaris making a bologna casserole for David? And would my e-mail be funny enough to make him go, "Get over here, Amy. This Wade Rouse is funnier than *Two and a Half Men*. We must blurb."

Of course not.

Burroughs's assistant kindly said he no longer provided blurbs.

I tried for six months to contact Sedaris, which proved more painful than giving myself rhinoplasty.

Kimmel kindly agreed to read my manuscript, *if* she had time.

I never heard from her again.

I assumed she despised the book and thus opted not to send, "This is the worst piece of crap I'll ever read in my life!" Which is a shame, because my publicist could easily have edited that to read: "This is the...piece...I will...read [all] my life!"

I harbor no ill will. They're busy, trying to lead normal lives, and I realize they're overwhelmed by such requests.

I guess I'd just like to see some publishing evidence that blurbs really help sell books, or if they are simply internal ego boosters, like literary Botox.

Ironically, moments after my April Fool's media debacle, a well-known author I'd asked for a blurb e-mailed—a year after my request—with a catty note, the basic sense of which was, "Do you know who I am?"

Yes. Which is why I had asked in the first place.

My April Fool's joke was no longer funny. Which is why my partner, Gary, dragged me to a psychic.

To undo the blurb curse.

Now, I don't believe in psychics. They are the equivalent of Ron Popeil in a turban.

However, Gary adores one particular back-alley medium who wears a pound of purple eye shadow and has more feral cats than teeth.

"She has 'the gift,'" Gary told me.

It cost me fifty dollars for a half hour, roughly what my dentist charges, money I'm convinced he doesn't spend on cat food and vodka.

When we arrived, the psychic led me to a dark room with incense burning, pushed me into a rickety chair in front of a cloth-draped table, and stared into a glass ball I'm convinced she bought at Spencer's.

She leaned dramatically across the table, grabbed my hands, and shut her eyes.

"I can feel your stress," she said. "I see great things in your future, if you can just transcend your doubt."

Gary whispered, "Concentrate, Wade. Unchain your baggage. Release the image of Augusten Burroughs. Let go of Haven Kimmel. Set the Sedaris spirit free."

Just like that, the psychic dropped my hands as if they were made of concrete and screamed, "Oh, my God, you know them? They're my favorite writers! Are they as funny in person?"

I clamped my eyes shut and concentrated. In fact, for once I swore I could hear the spirits talking, telling me something very specific:

"Start writing fiction. Perhaps novelists blurb."

The Wonder Years

Three days into spring, just as the mounds of dirty snow had melted into tiny rivers that forked through the hollows of our Michigan woods like country interstates, we found a dog.

Our neighbors, who own the blueberry farm and acreage that backs our woods, actually found it, calling us early that evening, just after daylight savings time, when the sun was still perched high in the sky.

"We just found a dog lying in our compost pile. Think it's dead."

Gary trudged over with a leash and a towel, green waders up to his knees, and a load of optimism.

Gary is an optimist.

One of those dirty stinking, the-sun-will-come-out-tomorrow optimists.

And, despite my tone, I love him for that.

He is the anti-me.

Ten minutes later he was back, leading the wobbly dog, which still had part of a rotting cabbage head in its mouth. The dog was a dirty, dingy, pee yellow, and there were burrs and cuts and dried blood strewn throughout its fur. Its nails were so long, they had curled and bent and grown into his pads, which were infected and raw. His eyes were matted shut. And the dog's ribs were showing—it was dust bunnies on bones, really—its midsection so thin, I could nearly encircle it with both my hands.

I wanted to cry, and puke, and scream, and immediately put it out of its misery. I wanted to strangle those who had done this, who could do this. But instead I said to Gary, "You'd kill for a waistline like that," because that's what he needed to hear at that moment, especially since he looked just like a kid who, for the first time, was seeing the grim reality of the world, of the woods.

Gary smiled through his tears.

Gary and I are country kids who moved to the city and then returned to our rural roots. We had grown accustomed to sprawling suburban yards and well-groomed purebreds with vanity collars who drank out of Pottery Barn ceramic dog bowls decorated with bones.

This dog was barely breathing.

Gasping for air.

Its teeth were chattering.

As it lay on its side we held some water to its face, and it smelled for it, its broad snout knocking the bowl from our hands. Its jaw released the cabbage head and its teeth began to chatter even more violently.

"Aren't you thirsty, boy?" I asked in a sing-song voice, my teeth chattering, too. "Aren't you thirsty, big guy?"

With every ounce of strength it seemed to possess, the dog willed its matted eyes open and looked up at me.

He was blind.

And then the dog licked my hand, rested his head on Gary's lap, and seemed to stare directly into my eyes.

He could see nothing, it seemed, but straight into my heart.

I named the dog Wonder, for many reasons.

Most obviously, it was a wonder he had survived, managed to

make his way through the woods, in the dark, dying, for God knows how long.

And he was blind, like one of our favorite singers, Stevie Wonder, whom I had, ironically, been listening to on my iPod when our neighbors called.

Everybody needs somebody
Everybody needs somebody—I need you.

Those were the lyrics to "Everybody Needs Somebody" that Stevie was singing when I saw Gary trudging back through the woods with this dying dog.

Never name a pet you don't intend to keep. That's the first mistake. It bonds you to it emotionally, in a way that seems forever.

But I couldn't help it.

Wonder.

It fit.

This wasn't the dog I wanted.

In fact, I didn't even want a second dog, much less one that was malnourished, mangy, and blind.

There were too many cute puppies out there. And we already had a very high-maintenance mutt, Marge, who was the love of my life.

Gary had wanted a second dog for a long time but I had nixed it, saying the timing wasn't right, or Marge wouldn't do well with another dog in the house, or it was too expensive, or this or that.

I am good with excuses. I am good at planning. I am good with spin.

In my former life I was a PR person. I can change the outlook on anything, make something awful sound good, make something good sound awful. What I've never been good at, however, is facing my own truth, dealing with my own emotions. I am a good burier, like—to pardon the obvious analogy—a dog with a bone.

Gary rushed Wonder to the vet after we found him, and when he returned he was crestfallen but hopeful. The dog was 40 percent underweight and had fleas, an infected paw, and, worst, the early stages of heartworm. Everything, he was told, however, might be curable. The vet wanted to see Wonder for a complete physical Monday: blood work, X-rays, a battery of tests to see just how deep his health issues were.

"This dog is a survivor," Gary said. "He will be saved."

Always the optimist.

I told Gary all the reasons why we shouldn't keep the dog. They were obvious. Too obvious. It just wasn't logical.

I told Gary the dog might not live through the weekend.

And then Gary spent the weekend ignoring those reasons. He took the dog to a groomer and had him washed and blown dry, Wonder standing under the dryer, his eyes shut, sighing as his matted yellow fur turned to fluffy gold.

By Saturday the dog was eating well, drinking water (too much, actually), and wagging his tail when he heard Gary's voice.

By Sunday, Gary had taught Wonder to navigate our stairs, to make his way around the house, to come to the sound of his voice.

Wonder could find Gary, walking directly to him—into his knees, actually—leaning his body into Gary's and sighing and wagging and smiling.

He would live.

When I woke Monday morning, I had made up my mind. We would keep Wonder.

That's the thing about living with an optimist: You realize you are one, too, somewhere deep down. You realize life and love is all about risk and doing the illogical sometimes.

Why must I always be the rational one, I thought all night. The sane one. Why do I always fight everything? I too often see the impossibility rather than the possibility. Why do we too often have to be adults, and see not the path but the obstacles? Our childhood wonder is knocked from us at too early an age. Act like a grown-up, do the logical thing. Even when your heart is telling you otherwise.

This was a dog that had lived a nightmare of a life and still never whined or howled or cried out of pain or discomfort. You don't make a sound, I learned from Wonder, when no one ever comes to see how you're doing.

So I decided: Gary and I would do everything in our power to give Wonder a few wonderful years. We would install a tether line so he could go to the bathroom and install gates by the stairs so he would be safe, and we would clear paths in the house so he could navigate. He would become part of our family, just like Marge.

On Monday we dropped Wonder off at the vet, me, for once, the optimist, thinking about what might be: Wonder by my feet, lying in front of the fireplace on cold winter nights; Wonder snuggling against me on the screen porch; Wonder feeling the sand in his paws when we walked him on the beach.

And then the vet called Gary a few hours later and gave us his report after viewing the dog's lab work: Wonder's kidneys were failing, his organs collapsing, his prognosis beyond bleak. He had a few weeks, a couple of months, tops.

We still considered taking him home for those final weeks, until we were told he was in pain. He may have been silent, but he was screaming inside.

So we did something we never thought we would: We put an animal to sleep. We took responsibility for someone else's irresponsibility. But we also gave Wonder a few days of peace, of home, of love. He did not die alone, abandoned.

When we arrived at the vet's office, we walked Wonder around outside for a final few minutes of talking, comforting, hugging, kissing, petting, and crying. He smelled the grass that was just coming to life, a few crocuses that signaled spring.

We reluctantly went back in, still crying, and into a private room with a nurse who asked if we were ready.

We said no.

"Do you know this is Prevention to Cruelty of Animals Month?" the nurse asked.

"I feel bad enough already," I said.

"No, no, it's just so sad that it comes to this. Over one hundred thousand dogs are abused every year in the United States. You didn't make Wonder this way."

Staring at this dying dog, it certainly felt that way, however.

And then the nurse brought out the needle and eased it into Wonder's fluffy arm.

At first Wonder fought the anesthesia, bobbing his head back and forth, "chasing the tennis balls," the nurse said. And then he closed his eyes. He fell asleep. He stopped breathing.

It was so quick.

But much too slow.

Gary and I kissed Wonder on the snout, crying, convulsing really, and I told him to go find my late brother, and that he would take him fishing, run with him through heaven.

Before we left Wonder, Gary leaned down and whispered into his ear, "It's spring, buddy. You've been reborn now. You're finally free. You can finally see again."

But really it was me who could.

The Quick Brown Fox Jumps over the Lazy Dog

I went through a brief bohemian period after graduate school in Chicago when I considered myself an artist. I was going to be a writer, nine to five be damned. I would *not* work for the Man or have anything whatsoever to do with the Man.

And then I got a call from the Man—my father—who explained in no uncertain terms that I wasn't earning enough to pay my phone bill, much less my rent, car, groceries, and utilities.

It seemed my job as a "serious writer" (read: freelancer who wrote five-hundred-word advertorials on car wax and home financing and got paid roughly a penny a word) didn't really qualify as a job.

So my dad told me in a very authoritative tone that this was a lesson in "trickle-down economics."

"The faucet," he said, "officially shuts off the first of the month. The gravy train is empty."

"You're mixing metaphors, Dad," I told him.

"And you're getting a real job," he replied. "Metaphors don't pay shit."

My bohemian period was over.

. . .

Though I did not want to work for the Man, the Man came calling.

Thanks to the parents of some friends of mine—parents who knew important people and who, more importantly, had deadbeat children themselves—I was able to snag an interview with a behemoth PR firm, an agency that was termed "the Wall" by the local media because reporters were unable to secure any information about anyone or anything of value until this firm commented or approved first.

I arrived at my interview to find myself confronted by an army of perfect pod people, petite blondes with tight chignons and tailored navy suits clutching too many pens, and tall, stone-faced anchormen with chiseled jaws, deep, serious voices, and really white eyes and teeth.

It was like being interviewed by an army of attractive wolverines.

Now, this was in the days before I was out and proud, when instead I was closeted and fat, so I arrived at my interview wearing the only nice clothes I owned that still fit: a blue blazer with loose gold buttons, a button-down white shirt that was beginning to pill and yellow at the collar, a pair of khakis the pleats of which were rendered invisible by my thighs, a scuffed pair of brown tasseled loafers (I had Scotch-taped the tassels on so they wouldn't fly off when I walked), and a red tie with yellow dots that looked like one of those 3-D card tricks where the woman looks old until you hold the card at a distance from your face.

Despite my interviewers' initial looks of shock at my appearance— "fraternity weight gain," I told them—I thought the half-day interview was going well: I had a credentialed background, great degrees from top universities, quality writing experience, and I engaged in thoughtful yet snappy repartee that elicited hearty laughs.

The snafu, it seems, came at lunch, a "required element" of the interview process at this firm, in which you dined on a preselected lunch at a private room near the top of the building. The lunch— which consisted of multiple, tricky-to-eat items such as salad with tiny diced vegetables, soup, and sauce-soaked pasta—was basically a white-collar boot camp that forced newbies to prove their mettle in front of a series of hard-edged scouts.

Still, I felt highly confident, especially since I had taken an etiquette class, when I was young and lived in the South, from an elderly woman who smelled like mothballs and constantly told our class of little boys and girls that each of us "needed to do all we could for the war effort."

As a result, I not only learned who Rommel was but also ascertained which silverware to use with each course, how to wrap my pasta in the big spoon, how to fold my napkin cavalierly on my lap, and how to chew with my mouth closed while smiling and nodding.

Everything in my interview, I thought, seemed to go swimmingly until lunch ended, I said my good-byes and thank-yous, and was waiting for the elevator. It was then that I noticed a trio of my PR lunch inquisitors—two men who looked like Charlie Sheen from *Wall Street* and a young woman who looked like a very angry Kate Hudson—doubled over in laughter, looking at me and pointing at their mouths.

Inside joke, I thought. Blowing off steam before getting back to work.

But when I returned to my car and pulled down the visor to check my reflection—just to see if I had survived the interview without becoming "too dewy"—it was then that I saw it: A shiny spinach leaf had tightly wrapped its way all around my front right tooth, making it look as if it were simply missing. In fact, I resembled a toothless extra from *The Grapes of Wrath*, or a fat boxer who couldn't protect his face.

I was humiliated, to say the least. I had done everything right—secretly shot spit between my teeth to clear potential peppercorns, rubbed my tongue over my teeth to remove foreign objects—but this single piece of spinach had somehow managed to adhere to my tooth like a bright, green cap, making it impossible to tongue-detect.

I never heard from the firm again. Not even a rejection letter. Which was the galling part: I realized that if a highly regarded PR agency didn't even bother with standard etiquette, I was pretty much unemployable, except for jobs that required no human interaction, minimal counting skills, or a series of vaccinations.

And then while desperately scouring the local paper, just days away from my father shutting off the faucet of gravy, I happened upon an ad for a junior account executive at a small integrated communications firm that did a mix of PR, advertising, and marketing.

"Great writing skills a must!" the ad proclaimed. "Outstanding opportunity for a hungry young college grad."

It seemed a perfect fit.

I mailed my résumé and list of references (i.e., friends and parents of friends who said they would lie for me) on a Sunday afternoon, and was called midweek by a woman who sighed after nearly every sentence.

"Are you Mr. Rouse?" Sigh.

"We received your résumé (sigh), and would be interested in speaking with you about the job (sigh)."

Although I became severely depressed midway through the call, I arranged an interview for Friday.

The firm was located in an old brick office building in a decaying section of downtown, one of those streets a few blocks off the main city strip that is lined with Rent-A-Centers and Quik Cash stores, storefront windows decorated with impenetrable steel bars.

I entered an empty lobby encased in decaying wood. I located the list of companies in the building, mostly small personal-injury-attorney firms, and found the agency.

I buzzed and heard a sigh.

An ornate but barely functioning elevator scooted me up to a midlevel floor, where I was dumped into another rotting wood lobby that smelled like floor wax. A huge airplane fern sat in a coppery container, the majority of its limbs picked clean of their leaves, cigarette butts smashed into the soil.

I opened the door and heard a sigh.

"Can I help you?" Sigh.

A middle-aged woman with helicopter-high silvery-blonde hair and one of those poorly drawn cartoon faces that would remain blank even after witnessing an airplane crash in her own backyard stared at me.

"Yes?" Sigh.

She was obviously no Angela Lansbury.

"Hi. I'm Wade Rouse. I'm here for the interview. You just buzzed me up."

Sigh.

She punched a number into her phone, the headset literally in her mouth. "Your nine o'clock is here." She looked at me and sighed. "You can have a seat."

I smiled at her with one of those too-toothy smiles, those big, creepy Garfield kinds of smiles, wondering if she might have been pretty back in the day before massive doses of honey buns and bleach did her in.

"Are you okay?" she asked, staring at me. And then she sighed and picked at a cruller with a red nail the size of a surfboard.

This PR office's reception area was decorated with a random assortment of couches, the worn, mismatched kinds my fraternity used to have in its vomit-strewn parlor, and they were all pushed against the walls of the lobby as if a street sweeper went through the middle of the place every night.

Each couch had its own glass end table, smudged with fingerprints, and there was a nearly empty watercooler that burped occasionally, and one of those coffeepots, sitting on a hot plate, that smelled like burning tires.

I flipped through a two-year-old copy of *Ad Age*, the most recent magazine on one of the end tables, and began to worry.

Fifteen minutes later, a nervous older man, a Barney Fife–ish guy, appeared and squirreled me into his office, a tiny interior square without windows. He kept looking around in a crazy-paranoid fashion the entire time.

The most discomforting part, however, and the feature from which I could not unleash my stare was the man's coffee cup, which was perched perilously high on a makeshift mountain of papers and magazines and faxes and binders, almost as if Christo had been commissioned to do the installation.

"Tell me a little about yourself," he said, having to stand in order to retrieve his coffee cup from high in the clouds.

I was, of course, a "hard worker," "quick learner," and "go-getter" who could "get along with anyone," I said with my freakish smile. "Even Idi Amin," I added before I could stop myself.

He did not laugh.

"What interests you about our firm?" he asked.

So I lied to him, trying not to sound too desperate, although I was about two weeks away from moving back to the Ozarks and becoming a carny.

"I am adept at all forms of communication, having majored in journalism, but I've had experience and internships in marketing, advertising, radio, and TV. I am simply fascinated with integrated communications. It's the wave of the future."

These were all lies. I thought "integrated communications" was an asinine buzzword, like "mission-based," "emerging technologies," "strategic planning," and "team player."

Uttering them made my colon spasm.

I really just wanted to write.

About myself.

Still, Barney Fife seemed intrigued enough to tell me about the firm's major accounts, which ranged from the awful to the pathetic: a small chain of quick-oil-change shops, a hard-rock radio station, a local developer of heinous homogenous subdivisions that featured faux gas lampposts and ranch houses with marbleized columns.

"Oh, and we just got a mall," he told me. "That's where we need the most help."

It was here that I finally began to get interested.

Saying "mall" to me was like saying "blow job" to a sex addict. Though I certainly didn't look like it at the time, I loved malls, lived for them, scoured them for skinny clothes, dreaming of the day when I could fit into anything tailored from Banana Republic. And then, depressed, I would hit Orange Julius and Sbarro's in the food court and end up buying something useless from Kirkland's.

"I am *very* interested in helping your company reach its potential, and, with your mentorship, I'm sure you will help me reach my own potential."

Had I just said this? Out loud?

I hated myself. But I couldn't move back home with my parents. That would be the ultimate failure.

"Okay. Good, good," he said. "I like what I hear. Let me go ahead and introduce you to the president of our firm. Follow me."

We walked down a long hallway that seemed akin to a gangplank to a closed office, from behind which was blaring the sounds of Michael Jackson's "Man in the Mirror."

Barney Fife knocked softly at first, then a touch louder, and, seeing no results, he banged the door with a bit more temerity.

"What?" a high-pitched voice boomed.

Barney peeked his head through a crack in the door and half yelled, "I have a candidate for the junior account position I'd like you to meet."

"Are you kidding me? I've got a meeting in an hour, and I need to psyche myself up for it. Give me a second."

"Wait here," Barney Fife said, his face twitching, before bolting away, simply leaving me to stand there alone.

"Good luck," he called out as he raced down the darkened hallway, and it was then I could have sworn he added, "You'll need it," but it was already too late: I was standing paralyzed, listening to a voice from behind the door parrot the high-pitched vocals of

Michael, when suddenly it flung open and I was confronted by a black behemoth wearing a touch of eyeliner, a super shiny suit, and a tiger-striped tie.

"Welcome, welcome, welcome, my little one."

He introduced himself with a flourish, bending forward, nearly bowing, like I was the queen. My worries, oddly, vanished. I felt flattered. Honored to be treated as the lady I knew I was.

He asked me to sit in a leather chair that fronted his giant desk while he continued to analyze himself in a large dressing mirror that was standing off to one side of his office.

"You have made it to the inner sanctum," he said. "Congratulations."

"Thanks."

He talked in a rather feline, feminine voice, and was very delicate with all of his gestures. And yet he was imposing in size, sort of the spawn of Eartha Kitt and Warren Sapp.

Instead of asking about my résumé, the firm's president eyed me over and stated, "Mmmmm, I like a boy with some meat on his bones."

The hair on my arms tingled.

I felt like that big girl in *Silence of the Lambs* who gets thrown down into the well and has to put on the lotion all the time.

And yet somewhere deep down I was oddly flattered, too. After my last interview debacle, it was nice to know my appearance wouldn't be cause for a never-ending corporate joke.

The president quickly segued, asking about my experience, and it became clear to me that I'd obviously misunderstood him, that he'd probably said, "I like a candidate with some meat on his résumé."

I talked about my journalism internships, and then he asked if I was creative, so I eagerly showed him my portfolio of writing and design samples.

He then asked if I could work under pressure.

I lied and said yes, omitting the fact that I flipped out if people watched me microwave.

"Can you start Monday?" he purred.

"Yes! Thank you for your confidence in me!"

I walked out into the hallway, the door closed, and Michael again began blaring in the background.

No salary had been discussed, no benefits, no vacation. I didn't even know what time to show up Monday, much less where I would be working.

But it didn't matter.

I had a job.

I arrived at work on Monday at seven fifty A.M. sharp, wearing exactly the same outfit I'd worn to all my interviews.

I was raring to get started, to prove my worth, to be a working man in the city.

But the door was locked, and I didn't have a key, so I waited in the hallway.

My watch rotated from eight to eight fifteen, to eight thirty, and still no one had arrived. I peed in a restroom at the end of the hall around eight forty-five and began to panic, standing in the stall, knowing in my heart this wasn't how a normal office operated.

Perhaps, I thought, as I stared at graffiti on the stall wall that disturbingly told me that CHE GUEVARA IS A FAGGOT!, working at a creative place, the office opened later in the morning.

But at nine I was still alone. I looked into a few other suites on the floor, and people were indeed answering phones and getting coffee, and businesses were open for, well, business.

Finally, at about a quarter past nine, the sigher showed up and asked who I was and what I was doing loitering outside her door.

"I'm Wade, the new hire."

"We hired somebody?"

"I guess you didn't get the memo?"

She polished off her cigarette, stamped it out in the fern, and sighed. "*Memo*? Ha! We're not real good communicators."

"But this is a communications firm?"

I intended for this to sound casual, like a joke, but it came out desperate, along the lines of yelling, "What do you mean I've woken up to find a bomb implanted in my anus?"

"*Mmm-hmmm,*" she said, sighing.

While the secretary sighed her way around the office, starting the coffee, booting up her computer, starting the printer, I stood and waited for her to show me to my office.

"Where will I be working?" I finally asked.

"Dunno," she sighed. "Both offices are filled."

Both?

And then I heard screaming outside. Barney Fife entered, holding a bag of Dunkin Donuts, followed by the president, who was berating him.

"You idiot! You never open your mouth at a meeting when I'm present, got it? I am the one the client is hiring. I *am* the firm. Got it?"

Barney Fife got a cup of coffee, looking around in his shell-shocked sort of way, and headed to his office.

"Who are you?" the president asked.

"I'm Wade Rouse. You hired me on Friday and told me to start today."

He wagged his big finger at me and I followed him down the hall.

He flung open a door, flicked on a light switch that triggered a dull fluorescent the strength of a dying bug zapper, and said, "Here you go."

And then he walked away.

My new "office" was a six-by-six storage closet cum office nerve center, a tiny space crammed with boxes of envelopes and stationery and promotional key chains and pens and tons of wires that snaked through the walls and ceiling tiles, as if I was being kept in the reptile house of a zoo.

Jammed in the corner was a tiny wood desk and chair, the kind a sixth grader might have in his bedroom to do his homework. My only office equipment was an ancient typewriter.

There was no computer or phone.

I sat in that storage room, idly, for hours, without anyone coming to check on me or talk to me or tell me what to do. I stacked boxes, rearranged wires, and cleaned off my desk, going so far as to place a fistful of promotional pens in a promotional cup and position it by my typewriter.

I sat and waited for an assignment.

I placed two pens in the back of my hair like chopsticks.

I played drums on empty boxes.

I cleaned out my wallet.

Around noon, on the verge of tears, I went to the lobby.

"Is everything okay?" I asked the sigher.

"Why do you ask?" she sighed.

"I'm just sitting in there...you know...alone. I don't know what to do. I don't have anything to do."

"Consider yourself lucky," she sighed.

And then her phone rang.

I got a cup of water and retreated to my coat closet. And then, as if my desk had a silent alarm system attached to it, the president sprinted down the hall and began screaming, "No drinks on the wood! No water stains! Use a coaster! Jesus Christ! This is a professional office!"

As he stormed away, I finally realized why Barney Fife had stacked his coffee on a cumulonimbus cloud.

I was working in a loony bin.

But just as I started to walk out, I thought: This has to be a joke. I am being tested. This is just like getting hazed in a fraternity; once I pass the test, I'll be let in on the joke and welcomed into the club.

And, still in the back of my head, lurked the reality: If you lose this job, you're moving back in with your parents. Talk about a loony bin.

Around four P.M., while nodding off in my David Blaine–sized torture box, the president appeared in my doorway, handed me a fifteen-second radio ad for a thirty-minute oil-change company, and asked for my thoughts.

"Well..." I started.

"Like I give a shit," he laughed. "Retype this. Cap every word and double-space every line so it's easier for the on-air talent to read."

"I don't have a computer," I said.

"There's a typewriter. That should be all you need right now."

"Are you pulling my leg?"

"I'd like to pull your chubby little leg," he leered, before departing.

Since, first and foremost, I'm a people pleaser, the type of guy who would pick Kirstie Alley up from food rehab and drive her immediately to a Steak 'n Shake, I typed the memo lickety-split, like I was back in high school finishing my typing final: *The quick brown fox jumps over the lazy dog.*

I ran the copy back to him.

While he looked it over, his phone rang. And rang. And rang. He looked at me before gesturing for me to answer it.

"Mr. X's office," I said. "How may I help you? Hold, please."

I looked at the big black man in front of me, who was loosening his tie and, I believe, leering at my ass.

"It's a Miss Q from the mall," I said.

He gestured to me in a highly dramatic writing motion, so I grabbed a pad and pen and took a note.

"She wants to discuss having a fashion show to showcase their retailers," I said excitedly after hanging up.

And then my boss said, "I'm getting a boner."

My mouth went dry, my heart raced.

"What? Excuse me?" I asked.

"I'll have to phone her," he said, laughing at me. "What did you think I said?"

The president asked me to meet him at the mall the next morning, an assignment that eased my troubling first day.

A mall.

A fashion show.

Models.

It was a dream.

However, upon my arrival the next day, the president not only refused to introduce me to the client, but he also didn't even acknowledge me. Instead he handed me his clipboard and a walkie-talkie. "Listen to every word I say," he instructed. "And take down pertinent points that we're discussing with the retailers, got it?"

I didn't.

"Why don't I come with you?" I asked. "Wouldn't that be easier?"

"Don't question me!" he bellowed.

And then he scurried away with a severe-looking woman who, it seems, had bathed in White Diamonds.

A walkie-talkie? I thought. Are we in third grade? Are we going to have Jeno's Pizza Rolls and watch The Goonies *later?*

I took a seat on a bench in the middle of the mall, where I quickly noticed I was next to a man in a wheelchair with an affixed oxygen tank. Upon closer inspection, I noticed that his body was directly under a giant plastic birch tree, the lower limbs of which were, literally, resting on his face.

I heard the walkie-talkie crackle and the president blabbering, but his words were garbled and disconnected, like when I tried to telephone my brother with a tin can when I was six.

"Gobble-dee-gobblezee-zook, sassamafrass-amatass."

This was what I heard on the walkie-talkie. So this was what I wrote.

I heard coughing and turned to see that there was now a leaf in the wheelchair-bound man's mouth. He was sort of gumming it, unhappily, and trying to spit it out, like I did when a piece of the plastic liner got trapped in the corn portion of my Hungry Man TV dinner.

"Are you okay?" I yelled at him, firmly but neighborly. "Can you talk? Do you need help?"

He didn't respond.

And then the old bastard started coughing and choking, which alarmed me, so I got up to push his wheelchair maybe two feet forward, to remove his face from the tree, and the once comatose man suddenly began to wail, screaming in an insane, *I'm being attacked by a fat man with a walkie-talkie!* sort of way.

Two women, holding denim vests with embroidered Holly Hobbie gardening girls on the back, sprinted to his aid from a nearby store. "What are you doing?" they yelled at me. "Leave him alone!"

"What?" I asked.

"What are you doing? Do we need to call security?"

"What were *you* doing?" I yelled. "He was smothering on a birch branch."

And, as fate would have it, just at that moment, the president and White Diamonds appeared out of nowhere, me fighting with two Holly Hobbie devotees over an incontinent man, my clipboard miles away.

"I'm so sorry," I said to them. "You wouldn't believe what happened."

"Can I see your notepad?" he said to me, while White Diamonds tried to stifle a laugh.

"*Gobble-dee-gobblezee-zook, sassamafrass-amatass,*" was pretty much what he read.

"You have some nerve," he said to me. "Who do you think you are?"

I tried to save face and began to introduce myself to the woman. "I'm sorry for the confusion. I'm Wade Rouse. I'm the new junior account executive."

"You're my *secretary*!" my boss laughed. "And you're not a very good one at that!"

The two of them cackled, and the president yelled, "Go back to the office. I'll deal with you later."

For some reason I did, always believing I could turn a situation around, make it better.

Near the end of the day, the president summoned me to his office.

"I don't know what kind of stunt you were pulling, but you humiliated me," he said, "Man in the Mirror" playing again in the background.

"I'm sorry, but I don't even know what's going on here," I said, my voice rising. "I was hired as a junior account executive, but I have no office or phone or computer or any real idea why I'm here. You've yelled and screamed, and treated me very poorly."

I wanted to sound James Bond, but it came out all Scarlett O'Hara.

The president leered at me from head to toe, his right hand crammed deeply in his pants pocket. And then it began moving quickly, back and forth, back and forth.

He was playing pocket pool.

I knew. I mean, I'd been an expert in the game ever since seventh grade, when I first saw Tommy Wilkins be skins during basketball in gym class.

"You're here to learn from me, be my secretary. I can take you places. It could be a win-win."

The president said this softly, throatily. Then he smiled and said, "You know, I like young men with a little meat on their bones. I'm a chub chaser. I bet you're familiar with that, aren't you, Wade?"

I wasn't. In fact, it didn't even sound flattering. I wanted to lose all my baggage, not be admired for having it.

I watched my boss's hand move more quickly in his pants. It looked like he was trying to start a fire.

Michael sang in the background: *"I've been a victim of . . . a selfish kind of love . . . "*

The president moved toward me.

Finally, after two days on the job, I did what I should have done from the very beginning: I ran, as quickly as any self-respecting chub chasee could, out of his office, down the hallway, through the lobby, down the stairs, out of the building, past the Quik Cash, and to my car.

The last sound I remember hearing—besides my heartbeat—was a sigh.

On the way home, I turned on the radio (this, mind you, was in the day before cell phones, before I could easily spread the word of my nightmare) and heard a local DJ announce, "Don't forget, tomorrow is Secretary's Day. Do something special for that one person who makes your life a little easier every day!"

And so I did.

After two full days of employment, I showed up the next morning around seven A.M., long before I knew anyone would arrive, and slipped an envelope under the door.

The envelope, addressed to the president, didn't contain an official resignation letter per se, but instead held a Secretary's Day card I had picked up at an adult novelty shop the evening before, just after I heard the local DJ's announcement.

I realized I would never be paid for my tenure, nor use anyone there as a reference, so I wanted to relay a sentiment that summed up my experience.

While I would never see my boss again, I like to imagine that he smiled when he opened the card, which featured a very obese white woman—her giant breasts flung over a typewriter, half glasses bouncing, taking a memo while she was getting barebacked by a black man in a three-piece suit.

The message inside?

"I may be a whore, my darling, but I'll never be your secretary."

Homo Depot

A few years back, when Gary and I lived in the city, we went to Homo Depot every Arbor Day to pick out a tree.

For gardening gays, like Gary, Arbor Day is a major holiday, on par with Christmas and Hanukkah.

I am not a gardening gay.

First, I don't like to get my nails dirty. I don't like the feel of earth under my hands and feet. That's why we build houses and sidewalks and have cute shirtless boys mow our yard. Second, I don't understand the importance of picking out and planting a tree, which will most likely just be cut down in three years when Gary decides he wants to blow out a wall and expand the master bath. And, finally, I don't get these Go Green urbanites who spend hours in Homo Depot acting all P. Allen Smith when they only have two square feet of deck space on which to pot some basil and oregano.

And yet every Arbor Day I must go with Gary to nurseries and landscaping centers, kind of like I must force myself to smile when I am presented a baby who looks like W.C. Fields.

Taking me to Homo Depot is the equivalent of having Michael J. Fox perform your Lasik surgery. I become immobilized as soon as I enter a home-improvement center and typically stop cold by the magazine rack at the entrance to peruse pretty pictures of and nice articles on people who have built water gardens all by themselves, or installed a designer kitchen, feats that simultaneously astound and baffle me, like Kevin Costner's career.

Most times, I gander at those magazines that show, in excruciatingly precise, step-by-step detail, how to wire an outdoor light or install a faucet and wonder if they were drawn and written in Mandarin.

While Gary wanders, I become bored, and I try to count how many gay employees (not counting the lesbians) work at Homo Depot and know absolutely nothing about home improvement. My personal record came at one of our city's newer stores, where I once counted sixteen and a half (the half being a rather straight-looking young man with a wedding band who, when asked by a customer which refrigerator was best, said, "The pretty one," and pointed at a stainless model).

Often I find myself looking around cluelessly in that gigantic aisle that features nothing but lug nuts, the four-mile-long row that has like four hundred thousand bins of bolts and screws, all of which look exactly the same.

My goal? To see how long it takes an employee to give up or strangle me to death.

"Can I help you with something, sir?" the screw guy will ask me.

"I need a bolt."

"What kind of bolt, sir?"

"A metal one."

"May I ask what you will be using the bolt for?"

"To hold something together."

"What exactly needs to be held together, sir?"

"This bolt-free item."

When I'm bored with this game, I wander into refrigerators and ovens and tell the appliance salesmen and kitchen designers that I have "an unlimited budget" and "a love affair with stainless and granite."

Occasionally I wander into those free seminars Homo Depot offers and stare at the freaks who feel compelled to learn how to spackle or lay tile or, worst of all, sponge paint.

"Don't you want to learn how to do it yourself?" a gay man will ask me excitedly as I stand in the back.

"Not unless it has to do with bronzer," I will reply.

I have a defective gene that kicks in during certain situations—like when someone raves about their stay at a La Quinta, or buys things with exact change, or wants to, like right now, learn how to stencil and border their scrapbooking room with windmills or watering cans—which makes me want to grab a straightedge and slice everyone's throats.

Gary's favorite trick, when I'm lost in my own world and away from him too long, is to go to the lesbian who works the PA in customer service—every Homo Depot has one—and have her announce, "We have a lost child in the store. His name is Wade. Wade, would you please locate a man in an orange apron and have him bring you to customer service. Your mommy is looking for you."

Lesbians will always play along.

"What kind of tree should we plant for Arbor Day?" Gary asks after I turn the corner.

We head outside to the gardening area, a football-stadium-size lot containing every flower, tree, fountain, and paving stone known to man.

This is usually my time to stop and tan my face.

Gary drags me to the tree section, where thousands of mini-saplings are flapping in that hair-blasting wind that always seems to whip through Homo Depot garden centers.

"What do you think?"

Every tree looks exactly the same to me.

Twigs in buckets with leaves.

"How about that one?" I say, looking at its tag. "It looks like it will be pretty one day."

"Oh, my God! That's a Bradford pear. It's the Calista Flockhart of trees. It'll snap in two in the slightest storm."

"How about this one?" I ask.

"Are you serious? That's a cedar. It's the ugliest tree in the world, and it'll dwarf our house one day."

By this time I have become shell-shocked and fearful of saying anything, like Julia Roberts in that movie where she runs away from her crazy husband but knows he's found her when all her towels are neatly folded.

I point at another tree.

"Sweetie, that's a sweet gum. Those are the ones that all the straight people in our neighborhood plant that drop those thorny balls that we trip over when we walk the dog."

I hear laughter, and we turn to find a man who looks like Rupert Everett.

"You have one of *those*, too?" he asks, gesturing toward me with his perfectly formed head.

One of those? What am I, a Weimaraner? And who says that out loud in front of someone? The trick is to belittle people quietly.

Rupert Everett's partner is a husky, balding man who looks a bit like a cage-fighting walrus. Obviously he's a brain surgeon or criminal attorney who makes tons of money and nabbed his dream man, who now wears the he-capris in the family.

Gary laughs. "Yeah, I have one of those."

"Hello!" I say. "We're standing right here. Talking in third person doesn't mean we're not here."

The cage-fighting walrus laughs.

"Are you here for Arbor Day, too?" Rupert Everett asks.

Now, this immediately qualifies as the stupidest conversation I've ever had in my life. And then I look around and see that Homo Depot is absolutely teeming with fags pushing carts loaded with saplings. Arbor Day is like Gay Pride with mulch instead of drag queens.

"Yeah," Gary says. "Every year!"

Gary is blinking his big lashes wildly, as if a sparrow just flew into one of his eyes. Gary was born with a double row of lashes, like a supermodel. I was born with albino-colored lashes. If I don't tint them, I look like those cave-dwelling beasts from the movie *Descent*.

Gary blinks again. *Jesus.* I know the signs: He's subconsciously flirting with Rupert.

"I just don't know what tree to plant. It has to be…right, you know?"

"I know!" squeals Rupert. "But *they* don't understand."

They?

"I'm thinking of a Japanese maple," Gary says. "I have a little Zen garden in our city backyard, and I think it would add a sense of dramatic tranquility."

Dramatic tranquility? That doesn't even make sense. That's like saying "peaceful war."

"Fabulous choice," Rupert says. "I'm thinking of a peony tree."

"Oh, my God!" Gary screams. "I didn't think of that. How stunning!"

Why don't you two get a room and jerk off while reading native plant guides to one another?

Then it hits me: I look around Homo Depot and notice that most couples are like us, one person interested in gardening, the other bored out of his skull. And then I notice that most couples are beginning to pair up, one of the men talking excitedly to a complete stranger about wood. It's like closing time at a gay bar.

I certainly don't need a do-it-yourself workshop to learn how to fight for my man, and I pride myself on the fact—at the very least—that I am way smarter and way more cynical than most men. I know

I can pull myself together in time to either bullshit myself out of any situation or bury my competition in bile.

"You know, honey," I say, putting my arm tenderly around Gary's waist, "I was thinking we should buy two dogwoods—one pink, one white—and plant them so they intertwine as they grow, as sort of a symbol of our love."

Gary is a weeper. He cries when a pigeon hits his windshield going under an overpass, while I scream, "Bam! Got the little germ spreader!"

He starts misting up, and Rupert glares at me.

I go in for the kill.

"But I don't know what kind of mulch we should use, since we'll have a pink tree and a white tree?" I ask stupidly. "What do you think?"

I ask Gary this question while looking at Rupert, who I know will interject in order to impress.

"Red mulch, no doubt," he answers. "It would complement the pink and white."

Gary lifts his hand to his mouth in horror and stares at Rupert as though he just poked a puppy in the eye with a sharp stick. Gary despises red mulch, loathes it, in fact, more than Ann Coulter or fat people in Crocs. He considers red mulch tacky, classless.

I knew what Rupert would say, of course. I'm a former journalist: I notice the little things. I can even read upside down.

Rupert's nails were rimmed in red. The tacky little jackass might as well have been branded with a scarlet *R*.

Rupert looks at me and then at his partner.

"Why can't you be like *him*?" he says to the cage-fighting walrus, nodding at me before storming away.

Gary and I buy two dogwoods, which he plants later that afternoon while bawling the whole time.

The next year, I suggest we go to Lowe's.

MAY

"All women become like their mothers. That is their tragedy. No man does. That's his."

—OSCAR WILDE

Fact or Fiction?

I was asked one spring, when I was in middle school, as my family ate Mother's Day dinner, if I was thinking of going out for Little League.

I laughed, thinking it was a joke, but when it was repeated, I began to smile prettily while shoving a forkful of roast in my mouth and bat my eyes, as though my beauty might blind my family from yet another follow-up.

My mother refused to let that happen.

"Why, yes, we are a family of very gifted athletes."

While I consider my mother to be one of the smartest women in the world, she has always had this odd habit of just making things up on the spot and then immediately telling them with complete conviction as if they were the absolute truth.

I nicknamed this habit "fact or fiction," a term she never found particularly amusing.

For instance, I have never been aware of anyone in my family ever playing a sport on a highly competitive level, unless Chinese checkers counted. Only my father, who was too small to play high school football, tried, and he played "little man" sports like tennis and golf, although he was a lightweight boxer in college and has the nose to prove it.

My mother, however, was never an athlete—it is impossible for her to make it to the bathroom without pulling a groin muscle—and my brother never played a sport in his life, unless you counted picking the tails off lizards or shooting squirrels as an organized childhood sport. I've seen pictures of my mom in athletic gear, such as the time she wore a football helmet to cover a bad blonde dye job, or a baseball jersey when it was Halloween, but it would be a stretch to say we were a family of athletes.

"Fact or fiction?" I yelled at the table.

My mother glared at me as I jammed another forkful of roast into my mouth and batted my eyes, and I immediately knew I would pay for this outburst.

"You are mistaken, sir! That is fact! James Wade, you have the genes of—*what!*—a great athlete residin' in your bones, isn't that correct?"

The only thing I had residing in my bones, if anyone in my family cared to open their eyes and actually look, was a lot of gay genes, considering I was a sixth grader who adored chokers, hemp bracelets, friendship pins, and mood rings. Never mind that I secretly pinched my cheeks to make myself look flushed and excited.

"You are mistaken!" my mother repeated, turkey-walking away from the dining room table to retrieve a collection of family photo albums.

One of my mom's favorite things to do, especially on Mother's Day, was to get out our old photo albums and pore through them, inventing happier tales than the ones depicted in the actual pictures.

The photo of me crying on Christmas because I had unwrapped a football instead of an Easy-Bake?

Tears of joy.

The photo of me fixing my hair while my brother tossed that football my way?

I was reaching high to make an amazing reception.

Just as my mom was saying, "Just before your hole in one!" and turning a page to display a photo of me applying cherry ChapStick while singing into a putter as our family played miniature golf, I yelled, "Fact or fiction!"

"Fact!" she screamed.

"It's too late anyway," I said. "Teams have already been formed."

And I was right. These were the important dates all tortured gay boys remembered from their country school days, along with how to skip class every time it was shirts-skins basketball day in gym class, or feign illness whenever the nurse announced it was scoliosis week.

To try and prove her point, my mother still checked around town, but was saddened to discover that:

Bob's Butcher Shop—whose uniforms featured a muscled pig swinging a bat—was filled.

The overall factory—whose uniforms looked, well, like overalls—was filled.

The Dairy Dip—whose uniforms featured a scoop of ice cream that looked like a dripping baseball whizzing into space—was filled.

And my favorite, Connie's Hair Barn—whose uniforms featured a comb dusting off home plate with a brush—was filled.

It seemed I could breathe another year.

But then my mother walked in one night after work, wearing her bloodied scrubs and a maniacal grin, and said, "Daphne Wilkins has saved the day!"

Her son, Willie, our town's equivalent of Robby Benson and Roger Staubach all rolled into one beautiful boy—had broken his arm over Christmas and was not expected to play baseball this year. But his family did have athletic genes, and he had recovered in time to play. Daphne had, at the last minute, persuaded her company to sponsor our team.

So, fittingly—the irony too much to take at such a young age—I lickety-split found myself standing in middle-right field wearing a skintight, bright-pink uniform that simply read "Mary Kay."

I looked like a bloated flamingo.

I stood out there as if under a klieg light and cursed God, who I did not realize until now had such a wicked sense of humor.

It was a nightmare, attending practices, dropping fly balls, whiffing at home plate, my family in the bleachers watching my every move, critiquing my play and the practices on rides to the Dairy Dip in the Rambler after we'd finished.

But what did they see?

Not the truth, obviously, as their love for me was blinding their vision.

What did I see?

I saw myself standing tense and motionless, holding my glove straight out in front of my body like Wonder Woman with her bracelets, looking as if I was trying to halt a runaway bullet. I saw myself standing at the plate, blowing bubbles with my gum, waving at people in the stands, staring dreamily at boys whose uniforms fit like gloves. I had no idea what I was doing out there, so most times I simply panicked, happy to strike out on three straight pitches.

Instead of even looking at the pitcher, I would stare at the vast expanse of pink fabric that funneled into my navel as if I were a pretty, pink, pregnant woman.

Though I had been forced to be on this team because I wanted to please my parents, to fit somehow into the fabric of rural America, I initially agreed because I believed that my team—apart from Willie—would comprise a band of ne'er-do-wells, nerds, and nincompoops, since all the good athletes in town had already been plucked to play for other teams.

In fact, I would dream at night that Willie would coach me every day, one-on-one, making me better, and then, of course, he would fall in love with me. And at the end of the season, as a thank-you and sign of my commitment to him, I would give Willie one of my mood rings over the red mosaic votive holder at Pizza Hut, pretending that we were canalside in Venice instead of sitting in a former Radio Shack eating iceberg lettuce.

But Willie, being the town's athletic god, had been able to persuade the best players to abandon their other teams and play with him, the promise of an undefeated team and league championship seemingly in the bag.

I was retained only because the team had to field ten players and because Willie's mother had promised my mother, and the team was not happy, to say the least, about this maternal verbal agreement, so I ended up being alternately abused and ignored like Dilbert Reynolds, the slow but evil kid in town who ate Elmer's glue, burned Hot Wheels on the sidewalk, and wrote dirty words on his Lite-Brite.

Thus I was quickly designated the team's "fourth" outfielder, a position I wouldn't realize until much later in life didn't even exist in real baseball, and so I was buried in deep right-center field, not far from the hurricane fence that served as the field's home-run wall.

Still, my team was confident early on, and it felt good to be around winners for once, naturally blond boys who didn't have to use Sun-In, boys who didn't eat Pop-Tarts or Funyuns and already had perfectly formed six-packs.

"Aren't you hot?" Willie would ask me at practice. "Why don't you take your shirt off?"

"Ummm, I'm good. Have a wicked sunburn on my shoulders," I'd lie, not wanting anyone to see the obvious: that I needed a training bra.

Eventually, I had to take the field in a real contest, and it was then I realized the hard truth: All the other teams in the league were pissed at Willie for stealing their best players, and so their anger fueled them, drove them—like revenge-minded killers—a long-standing vendetta waiting to be settled.

In our very first game we played Bob's Butcher Shop, and I remember going 0 for 4 and striking out looking every time, interested more in seeing how tan my hands were getting than in actually swinging the bat. Although my parents seemed to believe they were watching a young, albeit plumper, Mickey Mantle in action, snapping photos in the bleachers, my mother screaming, "Hey, batter, batter—yes, I'm talking to you, sir!—batter," my teammates comprehended my shocking lack of talent and interest. That's because with every ball that was hit even remotely in my direction, two outfielders would converge and call me off, yelling "Mine!" and leaving me to pedal backwards until my butt was pressed against the hurricane fence.

In our first game, we were leading, if I remember correctly, 8–7 in the bottom of the ninth, and Bob's Butcher Shop had a man on third and two outs when their final batter lofted a pop-up high into the sky, as high as a plane it seemed. I waited for my teammates to come running toward me, to help me, but I only heard, "I've lost it in the sun! I've lost it in the sun!" followed by the one word I never expected to hear: "YOURS!"

On a blindingly sunny day, I was the only one able to see the ball, thanks to the fact that I had tanned my whole childhood and was oblivious to the sun. I followed the ball's trajectory up, without the aid of sunglasses or eye black, high above the field's light posts and into the blue sky.

I remember holding my glove straight over my head, my left arm stiff like rigor mortis had set into my body. My right arm, tellingly, was held askew on my right hip as though I might be modeling capri pants or a jaunty summer bracelet. I felt dizzy and faint.

My hands were shaking, my body quaking. I could hear my mother yelling.

And then I had an epiphany: I can catch this ball. I can prove myself to the team. I can prove myself to this town.

But suddenly a lone cloud, puffy and white, happened to stagger by slowly, like a drunk cotton ball, and the baseball simply disappeared into it.

And then, forgetting what goes up must come down, the base-ball just as suddenly—*thwack!*—smacked me squarely in the face.

I went down hard, like a lumberjack's tree, but magically, ironi-cally, comically, the ball did not roll away. Rather, my girth held it in place, and the ball spun for a second between my pink breasts like a pinball before finally settling on the top of my belly, where it sat in my ample navel like a golf ball on a tee.

"Grab the ball! Grab the ball!"

My teammates all began running toward me, yelling. I could see Willie's face in the distance, screaming in slow motion, the words distorted, "The ball hasn't hit the ground. Just grab it with your glove and we win!"

I felt all warm inside; Willie was talking to me.

I had yet to realize that the warmth was due to a vicious nose-bleed.

I saw Willie coming toward me, yelling, "Don't move! I'll get it!" And just as he leaned down to straddle my body, to take me in his arms, I reached up in a dreamlike state to hug him.

"Don't!" he yelled, too late.

The ball rolled off my tummy and onto the ground.

We lost.

Willie removed his glove and angrily threw it at me.

"You stupid idiot!" he yelled.

I wanted to tell my soulmate his phrase was redundant, and that calling me either "stupid" or an "idiot" would suffice, but I knew that wouldn't do any good.

"There are other sports," my dad told me at the Dairy Dip after the game, "individual sports, like shot put and discus."

I knew these were dumb, fat-guy sports, ones where you could finish fortieth at a track meet and still get a medal. I didn't want that.

"Tough way to go down, huh?" Willie's mom said to my parents, licking a twist cone. "Maybe you need to work with Wade a little more...hit him a few hundred pop-ups every night."

I looked over at my mom expectantly.

I could see "fact or fiction" ready to roll.

Yes, like any good mother worth her salt, mine also refused to have her family belittled.

"We are a family of artists, not athletes, Daphne, didn't you know that about the Rouses?" my mother asked. "Our family's history is filled with famous painters and artists and inventors, isn't that correct, Ted? Those are the genes my son has."

Now, my father was an engineer who didn't have an artistic gene in his bones, unless you counted as art the fact that he outlined his tools on the wall of his work shed in blue chalk.

"I didn't realize that," Daphne said, rather sarcastically.

"We don't talk about it much," my mother whispered to her.

But others, it seemed, would.

Within a week, our family's fact-or-fiction faux-arts background had spread around town and garnered the attention of our middle-school band director.

Which is why, later that summer, I was specially invited to attend his band open house and instrument-selection night. I walked in to find that the windowless, egg-carton padded room was filled with our town's smartest and most sensitive kids—"the losers," as my brother called them. And yet I instantly felt more comfortable here, in a band room, than I ever had on a baseball diamond.

I scanned the room.

And winced.

There were Loralynn Jenkins and Vesta Rutini, big girls with even bigger moles, wearing winter coats even though it was ninety-seven degrees outside and 150 degrees in the room. Their greasy hair was slicked back and separated into two stiff braids that made it look as if they had just undergone electroshock therapy. They were fingering xylophones, and, from a distance, it looked as if they might be holding shiny pretzel sticks, the instruments dwarfed by their size.

There was Tabitha Buchanan, who was lovingly called "Tubby Buchanan" at school, and she was standing, fittingly, beside a tuba while smiling gleefully. From a distance it looked as though two very happy, very fat, very pale sisters were posing for a picture.

Ray Davenport, whom a couple of the mean boys called Gay Davenport as though that was his given name, was playing the piccolo. Really playing.

Ray had practiced, and it showed, notes floating forth that sounded like real notes you'd hear on the radio. Ray, unfortunately, drooled from both sides of his mouth when he played, like my dog did when I held a piece of steak in front of his face, and, considering the way he blew and went to town on his instrument, I had to admit his nickname seemed to fit.

"This is a house of freaks," said my brother, who had been forced by our parents to join us after he'd been caught chewing Skoal behind the high school bus barn. "Can't I wait outside? I don't want anyone to think I'm actually with these people."

But my brother was right. After he left, I focused on my primary purpose: to select an instrument less on its musical intricacies—the way its sound touched my soul—and more on how it would minimize my big-boy size while maximizing my reputation at school, not realizing at the time that neither goal was attainable.

I walked around the room and surveyed the instruments that were on display:

A xylophone? I glanced over at Loralynn and Vesta. Definitely not.

A piccolo? I looked at Gay, still sucking away. No way.

Tuba? I checked out Tubby and her sister. Next.

Drums. They would accentuate my stomach.

Trumpet. Not big enough, and too many people were already clamoring for it.

And then I saw it, the one instrument that stood alone. I walked over to it and ran my hands over its golden body, quickly becoming enamored by its uniqueness. I picked it up and blew through the large silver mouthpiece. A deep, bold blare shot forth.

Manly, I thought.

"This is it!" I yelled at my parents. "This is it!"

"A trombone?" my dad said. "Now why in the hell would you pick a trombone?"

I couldn't say the real reasons: that I thought its size and its big bell would make me look thin in comparison, that people would focus on the slide moving back and forth instead of on my girth, and that it sounded deep and commanding, unlike my real voice.

"It's the foundation for every piece of music," I said.

Our band director, a bouncy, thin man, rushed over and said, "He's right! The trombone is *the* key instrument to all musical pieces. It's rarely the lead, but it's always the key. However, we already have three trombonists coming back next year, and we really don't need another."

I looked at my mother, ready to cry, and she sensed I would be crushed if I couldn't play my instrument of destiny.

"How about the clarinet?" the band director asked.

"My great-great-uncle on my mother's side played trombone for the Count Basie Orchestra," my mother said. "That is correct!"

The band director looked at her, genuinely confused, wondering if she was really telling the truth, which, of course, she wasn't.

"Fact or fiction?" I mouthed to my mother, whose eyes widened with excitement.

"I guess a band could always use another talented trombonist," he said.

For the next six years, my mother and father would cheer me on from snow-covered streets as I marched by in epaulets, spats, and a two-foot-tall white fuzzy hat playing "Jingle Bell Rock." They would snap pictures from the bleachers as I played "Apache Dance" with the band, releasing the spit from my trombone between songs. They would even watch as I played Inspector Trotter from Agatha Christie's *Mousetrap,* poorly meshing an Ozarks accent with an English one. In fact, I would go on to do things my parents never anticipated, never expected. Their dreams of watching their son hit a home run, or make a game-saving tackle, or hit the game-winning free throw would be replaced by a son who would rather recite his own poetry.

And yet—always, always—my parents would be there to cheer me on, sitting in empty auditoriums or standing on deserted streets when other parents had long ago grown tired of the out-of-tune music and out-of-step marching of their dorky kids. I would look over and see my parents, clapping wildly, looks of absolute bewilderment frozen on their faces.

Years later over a Mother's Day dinner, just after my first feature story had been published in a fairly prominent newspaper, my mother proudly turkey-walked away to retrieve a photo album, carefully lifting the plastic to add my clip to our family history to proclaim, "I always knew we came from a family of artists, isn't that correct, Wade?"

Out of habit I wanted to yell, "Fact or fiction?" but instead I looked into her eyes, smiled, pulled her close, and hugged her, knowing that for once in her life she just might be telling the truth.

The Privileged Few

My grandma Shipman used to install twenty-foot inflatable reindeer on her roof, wrap our gifts in velvet bows, and bake and hand decorate hundreds of Santa Claus cookies, whipping and dyeing the icing so that Santa's coat looked red and velveteen, his beard white as snow, his eyes glistening from just that little extra coating of sugar.

Birthdays meant homemade cakes with mile-high frosting and colorful balloons filling the kitchen. Halloween meant carving pumpkins and laughing at witches that had flown directly into my grandma's light pole outside her home.

But when my grandmother became ill and her health slowly and methodically began to decline, our holidays became more minimalist.

It was too difficult for me to see my grandmother as some sort of ghost of Christmas past, so I began to stay away more and more during the holidays while she lived in a nursing home. What I missed during this absence, I would later discover, was the fact that my mom had taken on my grandma's role. In fact, my mother spent vast amounts of time in my grandma's nursing-home room re-creating those cherished holidays for her: She lavishly decorated her tree, she helped my grandma carve a pumpkin, and she walked into her room—ignoring all codes and regulations—with sparklers ablaze on the Fourth of July.

One spring evening, after I had not visited home in a particularly long time, my mother called and said, simply but directly, "I think it's time you visited your grandmother in the nursing home. I expect to see you here on Mother's Day."

"But…" I started.

"No buts," my mom said.

"But she's not my mother-mother."

And then my mom hung up on me.

I cussed my entire five-hour drive home, lamenting a lost weekend.

As a young man, I had so many better things to do than visit my grandmother in a nursing home. I had more important things to think about, other things to occupy my time and mind than the very real fact that my grandmother was dying and that youth was fleeting and that, sooner or later, this would eventually be my fate.

When I returned home that Mother's Day, I walked in to find my mother a changed woman.

She seemed harder, tougher, but more resilient. She didn't gush over my return like usual. She said, very directly, "It's about time."

That Sunday, my mother and I went to visit my grandmother on Mother's Day, bringing her a vase of hand-picked peonies from her garden, a heart-shaped box of chocolates, and a stack of elaborately wrapped gifts, ones that looked as if they might be photographed for a style magazine—hauling them into the very nice nursing home and past a few patients, some of whom sat motionless, wheelchair-bound, in the throes of dementia.

As we made our way past, a couple of the patients began to wail and flail, just like babies, unable to convey their emotions that visitors had come to call.

When I passed an ancient woman with a shock of white hair who was eating her lunch off the tray of her wheelchair, she suddenly stuck an arthritic hand into her compartment of corn and tossed a handful of kernels at me and said, in a disturbingly matter-of-fact way, "Well, look who the dog dragged in. If it ain't Sonny, home from the war."

And, just as quickly, she began screaming.

And crying.

Yelling, "Sonny, my baby!"

She was coughing up corn and ghosts from deep within her body.

I crumpled against my mother and we made our way to my grandma's room, which was marked simply and sweetly—like a kindergarten teacher might designate her room on the opening day of school—with only her first name, Viola, drawn in purple crayon, just like her floral namesake.

"I'll go in first," my mom said, taking all the presents. "I want to prepare her. It'll be easier this way, okay?"

There was something about the word *prepare*—prepare my grandma for what, I thought—that made me highly uncomfortable, made my teeth begin to chatter, which I tried to blame on the chill in the nursing home.

I waited outside the door a minute or two until my curiosity got the best of me, and then I peeked my head around the frame and saw not my grandma but a nearly unrecognizable version of her: bloated, pale, a mass of white, brushed-out permed hair, no makeup, no dentures.

My mother was hugging a ghost.

I retreated, standing flat against the blandly cheery wallpaper in the hallway. I tried to grip something to keep myself from falling and finally managed to grab the safety bar that served as the home's functional chair rail before I slid all the way to the linoleum floor.

I shut my eyes to stop the spinning and tried to remember my grandmother as she had been.

My grandma's sole dream in life had been to be a mother and a grandmother. Happiness pulsed from her body, joy radiated from her soul, when she engaged in the simplest of daily pleasures, the ones that made her family smile: frosting a towering, three-layer cherry-chip cake; making homemade pie crusts; pulling sugar cookies out of her oven; giving hugs; decorating for the holidays; simply listening to her family tell the tales of their lives.

My grandma was a simple woman, and—as I grew older and more bitter about my course in life, the fact I was gay, the belief I might never find happiness—I equated her simpleness with naïveté.

That was a mistake.

And when I longed to tell her the story of my life, to have her sit and listen to me around her Formica dining-room table like she did when I was young, it was too late.

"Wade?" I heard my mother say. "Wade, do you want to come in?"

I stood, rounded the corner, and my grandma looked at me, rather blankly, like a babysitter might look at a child they once cared for, with vague familiarity but no emotional ties.

"Mom? It's Wade? It's James Wade. Remember?"

I approached her bed gingerly, as if I were walking around land mines, and she looked at me, trying to fit the pieces together somewhere in her head, and when she did she began to bawl, to caress my face like it was a baby rabbit, as if I were the most tender and precious and beautiful thing she had ever seen.

And then she started screaming.

Always an emotional woman, my grandmother's illness had made her even more emotionally vulnerable, and my mother told me she would now start crying without reason at any minute of the day, unable to put into words her feelings of loss or fear or happiness.

I took a seat in one of those nursing-home chairs that looks inviting but is not comfortable, that begs you to sit but not stay, and listened to the roar of the TV infomercial my grandma had going.

My grandmother *never* watched TV.

I stared out the window and watched it rain, watched the wrens collect at the little feeder my mother had hung just outside of her window. My grandma's world was now this window.

My mom clicked off the TV, silencing the incessant noise and bringing blissful quiet to the room. A sense of calm seemed to envelop not only me but also my grandmother.

And then, out of the blue, my grandma began pointing at pictures on her wall and nightstand, at photos of her husband, her daughters, her grandchildren, of those who had died before her or those who rarely came to visit, and my mom would give one to her and she'd hold it closely, hugging the picture like it was the person, closing her eyes and remembering something from long ago.

My grandma would look at my mom, struggling to lift her hand to her mouth, and then point at the picture she was holding. She was asking my mom to speak for her. We sat for hours that Mother's Day, my mom telling stories of our family for my grandmother, and then at the very end my grandma pointed at me and then at a picture of me she had beside her bed, one of me when I was very little, dressed in a tiny bowtie.

"My baby!" she moaned, managing to find words from somewhere deep inside—words I thought she had lost long ago. "My baby Wade!"

And then it was me who began to cry, to bawl, my false bravado shattering, my gasps causing the wrens at the window to stop eating and take notice of the commotion.

My grandma lifted her fists and dabbed at my face, wiping tears, and then put her hands to her mouth, asking me to talk.

I scooched my chair up to her bed and held her hands, and it was then I knew that she knew me, truly knew me, because she just stared at me, smiling, like a baby at its mom, watching my every move, listening intently to my every word, like she did when I was young and we sat at her little kitchen table.

So I sat for an hour and finally told my grandmother about my life.

When we left her that day, I asked my mom on the ride home, "How do you do it? How *can* you do it? Every day? It's such an obligation."

"The question is," my mom answered, "how can I not do it?"

Her voice got a little shaky, and she said, "Do you know I visit nearly every person there? Their families and friends no longer come, because everyone is too busy to be bothered. Your grandmother spent her whole life sacrificing for me so I could be the first to go to college, the first to have a career, so I could have an easier life than she ever had."

And then my mom slowed the car, her hands trembling on the wheel.

"And it's not an *obligation,* Wade. It's a *privilege.*"

There was an awkward moment of silence. I looked down at the speedometer and noticed my mom was driving twenty miles per hour. Joggers were passing us.

And then my mom, the lifelong nurse who retired and became a hospice nurse, said, "When parents and grandparents age and become infirm, families no longer want to deal with it. They visit in the beginning out of guilt, and then it becomes a hassle, something they have to do between soccer lessons and work. People see these as 'the bad years,' but this is simply our time to take care of our elders, just like my mother cared for me when I was a baby. Those weren't such great years for her, I'm sure. She struggled to put food on the table. And I certainly couldn't talk. I could only tell her what I was thinking or feeling through my emotions. This is the same thing. She is the baby now. And I am the mother. It is my time to care for her, to let her pass on to God with dignity and love, to let her know during every single moment I spend with her these final days that it has been *my privilege* to be her daughter."

It would be the last Mother's Day of my grandmother's life.

And, as I learned that day, it was my privilege—not obligation—to spend it with her.

Pretty Pink Peonies

Many Memorial Days when I was a kid, I would accompany my mom and grandma around to the little cemeteries that dotted the Ozark countryside, the trunk of our car filled with miniature American flags, boxes of Kleenex, and a slew of fresh flowers from my grandmother's gardens.

While Memorial Day typically marked the end of school and beginning of summer vacation, our family would delay our departure to our log cabin on Sugar Creek until all of our "family visits" had been completed.

My grandma and mom would hit as many cemeteries as possible on Memorial Day with a great sense of purpose and a definitive agenda, like holiday shoppers the Friday after Thanksgiving.

My mom would slowly pull our car down the cemeteries' long dirt or gravel driveways and bicker with my grandma about who was buried where, my mom pointing this way, my grandma pointing the other, until both would give up and my mom would put the car in park and we would each grab a handful of fresh flowers, tiny flags, and Kleenex.

Ozark cemeteries were not lush, lavish, or large. Graveyards, as we simply called them, were usually compact and often rested on a rolling foothill or quiet piece of country land next to a pastoral pasture. They were not filled with enormous marble headstones. There were no mausoleums. They did not sit on breathtaking cliffs overlooking the crashing waves of an ocean.

But Ozark cemeteries were plentiful—almost too plentiful, like churches—seemingly one for every large family. We even knew families who would purchase a depository of family plots for sisters and brothers, moms and dads, aunts and uncles, a life-insurance policy, as it were, so the family could remain together in death.

The weather always varied greatly on Memorial Days in the Ozarks. Some days were hot and stifling, portending a humid, windless summer where the unified cry of the crickets could almost make a man go nuts. And others were wet and cool, a gentle rain softening the earth, chilling our bones, turning the green grass on the graves even greener.

But the weather never deterred my mom or grandma. They made their way in sensible, respectful heels over mounds and molehills, in the rain or sweltering heat, wending their way among the graves, their arms interlocked, purses notched in their elbows, their heels often getting mired in mud, me following to wipe them clean with Kleenex that were originally meant for mascara-strewn eyes and cheeks.

My mom and grandma would seek out sisters and brothers, cousins and nephews, friends and neighbors, soldiers and war vets who had passed before them or in service to the country, my mom and grandma sharing stories about the dead and what each had meant to them.

It was standing in these graveyards that I got to know many of those family members I never had the chance to meet. Sometimes my mom and grandma would laugh, sometimes they would cry—depending on the person and the length of time they had been gone—but they always ended with the same ritual: My mother and grandmother would kneel to say a prayer, pay their respects, and then plant peonies and American flags into the earth over the grave.

"See you next year," they would whisper, passing a kiss from their hand to the earth before standing again, interlocking arms, and slowly making their way to the next party guest.

But when I was fourteen, a litany of death strangled my family in short order like a swarm of locusts—starting with my brother, Todd, who was killed in a motorcycle accident weeks after he had graduated from high school and weeks before I was to begin my freshman year.

Todd's death was quickly followed by those of my aunt and my grandpa—my mom's sister and grandma's daughter; my mom's father and grandma's husband—and it was then that our Memorial Day visits abruptly ended.

We simply headed to our cabin, taking a circuitous route that bypassed all local cemeteries, a task, I now realize, that must have taken a great deal of forethought.

As I aged, I didn't consider Memorial Day much beyond the fact that it gave me a three-day weekend, a kick-start to summer.

And then I met my partner, Gary, who, in many ways, reminded me of my grandmother. Topping the list, he was an avid gardener, just like her.

I always admired those who tended to the earth—a gift I did not have—and I guess when I saw Gary work his garden, I saw my grandma. I also secretly believed if Gary could cultivate seeds in a dead patch of earth, then he could surely nurture me back to life.

And yet for years, when Gary would ask me to join him in his garden, I always declined, hiding in the house, behind a curtain, or just off to the side of a window, watching him work, weed, mulch. And seemingly every time Gary would begin to dig a hole in his garden, I would turn away.

One scorching summer day a few years back, around the anniversary of my brother's death, my parents drove up to visit Gary and me after we had moved to Michigan.

This had not been an easy visit for any of us, especially for me, since I found myself constantly preoccupied, even three decades later, with what my parents were still missing: my dead brother, his imaginary wife, the ghost grandchildren they would never hold.

Just before my parents were to leave, as I was dragging my mom's suitcase to the front door, I heard Gary ask her if she would like to go on a final tour of his garden. I hid behind a curtain in our cottage and watched Gary surprise my mom with a bouquet of peonies, along with a start of the plant in wet paper towels.

Suddenly my mother fell to her knees in his garden and started crying—convulsing, really—all the while hugging the peony start tenderly, as if it was an imaginary grandchild.

As my parents drove away, I said, "What was up with that? Are you the Flower Whisperer?"

It was my typical pattern: Sarcasm, like a good tan, could cover any defect.

"Those peonies," he said, "are from your grandmother's garden."

I stared at him. "What are you talking about? She's been dead for years."

"Just smell," Gary said.

He plucked a white peony with a pink center from our cottage garden and held it in front of my nose and, like some sort of scent therapy, the memories came flooding back.

My grandmother used to grow long rows of peonies on the back side of her Ozark house, a spot where the sun would bake them much of the day. She rotated bushes of white and pink, pink and white, and the flowers would grow so heavy that they simply exhausted the stems that valiantly tried to support them. Eventually her peonies would just flop on the ground like a tired, old dog, thick powder-puff blooms of soft pink and virginal white.

What I remember most was the flowers' fragrance, which would hang in the air like a cloud of perfume. For a few precious days, before a thunderstorm would come and knock off all the petals, I would rejoice in the peonies' thick smell, a fragrance so rich and deep, in fact, that it would scent the bedsheets that flapped on the nearby clothesline. I would fall into the pile of line-dried laundry when my grandma would bring it inside and roll around in crunchy, stiff sheets that smelled like heaven.

And it was then I remembered the conversations my mom and grandma used to have about these peonies as they drove to the cemeteries on those Memorial Days of my youth.

My grandmother intentionally planted two types of peonies, early and late blooming. The early-blooming peonies were planted for only one reason: so that she could decorate the graves of her family and friends on Memorial Day with not just real flowers but with flowers she considered to be the most beautiful in the world.

"I just don't understand how people can place plastic flowers on their loved ones' graves," she used to say. "Peonies are the perfect flower."

Which is why she always placed them on her family's graves.

And why I had buried that memory deep in the ground.

That summer day after my parents left, I stood in Gary's garden, remembering all this as he watered, and I started to cry, soaking his shoulder as the hose soaked the dry ground.

And it was then I finally accepted Gary's invitation: He asked if I would join him in his garden, and I—for once—accepted.

"The earth is what grounds us and connects us all for a very short time," Gary said to me. "That's why I like to grow and share starts of plants with others—like your grandmother's peonies—because it's like sharing a memory with the world. Did you know your mom saved peony starts from your grandma's garden after she died, and then passed them along to me? It's a way to keep family alive, to keep the memory of those we love in our home, no matter where we live or how much time has passed."

The next Memorial Day, I surprised my parents by driving eleven hours to visit them in the Ozarks, telling them I needed a few days by the water at our new cabin, despite the fact I had Lake Michigan and a beach less than a mile from our house.

The journey back home was never an easy trip for me: too many painful memories meshing with too many good ones.

Out of the blue on the Saturday of Memorial Day weekend, just as we had finished eating dollar-size pancakes with strawberry syrup, I gathered my courage and asked my mother if she wanted to decorate graves.

Her tears told me she did.

She reappeared moments later wearing a dress and a pair of respectful, sensible heels.

"We'll need to pick up a few things on the way," she said as we headed to my car.

I shook my head, popping the trunk, which I had already filled with miniature flags, a box of Kleenex, and, most important, peonies that had been born in my grandma's garden, passed to my mother, and then forwarded to Gary like precious, fragile cargo.

Though wilted, their beauty remained.

We stopped at my brother's grave first—just the second time I had visited it since he died—and then my grandmother's, where we told stories, and we wept, and we hugged.

I then knelt on my grandmother's grave that Memorial Day, my knees on the cool earth, and planted a flag and then said a prayer: a prayer that after I am long gone someone takes the time to share my story, to visit me on occasion, to pass along my legacy.

And then I scraped my hands into the wet earth, digging through new grass and mud and red clay, and planted some peonies.

JUNE

"When I was a boy of fourteen, my father was so ignorant I could hardly stand to have the old man around. But when I got to be twenty-one, I was astonished at how much he had learned in seven years."

—MARK TWAIN

Zooks, Cukes, Maters, & Taters

There once lived a family in my little town that I firmly believed had been in the circus. The husband was freakishly tall and thin, six eight, 160 at the most, while the wife was short and stout, almost like a footstool with hair. They had two children, a boy who, sadly, looked like Mom, and a girl, who, sadly, looked like Dad.

While my family ate TV dinners and watched *M*A*S*H*, I would often picture the circus family at dinnertime, the father and daughter consuming a single bean while plucking birds from the sky, the mother and son eating whole cows and hundreds of pies before going out back to roll around with their pigs.

Despite their differences and oddities, however, I always knew they were a family even though others seemed confounded. I guess I could just sense it, that familiarity that families have, the same way I could smell rain coming.

Ironically, though, I had trouble discerning that odor in my own family.

While strangers certainly never had any difficulty telling that I was my father's son—we're both little fireplugs of men, with sandy hair, occasionally clenched fists, and stomping walks—I always felt as if I were the illegitimate son of a circus performer.

Whereas my father is complete left-brain logic, I'm all right-brain creativity.

I'm a writer. He is an engineer.

My father couldn't care less about culture, fashion, trends. He thinks Warren Buffett should be knighted, while I believe Mary Hart should be granted sainthood.

Despite this, we have a wonderful relationship, forged through years of valiantly trying to build a bridge to span that personality gap.

Every Father's Day, for instance, my father used to emerge from the Ozarks and join me in the city, where I would immediately, upon his arrival, cart him around to different stores in the area—Trader Joe's, boutique delis, local farmers' markets—in order to prove that there were places to shop in this world other than Walmart or the Liquor Barn.

One Father's Day I took my dad to Whole Foods and had left him only briefly—in order to nab a box of Kashi Go-Lean Crunch cereal—when I heard my father screaming, "Where's the zooks, darlin'?"

I turned the corner just in time to see a produce clerk who looked like an earthy Cameron Diaz drop a pretty honeydew she was stacking.

She had obviously never seen a true man of the Ozarks.

There stood my father wearing his summer staples: jean shorts that were about to fall down, a horizontal-red-striped golf shirt that made him look like a pregnant barber pole, and a hat that said, GOLFERS HAVE BETTER BALLS.

"The zooks, hon'! Ain't you got no zooks?" my father asked again.

The clerk looked at me and I simply shrugged my shoulders.

I didn't know this man.

And though I hated myself for remaining silent, I didn't want her to connect us via our voices: Besides our stature, our low, rumbling voice was another physical attribute my father and I had in common.

But not our accents.

I had spent years trying to lose my Ozark twang and vocabulary, while my father still spoke Ozarks-ese.

Ozarks-ese, as I call it, is certainly not an officially recognized language like Spanish, French, or German, or even an important dead language like Latin. Instead, Ozarks-ese is like country rap, Nelly meets Paula Deen, a lexicon used in a seam of the American flag where Midwest becomes South.

In Ozarks-ese, words are shortened and slurred so the mouth doesn't really have to work too hard to enunciate them. If Ozark grammar were a food, it would be mashed potatoes. Ozarks-ese is like white man's rap, but instead of "boo," " 'hood," "peeps," "posse," and "shake that Laffy Taffy," we have my father's vocabulary.

When my father asks for "zooks," he's looking for zucchini.

When my father asks for "cukes," he's looking for cucumbers.

When my father asks for "maters" (long a), he's looking for tomatoes.

When my father asks for "taters" (long a), he's looking for potatoes.

Basically, if my father tried to buy ingredients for a salad outside of the Ozarks, he might as well be shopping for a vacuum in Guatemala.

When my father eats at a restaurant and orders "good meat," he wants steak. And he wants his steak "beatin'," which means bloody, heart-beating rare.

When he orders "fuckin' pluckin'," my father wants chicken.

Now, "telly" has many meanings. If an actor—any actor—is bald, my father calls him Telly, not caring less whether it's Ben Kingsley, Stanley Tucci, Bruce Willis, or Natalie Portman in *V for Vendetta*.

"Telly" is also my father's term for both the telephone and television: "What's on the telly?" or "Who's on the telly?"

I usually tell him that "Telly is on the telly," and that seems to satisfy him.

Despite my efforts, however, I never felt that I lived up to my father's expectations. Every gay son shoulders that burden, I believe.

So I made the mistake of taking Gary's advice one year and led my parents on a Father's Day trip to Ireland. Now, Gary firmly believed Ireland would be my father's promised land, a place where there was no language barrier, where golf was king, and where beer was as plentiful as oxygen.

"How can you go wrong?" Gary asked. "You will earn bonus points for life!"

But before we had even boarded the plane, my father pulled a three-day-old hoagie from his travel bag and began gnawing on its moldy remains.

I knew before we had even taken flight that my dreams were grounded.

"Ted, you old witch, I threw that hoagie out in Rolla," my mother yelled at him.

"I dug it back out of the trash at the Subway, hon'! *Mmmm,* damn horseradish is good. *Mmmm.*"

"That will rot out that fat iron gut you call a stomach, sir."

"I ain't the one who's already been to TCBY and Cinnabon, hon'!"

"Shut up, you old goat. After mad cow, airports forbid passengers from carryin' American lunchmeat products transatlantic, isn't that correct, James Wade?"

"What the Sam hell do you know about airport security, Geraldine? You're gonna set off the alarms with all the metal plates you got in that thick skull of yours!"

"You are fat and—*What!*—rude, sir! All my fellow passengers agree, don't you, ma'ams and sirs? Yes, yes, they are not fond of fat, bald witches."

By this time, Gary had moved to a neighboring concourse.

"Have you been on an Alaskan cruise, ma'am?" my mother continued, asking a woman who was fake-reading a book and wearing a sweatshirt that said ALASKAN CRUISE. My mother is a magician at busting people she knows are eavesdropping but pretending not to be. "I would love to go to Alaska, but Ted says it's too cold. Fat witches don't like the cold, do they, Ted?"

"Geraldine, it's too damn cold in Nome. I'd as soon cut my nuts off and serve 'em to the squirrels than freeze my ass off in the cold, yelling 'Fuck me, Charlie Brown!' into the arctic wind."

I smiled at the woman in the Alaskan sweatshirt, who looked from me to my parents and then back again, puzzled, wondering, I'm quite certain from her expression, if these were indeed the two who had given birth to me, or if I had happened to burst magically from my father's head like some sort of Greek god.

I passed out on the flight to Ireland and woke in the middle of the night, searching for my moisturizer and Purel, to find my father doing shots of Jägermeister with a group of college kids who asked for his phone number when we got off the plane.

I spent my entire Irish excursion watching my dad chug Guinness with the locals and make friends around the Ring of Kerry while I rolled my eyes.

By the end, I was mentally and physically soaked, sick of traveling around the beautiful countryside under a never-ending and constantly moving showerhead, but mostly sick with the uneasy realization that I really wasn't like my father—make that either of my parents—in any way: No, they were way more fun than me.

I was telling this Ireland story to one of my best friends from college, waiting for some sort of understanding response or equally horrifying story, but he said, simply, "Your parents *are* way more fun than you, Wade. I mean, no insult or anything. Remember college? They were who they were, and, well, you just wanted to change."

He was right.

Within the first thirty seconds of introducing myself as Wade to my new freshman college roommate, who was from the city, he asked, "Just how many syllables are in your first name?" At the time I was wearing my high school letter jacket—I "lettered" in the trombone—and I had an accent thicker than an eighties belt.

So I practiced my speech whenever I got a quiet moment, trying desperately to quicken the pace of my voice while losing my inbred Ozarks-ese.

"*Waaa-aa-aa-de,*" I would whisper in the toilet.

"*Waaa-aa-de,*" I would practice in my room when I was alone.

"*Waaa-de,*" I would say out loud as I walked to class.

And, ever so slowly, *Waaa-aa-aa-de* simply became Wade.

I was so good at mimicking others, fitting in, that I quickly mastered friends' accents and manners of speaking, focusing mostly on sounding "St. Louis," which I thought was truly metropolitan, working diligently on making my o's sound like harsh a's. If Abraham Lincoln had been a St. Louisan, he would have said, "Far scar and seven yars ago."

And then I worked on my walk, trying to unclench my fists and walk lightly and proudly, as if I were an Alvin Ailey dancer.

I wanted to change, to be somebody new, to not be the spitting image of my father.

But the more my parents visited me in college, the more I felt they defined me—my dad in his baggy jean shorts and hats with Reagan's face on them, going beer for beer with my fraternity brothers; my mother captivating a group who laughed like hell at a story that ended, "Well, sir, while he was asleep, all of us nurses tied his rather large and thick penis into the shape of a pretzel!"

The older I got, the more I began to intentionally hide my

parents, especially my father, from my friends, embarrassed by what they might do or say.

Every Father's Day after our Ireland trip, my father would tell me what a great time he'd had with me and Gary and hint strongly about how he'd like to travel somewhere with us again.

But I declined.

And then one Father's Day my parents came to St. Louis for a night, staying at our house before they were scheduled to leave the next morning for a vacation to Nova Scotia. It was a trip he'd desperately wanted us to be a part of.

When my father arrived, he did not look well: He was pasty, drawn, short of breath. He went to bed uncharacteristically early, without a beer and with very little fanfare. I thought he just wanted to rest before the early flight.

My mother woke me up at two in the morning in a panic, telling me that she thought my father was having a heart attack. I walked in to find my dad slowly pacing around the living room, gray-faced, gasping for air, clutching furniture for assistance. My mother, for once losing all of her nursing composure, not able to help him professionally, horrified but not wanting to show her husband or son how truly scared she was, reacted—holding back her tears—in the only way she knew how. "I told the old goat he can't just go on eatin' whole sticks of butter on his toast."

My father, for once, did not take the bait, could not respond to her barbs.

"Isn't that correct, Ted?" my mother yelled at him, trying hard not to bawl, shaking, her face twisted in agony. "You answer me, you old witch, do you hear? You answer me! Answer me, Ted! I cannot lose you!"

My father looked at my mom and, in a voice that was barely audible, whispered, knowing it was what he must say for her sake, "Shut the hell up, Geraldine!"

Here, now, my father dying, my mother yelling, the one moment in life when nothing was clear, I suddenly became completely sure of one thing: My parents loved each other more than I could ever comprehend.

And I loved them more than I had ever let them know.

I called 911.

The two minutes waiting for the ambulance were the longest in my life, the longest my father had ever been silent, and so I sat holding my father on the front steps of my house in the middle of the night, rocking with him, telling him I loved him, that it was going to be okay, not at all convinced that it was.

We were both wearing tattered sweats, and Gary, who was standing at the front door, watching helplessly, would later say he could not tell us apart as we rocked.

My father was carted into the back of the ambulance, my mother following, sirens blaring, lights flashing, neighbors watching. Even now, my dad was still the center of attention.

After what seemed like an eternity, my father's physician, a Pakistani doctor who looked like an Indian Don Rickles, finally emerged to tell us my dad had suffered a minor heart attack and that a stent had been inserted; however, he had suffered no heart damage and would be just fine.

In fact, it turned out that the most baffling and troubling aspect of my father's condition, the doctor explained, was the discovery of a tick on the head of my father's penis, which had been removed but needed to be "sent away for testing."

Following this announcement, a crowd of people waiting in the ER turned to look at my family curiously, as if we were dirty beggars in the street.

"So let me get this straight," I whispered. "My dad's heart is going to be okay, but he had a tick on his dick."

"That is a fairly accurate estimation," the doctor replied.

"He's just a filthy old man," my mother exclaimed. "I tell him to get in the tub and scrub those nasty old balls, but he never listens."

The doctor, along with about thirty people in the ER, stared at my mother. I was wearing sweatpants, my hair sticking straight up, Clearasil dotting the end of my nose. I now realized everyone here thought that my balls were probably dirty, too, that there was a good chance I might have a bloodsucking insect attached to my penis.

"So the old goat is not dead, doctor?" my mother asked.

"I'm sorry, Mrs. Rouse. I'm not following . . ." he said.

Their routine was still safe.

A short while later, we were allowed to see my dad. My mom went in first to spend a few minutes with him alone, and Gary followed. I needed some time. As I rounded the corner to my father's room, I stopped for a second in the hall and watched Gary holding the hands of my mom and dad, an unlikely family circle laughing. It was everything I had wanted in my life.

We were—despite our differences, our oddities—a family.

I was proud to be my father's son.

When I walked in, my dad was saying, "The doc couldn't understand a word I was sayin', and I couldn't understand a word he was sayin'!" His voice was weak but, again, filled with life. Just then a pretty nurse—a young blonde who looked like she might be hired to star in some low-budget porn flick like *Naughty Nurses* or *Fill My Prescription*—walked in to check on my dad.

"Geraldine, you've been replaced," he said. "You serve fried taters in this place, hon'?"

"Shut up, you fat old witch, you're done with taters for a while," my mother said, her facade finally cracking, tears welling in her eyes. She leaned in to hug my father and kiss him on the cheek. "You shut up now, sir."

Their voices were, at last, music to my ears.

My Plastic Peeps

I was hammering my mother about her smoking one summer evening while standing on the patio when she turned to me, taking a deep drag off her cigarette, and said, "We all have an addiction, Wade. If it's not smoking, it's drinking. And if it's not drinking, it's shopping. And if it's not shopping, it's sex."

She blew a gray-blue plume of smoke my way, and I coughed.

Just to piss her off.

Or perhaps it was an involuntary response, because I knew she was right.

Come to think of it, I knew one person who fit each of her categories. I had discovered porn videos in a shoe box in the attic of a seemingly straitlaced married friend whose house I was watching while he was on vacation; I had found empty vodka bottles in the trash bin of my ultra-Christian neighbors, who refused to even acknowledge me when I waved; I even spied the wife of a friend, who had recently been let go from his corporate job, charging oodles of skirts at Ann Taylor when I stopped by the mall to buy a latte.

Yes, my mother's words haunted me, deeply, and not just because I was a modern-day Gladys Kravitz, a defect I pawned off on my background as a journalist more than any psychological flaw.

No, my mother's words haunted me because I knew I harbored a secret addiction worse than liquor, sex, and shopping: Pez.

I began collecting Pez dispensers as a kid because they were an acceptable alternative to the Barbies I so desperately wanted. Although my Pez weren't realistic knockoffs of pretty girls who wore dazzling outfits, they were cute, colorful enough characters. I started simply, collecting angels and astronauts, before building to Bambi and Batman. I added Disney characters, and then one day my grampa gave me a rather battered Indian brave he'd had for years. My grampa gave me few personal gifts, so I cherished his Pez.

Most important, though, my Pez vomited candy. And for a fat little gay boy in rural America, that was better than having James at 15 come over to babysit.

I mainlined Pez candy because I was bored, and it was fun and addictive, not because I was ever really crazy about the taste: The fruity flavors were sweet, sure, but they were chalky and fake-tasting.

"Heavens to Betsy, Wade," my mother said, staring at me one afternoon as I overdosed on Pez in front of the TV. "It's like watching *Valley of the Dolls*."

But it wasn't the candy I was addicted to: The dispensers were the stars, my surrogate friends.

Eventually I gathered enough Pez to cover the top of my nightstand; really, I gathered enough Pez to serve as my army of bloodless buddies. They were cute and sweet, they always wanted to play with me, but, best of all, they were mute and couldn't talk back, couldn't make fun of me, couldn't call me "Turd Burglar."

Still, when junior high school came calling, Pez suddenly seemed a bit childish to collect. I hungered to have flesh-and-blood friends.

Sensing this, I was encouraged by my mom and grampa to switch to a more acceptable hobby for boys my age: coin collecting.

And it was a hobby that genuinely seemed to interest a number of local boys, albeit those who liked to go to the local grocery and Laundromat and ask customers and clerks if they could look through their change.

But for me, buffalo nickels, bicentennial quarters, and Susan B. Anthony dollars just weren't as much fun as my plastic pals. And money was too dirty to stick in my mouth.

Eventually, as we all do, I packed my childhood hobbies away and didn't really give my Pez much thought for nearly two decades, until I moved into my first home and my parents saw it as an opportunity to rid themselves of the junk I'd left behind at their house.

"We want to turn your bedroom into a study," my mother told me over the phone one night. "And we need to get rid of all the clutter. So we're bringing your stuff up next week, okay?"

For some reason this stung, even though I'd been gone nearly a decade and a half. My childhood home, without any trace of me in it? It seemed as wrong as the pope in an HRC tank top.

"What are you and dad going to *study*, mother?" I asked tersely. "Episodes of *Matlock*?"

"Sweetie, your room is still decorated as a tribute to our nation's bicentennial. Remember when your patriotic side meshed with your decorating side? I mean, the walls are red, white, and blue. Guests don't know whether to sleep or salute. You've got so much stuff here...boxes of coins, boxes of Pez."

My Pez, I thought, my mouth instantly watering. My friends.

As soon as my parents unloaded my memorabilia and left to turn my bedroom into a study that was part French countryside and part Gloria Swanson mansion from *Sunset Boulevard*, I slowly went through the boxes they had brought, lost in time, freeing my Pez that had long been housed in an army of tattered shoe boxes. Though they hadn't seen the light of day in decades, my dispensers still looked bright and cheery.

I pulled them out one at a time, remembering the lonely kid I had once been, thanking my Mickey Mouse, Spider-Man, and Bozo for being my friends at a time when I really needed them.

Like me, my friends had aged, grown a bit rough around the edges, but they were all still intact. All except, that was, for my grampa's little Indian brave. The feather that used to adorn his little plastic skull was no longer attached, and, no matter how hard I searched, or begged my parents to comb their home, it was gone.

I decided to display my Pez on a computer desk in the space that adjoined our bedroom, a sort of home-office-slash-closet.

But when we had sex, Gary freaked, thinking my childhood Pez were watching him deflower their friend. And when he worked, he said he could feel their disdain. And when he slept, he had *Trilogy of Terror* nightmares that my Pez were going to come to life, hide out under the bed, and then stab his feet with little knives when he put his tootsies on our wood floor.

"They've got to go," Gary said. It was his first few months of living with me, and he'd kept his redecorating bug under control. Until now. "And so does the recycling bin you believe is an end table."

I switched jobs a short time later to work as PR director at a prep school, and found that kids were constantly coming into my office with their moms and searching for something to do while I was being castrated. So I decided to showcase my Pez in an old wood cabinet in my office, and was pleased to discover—even decades later—they still had the same mesmerizing effect not only on kids but also on their parents.

"My God! Pez! I used to collect Pez as a kid!"

"Oh, my goodness! I haven't seen Pez since Jimmy Carter was president!"

Slowly, parents began to bring me Pez: one a month, one a week, until it became a steady stream. And then a flood.

I was awash in a river of candy.

Parents brought me newer Pez like Garfields, Muppets, action heroes, and the Peanuts gang. And then I began to receive Pez that parents had unearthed at their summer cottages or found at antique malls, like old Dumbos and Snow Whites. Even Gary's mom began to buy me Pez at every holiday: I received Pez chicks for Easter, Pez pumpkins and scary goblins for Halloween, Pez Santas and snowmen for Christmas.

But when I had finally accumulated a hundred or so Pez, my collection suddenly seemed puny and pathetic.

I wanted more. As many as I could get.

I wanted Pez no one else had.

I began to plead for Pez.

I began to shop online for Pez.

I realized that my pulse would race with each new Pez I purchased or received.

Something had clicked, something bad. Acquiring Pez was a rush, like porn, although the only hard things I was interested in seeing had bright plastic tubes and oddly shaped heads.

This obsession was silly, I realized, but in the blur of work and life I had trouble understanding why it had become so consuming.

Then, one Christmas, Gary's mother bought me a *Warman's Pez Field Guide,* a thick encyclopedia to all things Pez, including their monetary values and unique identifying characteristics.

I opened the guide and my mouth dropped, just like my beloved companions. I realized I was sitting on a fortune.

It seemed, according to my guide, that I had collected a lot of Pez without feet. In the early days of Pez, the dispensers were made without that little extra piece of plastic at the bottom; in the late eighties, the plastic feet were added to help the dispensers more easily stand upright without tipping.

Over the next few months I tried to calculate how much my booty was worth and came to the rough estimate that I was sitting on enough Pez to redecorate my dining room, or go to Punta Cana for ten days.

"Cash them in!" Gary said.

But I couldn't.

And then I heard on our local TV that the annual Pez Collectors Convention was coming to town.

My people! I thought. *This is a sign!*

I headed to the convention one June day—nervous, anxious, but excitedly toting a few of my most prized Pez. I walked inside and realized I had stumbled into Pez Paradise. There were Pez everywhere: locked cases of rare Pez dispensers worth thousands and thousands of dollars; old, uneaten candy packs worth thousands and thousands of dollars; antique Pez that were being sold for thousands and thousands of dollars.

Things that had been purchased for pennies were now virtual plastic Picassos.

My mouth watered. My eyes glazed.

I was a genius!

Perhaps, I thought, as I stared at a rare soft-head version of Dumbo on display in a bulletproof case that was more highly valued than my car—and, most likely, my home—Gary was right.

I should sell.

And then I heard:

"Hi! I'm Judy from Illinois, and I'm a Pezhead too!"

A mammoth woman with frosted hair, sporting a formless shift, was screaming at me.

"Hi, Judy."

"You're a Pezzer, I'm a Pezzer, he's a Pezzer, too!"

Judy laughed and offered me some candy.

"We're all Pezzers! Pez people are perfect people," she yelled.

Judy, it seemed, was insane.

"Dumbo's something else, huh?"

You sure are, I thought.

I was saved from Judy by Bill, who was also a screamer.

"Hi! I'm Bill from Kansas, and I'm a Pezhead!" yelled a man in a Pez sweatshirt. "I'm kinda the king of Pez! Are you new? Are you staying for dinner, Pez bingo, and late-night room hopping?"

There comes a point, I realized, when every person with an addiction reaches bottom and finally has a clear vision of what he has allowed himself to become: Looking around at this group of crazies, I shouted to myself: *My name is Wade, and I'm a Pez-o-holic!"*

And yet I came with a mission, and I couldn't leave without fulfilling it.

"Bill?" I asked. "Could I ask you a question? I've been a collector since I was a kid, and I brought a couple of things to price..."

"Hit me, my new Pez peep!"

I yanked my Indian-brave Pez out of a Gap bag I was carrying, and Bill gasped.

"Oh, my God! You're carrying the chief around in a bag? Why isn't he in a protective case?"

"My grampa gave him to me when I was little. He's never been covered. I used to play with him. He was my friend."

Bill covered his mouth with his hand and screamed, as if I'd just set a kitten on fire.

"And where's the chief's feather?"

"I can't find it," I said.

Again Bill screamed, this time even more dramatically, as if I'd just set two kittens on fire.

"Oh, my God!" he gasped. "You're a...*collector*?"

"More of an enthusiast, I'd say, if you want to nitpick."

"Well, I do. I mean, if you'd been a *collector*, you would have known to protect your Indian. And if you'd been a *collector*, he would still have his feather, which would have made him worth, I guess, a few thousand dollars."

"Holy Sacagawea!" I yelled at Bill.

"But he's not. He's worn. And damaged. And kind of useless..."

I had a feeling Bill wanted to add, "Just like you."

I walked out of my first and last Pez Collectors Convention that day much like a girl who loses her virginity to the cute boy who will never call her back: crestfallen, a touch sore, but wiser.

To this day my Pez sit—out of boxes, out in the open—on a low-slung bookshelf that faces my writing desk.

About a hundred times a day, I look over at Charlie Brown, Marge Simpson, and my little Indian brave, and I smile every time.

JULY

"You have to love a nation that celebrates its independence every July Fourth, not with a parade of guns, tanks, and soldiers who file by the White House in a show of strength and muscle, but with family picnics where kids throw Frisbees, the potato salad gets iffy, and the flies die from happiness. You may think you have overeaten, but it is patriotism."

—ERMA BOMBECK

Gutting Gary

I spent the Fourth of July holidays of my youth at our log cabin on Sugar Creek.

There, enveloped by the sandy bluffs and ice-cold water, my family would swim, shoot off bottle rockets, and throw smoke bombs into the water.

At night we built a giant bonfire on our rocky beach and roasted hot dogs and toasted marshmallows for s'mores. Our Fourth of July beach bonanza culminated with a spectacular fireworks display that would run nearly an hour and feature extravagant bursts of purple and gold comets, green palm trees, and giant red chrysanthemums.

I used to sit back, my mouth stuffed with a s'more, and watch the explosions in the blue-black summer-night sky—the echoes booming off the surrounding cliffs, the colors reflecting off the burbling creek.

They were amazing, yes, but I also knew the best fireworks were yet to come when my family would scamper up the stone steps that dotted the hillside to our cabin and huddle together to kick off our annual Fourth of July Game Night. This competition involved every member of the family, young and old, in a series of card and board games, the last man standing the winner.

Fourth of July Game Night was sacrosanct at our family's old log cabin. In fact, looking back, those contests seemed to be held on an even higher level than births and major surgeries that involved the removal of important organs.

The Rouses battled in Battleship and contested one another in canasta and Chinese checkers for two main reasons: boredom, and a genetic defect that made us want to crush the competition, like today's New England Patriots.

Truly, there was little to do at our cabin besides eat, swim, or fish. We didn't have a TV, only an ancient radio the size of a Buick that received faint, scratchy voices that sounded like mice trying to claw their way to freedom. We were also a gene pool not blessed with speed of foot, great coordination, or even passable singing voices, so, as a result, we were forced to entertain ourselves with games.

While our annual Game Night was titled something different but dramatic every year—the Summer Showdown, the Duel to the Death, the Blood Match, the Rouse Rumble, the Ozarks National Board Championship—one thing was always certain: My father would win, no matter how much my family teamed up to slay the dragon.

In fact, he never lost.

But it wasn't just the fact that my father always won, it was the *way* he won that upset the family: He crushed his victims, and did it with such spiteful glee you would almost swear he was spitting venom. My father, an engineer and mathematical whiz, could count cards and memorize players' bad habits. He was invincible.

One of the earliest Fourth of July memories I have of my dad was playing Operation with him as my teammate. Though I was still too young to be much good, my father single-handedly whooped family members, badly, using those little tweezers like a scalpel, plucking organs willy-nilly from that clownish body like a skilled surgeon.

As a result, I was trained from an early age to be deadly, to strike without feeling, like a child soldier. I learned that humiliating others in board games was a way to prove my dominance, and I loved that passive-aggressive approach to life. I learned it was wonderful to win, but one got even more pleasure if he was able to crack Professor Plum over the head with a candlestick in the conservatory—over and over and over again.

"Life is like a board game," my dad would always tell the vanquished, holding tweezers or dice or cards over his head in a victory dance. "There are always winners and losers. And I'm always the winner!"

And then I met Gary and fell deeply, madly in love. He was funny, handsome, warm, nurturing, talented, adventurous.

But, as fate would have it, horrific in board games.

I uncovered this important fact quickly—like a woman might discern up front if a prospective husband truly wanted children—by whipping him in every board game we could possibly play: Scattergories, Scrabble, Cranium, Trivial Pursuit. Even Candy Land and pick-up sticks. Playing board games with Gary was like playing board games with a stroke victim. In fact, a stroke victim could take Gary because his attention span would be longer and deductive reasoning better.

Which is why I was consumed with fear the very first Fourth of July I brought Gary back to my family's cabin.

I knew my dad would eat him alive.

I tried to fill the holiday with nervous chatter and activities: float trips, bottle rockets, fishing, sunning, berry picking.

But I could not outrun the inevitable, and the moment I had long feared, the words that had caused my colon to cramp in the wee hours of the morning were uttered by my father at sundown after we'd eaten barbecued ribs and watched the fireworks: "Gary, are you up for the traditional Rouse Fourth of July Game Night?"

I had warned Gary.

He knew what he was in for.

He had even witnessed my own brutality with his family, who played board games without any rules so that everyone won. After playing Tripoli for hours the New Year's before with his family, without any clear set of rules or winner, I finally screamed: "This isn't Neverland, people! Board games are like life. There are always winners and losers. And I'm always the winner!"

We had survived that low point in our relationship, which gave me a glimmer of hope that we could survive our first Rouse Game Night, which my dad sweetly titled the Fourth of July Massacre of the Newbie.

I suggested that we start with something friendly, like Monopoly or Cranium.

But my dad suggested we go straight for the heart with hearts, the card game where the queen of spades is the old biddy, the game where you try to shoot the moon and instantly give opponents twenty-six points, the game my father has never, ever lost.

Watching my father shuffle the deck and deal the cards while smiling and staring down Gary like Paul Newman in *The Sting,* I honestly believed my father had sold his soul to Satan for one simple thing: board-game invincibility.

I mean, the man counted cards like Rain Man. He once made an aunt cry by shooting the moon four consecutive times, thus ending the game in under fifteen minutes. Another family member, who refused to play with my father after being publicly humiliated one too many times, had called my dad "the most vicious man alive."

Tonight wasn't really a fair fight from the start. My father sat Gary to his immediate left, kind of the way a lion might seat a water buffalo next to him at a safari dinner party. And then my dad shot the moon on the first hand, handing us all twenty-six points. And then my mom shot the moon. And then my dad shot the moon again.

I looked over at Gary, who was over the moon. He sat lifeless, shell-shocked, his double row of eyelashes soaked, close to tears.

I glanced over at my father. He winked at me.

Jesus Christ, he's going in for the kill, I thought. The only successful relationship I'll ever be able to pull off with my family is if I get involved with a professional poker player, or someone creepy smart like Bill Gates.

But then something miraculous happened.

Gary shot the moon.

Despite the fact his hand was rife with losing cards: an eight of diamonds, a six of hearts.

He won hands he shouldn't have won.

My dad threw away cards he should have kept.

And my mom followed his lead.

At that moment—on a stifling July night, despite bottle rockets still popping in the distance—I knew my family's fireworks had officially ended: Gary was loved. He had been accepted into our family.

Gary smiled triumphantly, but I knew my family's one good deed was done. After that, my father proceeded to gut Gary like a fresh bass.

About fifteen minutes later, my dad pushed his chair back after winning and stood to taunt my partner. "You know, Gary, life is like a board game," my dad said, twisting around in his victory dance. "There are always winners and losers. I'm always the winner, and you'll always be the loser! "

Gary would cry later that night, softly, out of humiliation, as every Rouse had done at one point in our lives. But before he fell asleep, I pulled him into my arms and whispered, finally remembering the reason my family loved Game Night: "You shouldn't be sad, sweetie, you should be honored. It's the only way we know how to show our love to one another."

So, a Gift Card to
Trader Joe's Isn't Romantic?

G ary and I once took a loaf of Amish friendship bread to a new neighbor, a kindly, older, sassy woman who looked a lot like Shirley MacLaine and always waved to us from her front porch.

She thanked us profusely for the bread by asking us in for a cup of coffee and depositing us in her dining room, the walls and cabinets of which were lined and stuffed with commemorative anniversary plates and dishes. There was seemingly a teacup, goblet, dessert fork, and sherry glass for every anniversary up to number sixty.

"You've been married sixty years?" I asked, nodding my head at the walls as she walked back in with a pot of coffee. "Congratulations! What's your husband's name? I don't think I've seen him yet."

"All that shit belonged to my parents," she said coarsely, pouring us cups of coffee. "I've been divorced three times. Not a big fan of marriage...or anniversaries. Just makes me feel good to know someone made it work. And all this crap will be worth a fortune, too, someday."

Gary promptly poured the coffee into his lap.

"I should've taken my Amish bread back!" Gary said, charging back across our street when we were done. It looked like he had wet himself.

Incidents like this shake Gary to his core. He believes they serve as signs: signs of impending doom. "She was so negative about relationships and romance. She might as well have spit in our faces."

"Can it still be considered Amish friendship bread since you didn't bake it in a bonnet over a copper urn, and you no longer like her?" I asked.

I knew I needed to change the subject before this ended up turning bad more quickly than a cup of clam chowder in the Sahara.

But it was too late.

"I'm serious," Gary said. "It's sad. But then again, you don't believe in anniversaries either, do you?"

Ahh, the question that had no answer, like "Do I look fat in this?" and "What do you think of my mother?"

But he was right. I didn't. I believed in marriage. I believed that my parents and grandparents stayed married for fifty years because of the simple yet undeniable fact that they worked like hell at it every single day, not because they bought each other a commemorative teacup every year.

I mean, I had worked in retail. I saw what men did: They used gift buying as a ruse. Buying a gift bought them time. They were perceived as romantic. And so they could slide.

I believed that if you loved someone, you showed them every day. I believed that it was the small gestures—opening a door, taking Gary's hand in mine every night before we fell asleep—that meant the most. You didn't buy the one you loved a happy-anniversary spoon rest and then receive a free pass for the next 365 days.

Gary was my antithesis. He had also worked for a number of years in retail, selling Tommy Hilfiger and Polo in a large department store. He believed that a $145 cotton summer sweater with an American flag on the front not only conveyed love but also had the power to change a man's life.

Gary believed that gifts, the bigger the better, spoke volumes.

What made our schism even more cavernous was the fact that Gary knew every single anniversary, kind of like he knew the names of every member of DeBarge. It was an odd ability, but one that came in handy every so often. Especially when he wanted to drive home a point.

"Do you even remember what anniversary gifts I've gotten for you over the years, while you've gotten off scot-free?"

For some reason I pictured Gary as an Amish woman, in a bonnet, getting banged over a hot copper urn by a man with one of those freaky Amish beards that for some reason is always missing the mustache part.

Free association and fantasy: That's how I—and prisoners of war—survive.

"Let me remind you," Gary said, "since you seem at a loss for words."

We stopped on the sidewalk in front of our house and Gary began recounting his anniversary gifts to me:

"First anniversary...paper...I got you a journal for your writing. Second, cotton, romantic sheets for the bed. Third, leather. You got Kenneth Cole slides and a Dolce belt. Fourth, flowers. I planted an entire anniversary garden of your favorites, from peonies to hydrangeas. Fifth, wood."

Here I interjected. "I'm sure I gave you some wood on our anniversary."

Gary didn't laugh.

"You're disgusting. I planted a birch in the front yard in your honor."

"Okay, okay, I get it."

"Do you? Do you know what anniversary this is for us?"

"Yes. Eleven."

"Very good. Do you know what the theme for eleven is?"

"Rubies?"

"No, steel."

"Steel? What are we buying each other this year, rebar?"

"Use your imagination," Gary said. "Surprise *me*...for *once*."

He walked inside, looking back at me for dramatic effect. Still, I hated when he told me to surprise him. It meant his expectations would be elevated, on par with Mars—when shooting for midcalf, whenever surprise and I were involved, seemed much more appropriate.

That week, during my lunch breaks at work, I began shopping to find inspiration.

I looked at watches and stainless-steel appliances. But those seemed either boring ("A *watch*?") or exploitive ("You just want me around to bake for you?").

So I shopped for myself, a bad habit of mine. Whenever I did something nice for somebody else, I usually did something even nicer for me.

Which is why I was browsing through too-tight T's at Abercrombie & Fitch when a clerk approached and asked if I needed help picking something out for my son.

Now, if I hadn't been so absolutely mesmerized by the clerk's youthful splendor, stupefied by his tousled blond hair, and intoxicated by the Abercrombie scent that made him smell like beach, sweat, and denim, I would have bitch-slapped him into next Tuesday.

The clerk was, of course, beautiful—just like every Abercrombie clerk, just like every Abercrombie model who smiles flirtatiously and flashes one perfectly pert, tan nipple from the side of a shopping bag.

So I assumed this pretty-boy clerk was stupid, simply because I needed something—besides the fact that I had health-care coverage—to make me feel superior.

"What size is your son?" the clerk asked me again.

"I'm shopping for *myself,*" I said indignantly, but in a whisper.

"There's, like, a Macy's at the end of the mall, and, like, a Brooks Brothers just across from us," he said to me.

"*Brooks Brothers?*" I hissed.

"Umm, yeah, you know, for, like, guys...your age."

I stormed out of the store, out of the mall, and into the parking garage, lost in my own world of misery, when a sleek, black, brand-new Honda Pilot honked before screeching to a stop inches from my aged face and brittle bones.

It was a sign.

Steel.

Anniversary.

Car!

For once, I thought, I would go big or go home.

So I decided to play hooky from work one day the next week, telling everyone, including Gary, that I was sick. And, as fate would have it, I indeed got sick, a hideous summer flu that invaded my lungs and turned my once tan face into some sort of swollen mass. I was a hacking human tick.

In the midst of my Ebola outbreak, I sneaked to a local Honda dealership after Gary had left for work, looking as if I had left my oxygen tank at home.

Now, I am not a car man. I do not believe they connote status of any kind. I view cars as purely utilitarian. I want one that works. I don't need a leather interior, a sunroof, a jazzy stereo, spinning chrome hubcaps.

We have a friend who owns two Vipers—one red and one yellow. I thought, until he told me, that they were Camaros. He wanted to punch me in the sternum.

I have driven, since I was twenty-two, just three cars: a white Toyota Corolla with cloth interior and no power anything—windows, car seats, locks. It had only AM/FM. I traded that in for a forest-green Honda CR-V with cloth interior. I would still be driving it today if it hadn't been totaled by hail. I now drive an orange Honda Element, which you can literally hose out. It's my dog car.

It's my beach car. It's covered in sand and filled with workout clothes and bottled water and dog toys and hundreds of Post-It notes filled with spur-of-the-moment writing ideas.

Now, in the eleven years Gary and I have been together, he has had six cars. He has been robbed and screwed by more bad cars than a Vegas hooker. But his obsession continues. He now desires an SUV that connotes luxury but isn't ostentatious. He wants it in black to connote mystery and sexiness. He wants leather because he deserves it. He wants XM and a nine-hundred-disc CD player and surround-sound stereo and conversation mirrors.

So I decided to get it all for my man.

I stepped out of my Element at the local Honda dealership and was immediately greeted by a young man with all the teeth and annoying earnestness of Matt Damon.

"Hello! I'm Dave! Looking to buy a car today?"

"Yes, I am."

"That! Is! Terrific! You've! Come! To! The! Right! Place! Great! Weather! We're! Having! What! Can! I! Do! You! For!"

Everything! Dave! Said! Ended! With! An! Exclamation! Point!

I had never been this excited in my life.

"I want to buy my partner a new Honda Pilot," I said.

"Your business partner?"

"No, my partner partner. My lover. My husband. My boyfriend."

"Oooohhhh, well..."

At least Dave's enthusiasm had waned.

"Your partner..." he said again to himself.

"Yes."

Dave looked as though he just learned that babies aren't delivered by storks.

"Your partner..."

At this point I wanted to scream, "Yes! Dave! My! Partner! My! Boyfriend! My! Husband! My! Better! Half! The! One! Who! Will!

Most! Likely! Bang! Me! In! The! Third! Row! Seat! When! He! Sees! I've! Bought! Him! A! Car!"

"Can you excuse me for one second?" Dave said.

I watched Dave disappear into the dealership, where he proceeded to stand in the center of the all-glass showroom and tell his associates that He! Has! Been! Talking! To! A! Faggot!

A pretty but hardened woman—think Lynda Carter but with way more makeup—approached me next.

"Good morning, sir. Dave had to deal with an emergency. My apologies. But I'm Margot, and I'm here to help. What are you looking for today?"

"A new Honda Pilot for my partner."

Margot was dressed in a sleek black pantsuit, heels, and loads of gold. She never made it out of the *Dynasty* era, it seemed. She smelled like Paloma Picasso.

She looked me over, slowly, from head to toe, in a dismissive sort of way.

I looked down. I had forgotten that I was wearing a mustard-yellow sweatsuit that my parents bought me that made me look like a walking hot dog, and a South Carolina ball cap a friend gave to me that simply said COCKS on it.

"You want to look at Honda Pilots?" she asked.

"That's right."

"Do you know how much Honda Pilots run?" she said, as if I was a third-grade girl who wanted to buy a Vera Wang wedding dress for her Barbie.

"Yes, ma'am. I'm well aware."

OMG! She thinks I can't afford it because of how I'm dressed.

"Why don't I show you some of our used Civics?" Margot suggested. "They have a few miles on them, but they're great, affordable, reliable cars."

I suddenly thought of the story a friend of mine—a retail lifer who now worked as a manager and buyer—once told me, a story she liked to share with her new employees. It seemed a man in dirty jeans, muddy boots, and a ripped T-shirt had walked into a Jag dealership one afternoon to look at cars. After cycling through three or four sales associates, all of whom dismissed him because of how he was dressed, he left, went home, and bought the dealership that night, firing everyone who had refused to help him. Turns out he was one of the richest men in America, had been working at his ranch all day, and had gone out to buy his wife a new Jag as an anniversary present.

Folklore or not, it was a great story.

"Would you mind if we went to your office and talked for a moment?" I asked.

Margot looked me over again, head to toe, very slowly and cautiously, but agreed.

I walked into the showroom, sunlight streaming through the clean windows, pulled out my checkbook, and began waving it about while saying very loudly, between coughs, "I was going to buy a new Honda Pilot today, but no one wanted to help me. I was going to write a check. Cash deal. No trade-in. No bartering. Easiest transaction you would have had all year. But I'm going to leave now. Have a wonderful day."

As I retreated to my dirty Element in my yellow sweats and Cocks hat, I heard Dave yelling, "Gays! Always! Have! The! Money!"

I headed directly to see my retail friend—the last remaining great retail person I knew in the world—and she helped me pick out a stainless-steel watch at a great price, which I wrapped up beautifully and gave to Gary on our anniversary with a card that stated, "IOU...One Honda Pilot."

To say he was surprised on our anniversary would be a mammoth understatement.

And Gary did get his dream SUV the next year, just prior to our silk/linen anniversary. But I knew the stickler for anniversary themes didn't mind the confusion: He liked his delayed steel way better than linen pants from J. Crew.

SEPTEMBER

"Yes, it was only a dog, and dogs come and go in the course of human life...It was a dog, and yet every time I tried to talk about Marley to them, tears welled in my eyes."

—JOHN GROGAN

Isn't Our Daughter a Doll?

One of the first things that Gary and I purchased together as a couple was a Barbie doll.

It was a mutual investment, and one that made us both very, very happy, more so at the time than, say, a new Land Rover, or even a trip to Greece.

It was the one gift we had both always wanted but never bought on our own.

So we walked into Target one evening after work—Gary miraculously bypassing every endcap and table runner and flannel sheet with prancing deer—both of us expecting to stroll into the toy aisle, pluck a Barbie, and exit in under five minutes.

But we quickly discovered the world of toys had changed dramatically since we were children and dreamed of owning a Barbie. There were, seemingly, billions of Barbies: black Barbies and wedding-day Barbies, roller-girl Barbies and Hilary Duff Barbies. There were even career Barbies, brainy Barbies who—for some reason—did not find it fulfilling enough to live off their beauty alone; no, they had to attend med school and become surgeons and pet doctors, a notion that unnerved me greatly.

We kept searching until we finally found, sitting at the end of the row with their tans, white hair, and electric-pink go-go outfits, the Barbies Gary and I had desired since childhood, the ones who were just fine getting by on their girlish looks, gigantic breasts, and fake smiles.

"Oh, my God! She's perfect!" Gary squealed, picking one who somehow managed to have even bigger boobs than the others.

And then he rattled the box. Hard. And held her out for me to see.

"Look, she's still smiling!" he said. "Even with a concussion! Barbie, I love you!"

Gary loves blondes.

He loves me.

But most of all Gary loves Barbie.

And so do I.

Gary and I had both been robbed as children. We grew up in rural America in the 1960s and '70s, at a time when boys were boys and girls just looked like boys. Which is why every Christmas and birthday I received a Daisy BB gun or train set instead of the Barbie doll I desperately wanted, and Gary got a baseball mitt or football instead of his cherished gal pal.

Our holiday photos showcase our disappointment: me, my hand on my hip, watching my dad cock my BB gun and fire at a beer can sitting on a fence in the distance; Gary, his baseball mitt firmly on his angled hip like a supermodel, watching the ball zip right over his head.

Over the years we held out hope that parenting had evolved, mostly because we had a very good friend who seemed like a hip and with-it dad. He bought dolls for his son when the little boy begged for them.

All of this gave us hope for the future generation.

Hope that grown men wouldn't have to sneak into a Target and buy a Barbie in their thirties.

And then our friend called to tell us, proudly, that his little boy was "over dolls."

"I walked in and Junior had yanked all the hair out of Barbie's head, pulled off her legs, and was trying to crush her head in his underwear drawer. I'm so damn proud of that kid. And I think he's over all his issues, don't you?"

"I do," I said, wondering how many years it would be before Junior was in juve hall for torching my car.

Unlike our friend's little boy, however, Gary and I never, ever seemed to tire of our new Barbie once we got her home, and we took immediate and great strides to make up for all of our lost years of enjoyment. We included Barbie in our everyday lives, as a parent would a baby, or one might a puppy.

Barbie joined us at breakfast, where she enjoyed something light and nonbloating, before Gary sat her in his passenger seat to ride along with him on sales calls.

Barbie tanned with us on our back porch and joined us on the couch to watch TV. (She loved Lifetime and anything with Susan Anton or Loni Anderson.)

We took Barbie to nice restaurants. When we were asked, "Table for two?" Gary and I would gently reply, in a tone of embarrassment and irritation, "No, three," before yanking Barbie out of a pocket.

"Something to drink?" the waiter would ask a few moments later.

"Barbie?" we would say, looking over to our dinner companion propped up in the third seat. "Ladies first."

People thought it was a joke so we had to act like it, too, but the reality was that we bought so many clothes for Barbie that she ended up with her own drawer in our dresser. Gary and I had to merge all of our underwear just to make room for her skirts and capes and boots and sunglasses and hats.

The thing Barbie loved most, however, was travel. Since she had lived most of her life on a shelf in a cardboard box with a dust-covered plastic window, getting out in the world thrilled Barbie, just as it had us when we finally left rural America.

We showed Barbie her hometown of St. Louis first, taking her up in the Arch (she got dizzy), to a Cardinals game (she still wore pink instead of red), and then to the Mississippi River, where we removed her pumps and dipped her plastic toes in the water (too muddy).

Barbie's first out-of-state trip was to Memphis to see Elvis's grave. We carried her around Graceland, photographing her in the Jungle Room and then at Big E's grave site. It was a hard trip for her ("They ruined my baby!" her blue eyes seemed to moan), so we took her to Beale Street to drink away her blues while she listened to some.

Barbie loved the all-inclusive at Punta Cana, though she barely made it through customs ("*¿Los muchachos tienen una muñeca?*" the airport security guard bellowed to his compadres, laughing, pulling Barbie out of my suitcase and then holding her high in the air like some sort of spectacle. "It's not a doll," I exclaimed in horror, my four years of Spanish in college finally coming in handy. "It's Barbie!").

Our new-age thripple traveled the world, went to plays and movies, and took baths together. Gary and I admired her hard plastic breasts and impossibly shapely body, her naturally blonde hair and sunny disposition, her too-white teeth and button nose. We both spent thousands of dollars and hundreds of hours with personal trainers and therapists to achieve that same body and outlook, only to fall woefully short.

And then, one night, about two years into our relationship with Barbie, Gary and I were having sex and rolled on top of our girl, who entered a part of our bodies where women had never gone. It made us finally realize, "You know what? This is kinda creepy."

So we got a puppy, Marge, a new toy to obsess over and play with and dress up. It seems we had tired of Barbie; we had grown up; we had made up for our lost youth.

At first, out of guilt, we stuck Barbie in the dresser drawer with all of her clothes, and then, over time, we needed the space back for our own stuff and Barbie moved into the basement, where a blue plastic crate from Organized Living became her new home. The last words I said to Barbie were, "Think of it as the *Sex and the City* singles pad you always wanted."

I swear I could hear Barbie scream as I snapped the lid shut.

Gary and I didn't think of Barbie for years, until I heard on TV that she would celebrate her fiftieth birthday on September 6, 2009.

We had moved since we had last seen our girl, endured much stress and happiness, and celebrated numerous birthdays, too. I went down into our basement one evening, searching through our color-coded crates and bins, until, trapped there, under a mix of Fourth of July flags, Christmas lights, and some pink taffeta, I found Barbie.

Her clothes were a bit flattened, her hair a touch more ratted, and one leg looked as though it might have been truncated after being wedged under a concrete garden gnome for years.

Still, I dusted her off and took Barbie upstairs to our bathroom, where I held her under the strong light. I turned her toward the mirror so she could see her face after all these years, and even I was stunned to see that Barbie looked as fresh, young, and pretty as the day we tired of her.

"Happy fiftieth, Barbie!" I said. "You haven't aged a day."

Her silent response—prompted by the reflected visage of my now forty-three-year-old head resting against hers—was not nearly as kind.

Margie and Me

"**D**uck, Mom!"

I was standing in Dillard's one fall afternoon a number of years ago about to throw a $150 crystal punch bowl down the escalator and into women's fragrances.

Luckily, a severe-looking woman with an asymmetric bob who was just about to assist her aged mother off the escalator sobered me up.

The punch bowl was going to be a wedding gift for a woman with whom I worked and despised. She used to sneer at me, for God's sake, something I hadn't seen anyone do since Alexis Carrington, and she always asked me condescendingly to "tidy the mess" after a staff luncheon. She lived in a hideous beige cookie-cutter condo near a mall, and she was marrying a man who told me once at a work party that he "gave generously to the Republican Party." I Googled him, naturally, only to find he'd donated a whopping $50.

And yet their wedding registry contained pricier gifts than a Saudi princess's sweet sixteen.

The thought of this—along with the fact that the old woman and her daughter were now safely off the escalator and hiding in linens—reignited my rage.

"This is ridiculous," I yelled at Gary, again holding the glistening punch bowl dramatically over my head. "Why don't we just get the vampire a garlic press?"

"We can't do that. We'll look like cheapskates," Gary said in his calm voice, the one he used when I was enraged or on Ambien. "They're getting married, Wade. It's a special occasion."

"I'm special occasioned out!" I yelled.

And I was.

Within this very same calendar year, Gary and I had attended three weddings, a christening, four children's birthday parties, two anniversary parties, and three baby showers. This on top of the innumerable coworkers' birthday parties and baby showers we had been required not only to attend but also to support generously.

When I got home, I yanked out our calculator and did some cipherin', as Andy Griffith used to say. Between the boxed sets of Baby Einsteins and the gift cards and the crystal punch bowls, we had spent a few *thousand* dollars.

"Can you believe that amount?" I yelled, coming down the basement stairs, in a distressed voice better suited for saying, "The sky is raining Skittles!"

I found Gary sitting knee-deep in wrapping paper. "What are you doing?" I asked.

"The department store paper is just tacky," he said, encasing the punch bowl in a blanket of expensive, thick white paper featuring blue velveteen wedding bells. "I'm sorry, but what's your point?"

I stared open-mouthed at Gary, who was now scooting a pair of scissors down a foot of satiny, pastel ribbon.

"Didn't you hear me? We've spent thousands of dollars on people—many that we despise—and we have never gotten anything in return."

Gary yanked some foil ribbon out of another drawer in his "Martha desk" and began making his own bows.

"I mean, just look at you! You're creating a work of art for a woman who hands me her dirty coffee cup at the end of every staff meeting."

"But that's a reflection on her," Gary said. "This is a reflection on us."

"Have you been reading Deepak Chopra again?"

"Wade, we live in middle, red-state America. We live in a flyover zone. We work mostly with straight people and have mostly straight friends. I'm sorry, but that's the price of our conformity. We have decided to live as window dressing in straight America. When are you going to realize that gays will never be treated equally?"

Gary's speech stunned me, to say the least. Perhaps because it came from a man who typically preferred watching *Facts of Life* reruns over CNN, or perhaps because it was the shockingly emotionless way in which it was delivered.

We went to our frenemy's wedding, where we were served chicken that smelled like a condom. There was actually a *cash* bar. Between the punch bowl and the dry cleaning and the new tie and the liquor it took to get me drunk enough to do the macarena with a bridesmaid wearing a ruffled rose-colored dress with a giant bow on the belly that made her look like she had a painful goiter, I figured I came out four hundred dollars in the red.

"When do we get *our* day?" I screamed to Gary while "Eye of the Tiger" played in the background. "And you *cannot* dance to this song, people! It's impossible!"

Yes, I was drunk. Crazy, room-spinning, pull-my-pants-down drunk.

Gary grabbed me by the shoulders to calm me.

"Everyone gets their big day except the gays," I slurred. "We don't get 'societally accepted' weddings, or baby showers, or anniversary parties. We don't get big stuff, like each other's social-security or health-care benefits. We don't even get little stuff, like blenders and toasters. We get nada. I want my stuff. I'm sick of buying silk scarves for women who have Rush Limbaugh stickers on their SUVs. I'm sick of buying baby gifts for babies we'll never be allowed to hold. I'm sick of buying anniversary gifts for couples who despise one another."

Gary dragged me out of the Charles Lindbergh Room and into the lobby of the Holiday Inn.

He hugged me.

I looked over his shoulder, and an old couple sporting tight perms and matching FREEDOM ISN'T FREE! T-shirts looked at us like we'd just grown forked tongues.

"I…WANT…MY…SHIT!" I screamed at them as they retreated into a sixtieth high school class reunion. "I…WANT… MY…HUNDRED-AND-FIFTY-DOLLAR CRYSTAL PUNCH BOWL BACK…SO…I CAN…PUT IT IN OUR CORNER CABINET…AND JUST STARE AT IT! I…WANT…YOU… TO GET EMOTIONAL ABOUT OUR LIVES AGAIN!"

This time, instead of talking me off the ledge in his calm voice, Gary stared into my eyes and said, "You want your shit. I'll give you shit. We're going to adopt a puppy and throw the most fabulous puppy shower ever known to man. And we'll ask for gifts…It'll be better than any wedding the straights have ever thrown."

So the next day—hungover, seeing double, my tongue stuck to the roof of my mouth—Gary and I had a baby, just like most couples do the morning after their wedding night.

Except we adopted ours from the humane shelter. She came from a litter of twelve, and we picked our puppy because she looked like a baby Scooby-Doo and because she had enough moxie to pee right on the newspaper.

Her given name was Maria.

But she didn't look remotely Latina, so we changed it to Marge, a sturdy, hardworking American woman's name.

Like Marge Simpson.

And nearly instantaneously, Marge did something every baby does: She changed our lives.

She snuggled with me when I was cold. She licked my face when I would get angry or cry. She lay on my feet, never leaving my side, no matter how many hours I wrote.

Marge would stare at me with such intensity and need and love that my heart melted about fifty times a day.

More than anything, she was happy to see me when I got home. She loved me unconditionally. She didn't care if I was gay or straight.

And when it was time to share our joy with the world, Gary made good on his promise and began planning our puppy shower.

Fittingly, we didn't do this as payback: We did it out of joy. In addition, Gary and I had just approached another anniversary together. It seemed a wonderful moment to celebrate and share all that was good in our lives.

So for once I let Gary, the quintessential party planner, go wild, giving him full access to our bank accounts, something I normally wouldn't even do for Suze Orman.

Gary not only has an eye for detail, but he can spend money like a crack-addicted socialite. He could make David Tutera pee his pants in envy.

Gary spent nearly a month planning our puppy shower, obsessing over every detail. He was going to create pup-cakes, cupcakes with Marge's face on them, and serve pup-corn out of little dog bowls; our drink options would include Salty Dogs and Red Dog beer; Gary made mix tapes with "You Ain't Nothin' but a Hound Dog," "Puppy Love," "Atomic Dog," "How Much Is That Doggie in the Window?" and songs by Three Dog Night. As party gifts, Gary planned to give out dog tags engraved with the date of our party.

Our invitations *were going to bark!*

We proudly registered at PetSmart and PETCO, and—just for fun—at Banana Republic and Pottery Barn. We didn't ask for gifts per se, but we did hint that it was a puppy shower and anniversary party. We meant for it to be fun, a celebration.

But something strange happened.

We began to get a lot of phone calls but very few RSVPs.

The tones of some people's voices bordered not just on irritation but outright outrage.

"Is this supposed to be some kind of a joke?" one person said. "If so, I'm not getting it. Okay, guys, what am I missing?"

"Why would I bring a gift for a *dog*...or for *you*?" another remarked. "You're not married."

"Is this really a wedding disguised as a dog party?" an acquaintance remarked. "Anyway, I think we'll be out of town."

We *never* had cancellations to our parties. In fact, we always *overestimated* when planning a party, because our guests always asked if they could bring their friends because they knew what was in store: innovative theme, fabulous food, lots of liquor, great guests, one-of-a-kind party favors, scintillating dance CDs.

Now, I don't want this to sound overly stereotypical—too *Queer Eye*—because we have gay friends with no taste, just like we have straight friends with better taste than we have. But we can throw one hell of a party.

"I don't understand," I said to Gary as our guest list bordered on a number best suited for women's dresses.

"We're window dressing," Gary said robotically, just as he had stated before. "The giving...we're not doing it for once. We're asking to receive something."

"A dog toy, for God's sake," I said. "And maybe a nice belt."

"You still don't get it, do you?" he said. "We're not just having a party, we're seeking acknowledgment. We're asking for affirmation. We're asking that people join us in celebrating the fact that our lives and relationship are just as important as theirs."

I couldn't accept this was true.

But it was.

I ended up downsizing our party. It returned to being a simple puppy shower on a quiet Sunday afternoon, a concept people now seemed to grasp.

The fallout from our puppy shower kicked off a long, deep funk in my own life, culminating a few years later when our home state of Missouri ended up confirming what Gary had been telling me all along: People did not want to acknowledge gays as their equals. Which is why voters passed a constitutional amendment to ban gay marriage by a whopping 70–30 margin.

The campaign was vicious. The end result expected but wholly unnerving.

I retreated into myself and became window dressing once again.

But over this time something magical occurred. Love blossomed between one of my best friends from college—in fact, we had been in the same fraternity and graduated together—and one of Gary's best friends, a woman with whom he had previously worked.

"I think they're in love," Gary told me one day. "You've just been in too much of a dark hole to notice."

When I asked one day when this all began, Gary told me their puppy love began to wag its tail at our puppy shower, where the two first met. It seems they bonded over their love of animals before bonding with one another.

And then this couple did something—just like our puppy shower/anniversary party had tried to do—that was not considered "normal": They broke all the staid, conventional rules of a wedding. My friend asked me to serve as best man, and Gary's best friend asked him to serve as gentleman of honor. When we walked down the aisle together, people whispered, "What's he doing with...him? Is this a...mistake? Are they...?"

And then we danced together, right after the bride and groom, spotlighted, with my parents present.

In the end, people said it was the best wedding they had ever attended.

Our baby, Marge, is now thirteen; she is an old woman. She has leapfrogged past us in dog years. She still lies on my feet every day as I write—sighing, grunting, kissing, loving—grounding me.

She is looking at me right now, contented, her chin on my thigh, her brown eyes filled with as much love as I've ever known in my life.

Yes, like every child born changes every parent's life, Marge has changed mine, and I believe her birth helped change this world in a small way, too.

She not only brought two friends together in a wedding that redefined marriage to me, but she also reminds me every day that there is still incredible love and possibility in this world if we only choose to embrace it.

Which is why on our tenth anniversary—in the midst of all the state votes and Supreme Court rulings over gay marriage, in the middle of all the protests and anger and bile—Gary and I simply grabbed hands on a beautiful summer afternoon and walked into the open field that backs the woods behind our Michigan cottage.

We had moved to Michigan, uprooted our lives, so I would no longer have to serve as window dressing.

On our tenth anniversary we invited no guests, and I expected no gifts in celebration of our decade of marriage.

Rather, I picked some bright orange Indian paintbrush, a warm lake breeze blowing the field around us, and tied the flower around Gary's finger, thanking him—in front of God, in front of nature—for being my partner, my life, my love.

"Who gives this man to this man today?" Gary said, laughing.

We heard a bark and turned to look at Marge, our baby, our sole witness, wagging her approval.

Sold!...to the
Woman Holding Her Teeth!

I used to march in small-town holiday parades, playing the back-beat of some Christmas or patriotic tune on my trombone while attempting to march my chubby body in a straight line while wearing a twenty-pound polyester band uniform with epaulets and a two-foot-tall fuzzy hat.

When I would finish, I would stand on the fringe with my friends, soaked with sweat, holding my fuzzy white hat and fighting the crowd for the hard candy that was tossed onto the street and flattened by the Shriners. Rural holiday parades were pure American kitsch, and they seemingly always culminated with the crowning of a festival queen, a coronation that involved a plastic crown and a farm girl with a nasty overbite whose father owned the local tractor supply.

I would watch all this wondering where, exactly, if at all, this big boy fit into small-town America. Everything just seemed so much easier for everyone else: the football team, filled with confident boys who had broad backs and chiseled faces and who owned the town; the pack of blonde cheerleaders with braces and boobies who seemed to be living the American dream.

There was a touch of nostalgic bittersweetness that glazed every

Labor Day parade, however, because townsfolk stayed home, readying themselves for the start of school the following Tuesday.

The parade signaled that summer was over, sighing its final breath.

Oftentimes, my family would load up after the Labor Day parade and meander along the hilly, winding side roads in the Ozarks, searching for yard sales.

The best yard sales always seemed to take place on Labor Day weekend, since most families held their best stuff back so kids could earn a little extra cash for back-to-school clothes and parents could rid themselves of a lot of crap before even more came rolling in.

As a child, I never understood why we hit yard sales, because we *never* bought anything; but as I grew older I began to understand this routine was more a venture in economics and psychology than shopping.

"Look at all this shit!" my dad would announce to us as we pulled in front of a decaying bilevel whose open garage belched the embarrassing remnants of some family's lives. "Who lives like this?"

We didn't.

Not by a long shot.

Rather, the Rouses hid our dirty laundry in an outbuilding on the edge of our woods, or in a crawlspace under the house. We didn't part with it—no, not ever—because a depression or nuclear war always seemed to be just on the horizon.

My father would spill out of our white Rambler on Labor Day and immediately begin pawing through some family's old bathroom cabinets, fishing lures, lamps, or shoes, saying a bit too loudly as he went from item to item, "A buck fifty?...A quarter?...I guess they need the money."

Or he would comment, standing next to the sellers, "It's a damn shame. A little TLC and elbow grease would've kept this trash compactor working for years."

Yes, yard sales served as sort of a psychological *Family Feud* for the Rouses, my father's inner Richard Dawson telling him:

My family is better than this one. And smarter. And richer. Oh, and we horde way better stuff than we'll ever find here...I mean, who would sell worn bowling shoes or charred oven mitts for a mere pittance?

And then I met Gary's family.

And discovered they were the family that my family had pitied all those years.

"Oh, my God! We live for our yard sales!" Gary told me excitedly before we were to make the two-hour drive to his family's house on Labor Day. "It's tradition. Who doesn't like a good yard sale? It's easy money."

I smiled, my stomach clenching.

I felt like a Kennedy who realized he just married a Clampett.

I arrived in remote corn country to discover a two-car garage attached to a ranch house that was bursting at its bricks and overflowing into the driveway with folding tables sighing under the weight of used potpourri, Yankee candles, and magazines from 1974 featuring Brett Somers. There were retractable clotheslines lined with harvest-gold pantsuits and ties wider than a four-lane highway.

"Isn't this awesome?" Gary asked.

Gary's family believed a yard sale was a saner and safer way of earning money, say, than investing in stocks or a 401(k). They believed a garage sale to be the equivalent of purchasing a lottery ticket, firmly believing in their hearts that this Labor Day garage sale would finally be the motherlode of all garage sales—the one in which they unloaded the Zenith from 1968 with no picture tube, the white pumps that smelled like death and baby powder, the Lady Bird Johnson power suit with the grease stain on the lapel—and that they'd cumulatively collect enough dimes, quarters, and dollars to not only pay off their credit cards and mortgage but also have just a touch left for a dream vacation.

Gary's mother, in fact, had—like her lipstick procedure—honed economics down to a simple two-step process: Spend the money quickly, no questions asked, and then hold a garage sale to recoup the cash.

On the flip side, my family's solution to handling money was to invest it immediately and simply never spend it—on anything.

As the child of a Depression-era mother who collected tinfoil like it was gold and stole the condiments from every restaurant west of the Mississippi, my father bought used cars and mowers, used dishwashers and fireplace inserts. He simply refused to buy clothes. He wore the same things he wore in high school and college, no matter how much his body defied the fabric. "You look like Fat Boone," my mother would say to him when he'd come out for a wedding dressed in an argyle sweater and penny loafers.

The few times we did spend money, my dad went through a very specific series of stages, much like the stages someone experiences when a loved one dies.

His first reaction was to fight the need to spend money.

The second was to deny he might have to spend money.

The third was to mourn money's loss.

The fourth was to bargain as hard as possible to spend as little money as possible.

The fifth was not to use the newly purchased item, in order to keep it special and unused.

And the sixth and final step was to vow never to spend money again.

I remember when my parents' first washer broke down; it was a hand-me-down they had gotten from my grandparents when they first married. It was meant as an interim piece of equipment to get them through a couple of years until they could afford to buy a new one on their own. That washer lasted them twenty years, until I was in high school. For weeks after it broke down, my dad tried to cobble the original back together with duct tape and tube socks. "That should hold it for a while," my dad would say. "I've saved us a pretty penny. I don't think we really need a new warsher, do you, hon'?" he would ask my mom, who would be on her hands and knees mopping up water.

Then my dad would open his checkbook and stare at it as if it was a crystal ball, waiting for a sign only he could interpret that would grant him the go-ahead to spend the cash. He would mope around for days, poring over issues of *Consumer Reports*, yelling at the dog, not giving me my allowance, until he finally came to terms. When it was time to buy, he scoured every appliance store in a hundred-mile radius looking for the best deal. He would barter and beg, lie and charm, ultimately pitting rural appliance salesmen in white, short-sleeve dress shirts and polyester ties against each other so he could get the biggest bargain. He actually cost a rural appliance salesman part of his paycheck for getting the washer below whole-sale. The salesman called my father and told him that his manager was forcing him to kick in part of his paycheck if he couldn't get my dad to go up seventy-five dollars to the break-even price.

"A deal's a deal, hon!" my dad yelled into our giant red rotary phone. "Ain't you never watched Monty Hall?"

When the new washer finally was delivered, my parents steadfastly refused to use it, leaving the tags and instructions on it for weeks, my mother washing all the clothes in the sink, afraid to spoil the newness of this rare gift. Finally, once my parents broke down and used the new machine, my dad would firmly announce, "That's the last family expense for a while. Everyone get ready to buckle down! Times are gonna be tough!"

I guess this is why it was difficult for me to part with any of my belongings my first Labor Day garage sale with Gary's family. I wanted to mourn my stuff, while Gary just coldly and callously piled it in the living room.

"We are going to make a haul!" he said, dragging my old clothes, broken toaster, and malfunctioning microwave out of the basement.

"I can't get rid of that!" I'd say, pointing at a size 44 mint-green suit I wore when I was not only fat but obviously myopic. "Or *that*!" I'd yell, grabbing a recycling bin I used as an end table, or a blender that could no longer puree water.

But Gary was undeterred. "You're not fat anymore. You're not poor. You have clothes that fit. And an end table."

I looked at him skeptically.

"And you're not your father. You're a different person than you were growing up."

We arrived at Gary's parents' a day early, because holding a garage sale in rural America takes as much care and planning, it seemed, as staging the Super Bowl.

Upon arrival, I was first immersed in family strategy: Flyers and signs were made and then posted, strewn and planted around town. Balloons were blown and attached to anything that could move. Phone chains were enacted as if a natural disaster was imminent.

In order to keep track of the money, each person with merchandise for sale received his or her very own specially colored Magic Marker—Gary was orange, his mother red, his father brown, and I was given green—in order to make price tags out of masking tape. As items were sold, the tags were removed and stuck onto notepads, the color-coded sales calculated at the end.

We woke Labor Day Saturday at four A.M. to begin setting up.

"This is insane!" I said, bleary-eyed.

"Just wait," Gary's mom replied.

The hard-core buyers began showing around five, while the streetlights were still casting an ominous glow.

And by hard-core I mean hundreds of people, some still in pj's or robes, descending in droves upon us like locusts on helpless townsfolk.

As I sipped coffee in a cool garage in the middle of the night, I felt a bit like Jane Goodall studying apes. I watched these hideously magical creatures crawl out of their cages at sunrise to gather at the local watering hole.

By five fifteen A.M., the apes were animatedly fighting over the merchandise, the stronger animals able to pull pee-rusted bathroom magazine racks and half-melted cookie cutters from the arms of weaker prey.

And then they began to approach us, their fangs bared, ready to barter. And Gary's family was ready, ready to fight in order to protect their lair.

"No! I will not, under any circumstance, take a quarter for those stained, torn tube socks. Oh? Fifty cents? Sold to the lady with the wandering eye who smells like a horse barn!"

"You want to buy only one shoe? No, ma'am, we have to sell them as a pair. Oh, I'm sorry . . . I didn't see your seven-hundred-pound husband coming up the driveway in that motorized cart drinking a Mountain Dew. Diabetes took that foot? Such a tragedy. Are you sure a single ladies' size six will work for him?"

"It is lovely, isn't it? Why am I getting rid of it? Well, to be honest, I just redecorated and simply didn't have a place anywhere for a faux-marble kitty that looks like it's had breast implants and is holding a bottle of moonshine. Oh, you think you've seen it on the Antiques Roadshow? *Well, I think seven fifty is a steal, then!"*

"No, ma'am, that's a spatula, not an eyebrow stencil . . . although, for a buck fifty, I could be wrong."

Though my career was in public relations, I couldn't locate my inner media man this early in the morning. I couldn't summon the strength to deal with this group of bargain hunters looking to fill their empty lives with junk, so I instead channeled my father and, as a result, my conversations were considerably more direct:

> *"It's only a quarter, for God's sake! No, I won't take a dime. Where are you going to find a T-shirt with yellow armpits for a quarter?"*

> *"It's a lamp. When it's on, the angel looks like it's getting a well-lit colonoscopy."*

> *"Does it look like it works with the frayed wire and no plug?"*

Some fourteen hours later, around six P.M., we pulled the signs, closed the garage door as best we could, and ordered a pizza.

Gary's family energetically gathered their masking-tape receipts, pulled out a solar-operated calculator the size of the sun itself, and began hunting and pecking.

Grand total earned: $304.75.

They jumped and screamed and hugged as if they had just gotten off the phone with Warren Buffett and discovered he was dying and they were his sole heirs.

I began to do my own mental math:

Ad in the newspaper: $50
Lattes to keep us alert: $30
Signage on all the street corners: $25
Hangers for stained clothes: $15
Wide variety of colored magic markers to ID the items: $10
Having crazy people inside your garage and children peeing in your yard: priceless

Sum total, the net gain was really about two hundred dollars for twelve hours' labor divided among the participants. That rounded out to a little over four dollars an hour per person.

I could've earned more cash and respect begging.

And then, just as we were cracking the garage door to retrieve our pizza, two sturdy country men with steel-gray mullets came storming into the garage eating a carton of donut holes.

"I'm sorry. But we're closed, fellas," I said.

Then I noticed the fellas had breasts.

And mustaches.

The gals beelined to the clothes in the back of the garage, directly to my old size-44 men's fat suits, which, naturally, had not sold.

"Please. Please. Just a minute," they begged.

Then they whispered to one another, pumped their fists, and bought all ten of my men's fat suits for five dollars each.

"Easiest fifty bucks you'll ever make," Gary said to me.

I helped the gals out to their rusting pickup with my clothes, and they continued to whisper to one another nervously. Finally, the one who looked like Charles Durning turned to me and asked if I would "give 'em a ring" if I was ever back "in these parts" and had any more "fancy fella suits" for sale.

And then the other one, the one who looked like Dom DeLuise, asked, "You live in the city?"

"Umm...yes," I said.

"Is that guy in the garage...your...you know...*friend*?" she asked.

"Umm...yeah," I said.

"Are those his parents?"

"Yes."

"What's it like?" she asked.

"Well, St. Louis is a pretty big city..." I started, not following her lead.

"No," she said nervously. "What's it like to...to...you know..."

"To have a...*special friend*?" I answered.

She leaned into me and whispered, while hugging one of my fat suits. "No. What's it like...you know...to be...yourself?"

I felt as if I'd been punched in the gut.

She waited for my answer, literally standing on her tiptoes for me to respond, her friend looking around nervously as though the gay police might pull up at any time.

It took me a moment to respond because I kept hearing the distant but very loud backbeat of a trombone ringing in my head this Labor Day.

"You know what, I'm just finding that out," I answered, as honestly as I could. "It's taken a long time."

And then the two "friends" got in their pickup, hauling away ten suits and a lot of my old baggage, and I stood in the driveway outside the garage sale, waving good-bye to the truck, to my stuff, to the boy I used to be, and the man I had too long feared of becoming.

OCTOBER

"Halloween is the one night a year when girls can dress like a total slut, and no other girls can say anything about it."

—LINDSAY LOHAN, *MEAN GIRLS*

Ubangi in the Ozarks

There used to be a girl near my brother's age in school who dressed as a cowgirl every single year for Halloween.

She wore boots, a brown suede skirt with country stitching, a denim shirt, a cow-print vest and a cowboy hat, and she carried a lasso.

After a few years the costume began to look worn, yellowed, dirty, and by the time she reached middle school, the girl had developed a paunch and a slight mustache.

Being a cute little cowgirl just didn't work anymore, especially since she looked like Hitler.

Worst of all, a few mothers in town would whisper viciously about the cowgirl's mother.

What kind of mother would send her daughter to school in the same old costume every year? was pretty much the running theme.

Any good mother worth her salt made her child's Halloween costume in the 1960s and '70s. A great mother, in fact, knew the endless possibilities that an old bedsheet, empty egg cartons, wire hangers, and her makeup could provide.

In small-town America, the pressure to achieve Halloween perfection was even more intense because everyone trick-or-treated at everyone's house, so everyone knew which mothers could sew and, therefore, deeply loved their children, and which neglectful moms covered their kids' left eyes in duct tape, called them pirates, and sent them out with a steak knife.

Halloween presented an ethical dilemma for my mother, an educated woman who worked full-time, watched the evening news, and had the gall to question what she read in the paper. My mom was a nurse. She stitched people's wounds. She didn't hem.

While she enjoyed Halloween, I think she felt it was frivolous, wasn't as important as, say, saving a life.

I always had nice costumes, considering my grandmothers were both accomplished seamstresses—I made an adorable little green bean as a baby and a passable vampire—but my costumes always lacked a certain Ozarkian je ne sais quoi. Which is perhaps why I yanked on my mother's bloodstained scrubs one fall evening when she got home from work and begged, "You have to make my costume this year!"

I think I knew she needed the challenge and that I needed to take more of a risk.

Now, I was certainly a boy with a high sense of drama. I mean, I gasped when a classmate misconjugated a verb. But I also felt as though—for a boy with a tendency to wear too many ascots and starched pink oxfords—it was my responsibility not to stand out too much in a part of the world whose people, food, and houses tended to be a bit too gray for me.

I guess I finally yearned for a costume that was *me*, a costume that would stun the crowd as I marched around the school gymnasium in our annual Halloween parade.

I wanted *Wow*!

My mother seemed to sense this, and she thought long and hard about what to make for me. And then one evening I walked into our den to find her lying on our chic, black-and-white-plaid ottoman perusing the latest issue of *National Geographic*, a subscription to which she had received as a Christmas gift the previous year. Once my mother discovered she could learn about Venice and Machu Picchu, or read about Hindus and vineyards in France, she turned her back forever on *Better Homes and Gardens*.

"Come here," she said, wagging a nail.

She held open the magazine to display a shocking spread of frolicking nude black men and announced, "*This* is your costume. You will go as a Ubangi tribesman."

I stared at the photo of a naked, sinewy black man with a schlong the size of our Oster blender and felt a twinge down south, in a place where I'd never felt such a twinge.

My mother smiled.

Even as a child, I knew her motives: Not only would she be able to show off her caretaking skills by making me a costume that would be the envy of the school for years to come, but she could also educate our local community about the world at large.

Although the sensible part of me screamed, *Danger!* the dramatic part of me was fascinated with this option, knowing that no other Ozarks child in his right mind would dress as a Ubangi tribesman for Halloween—much less even think of such an idea.

Based on the photo my mother showed me, I did, however, outline a few immediate costume demands of her: I would not, under any circumstance, go completely topless, considering I had ample boy breasts instead of chiseled pecs; I would not stretch my bottom lip with one of my mom's ashtrays; and, considering my love of candy, I *had* to carry a pillowcase to haul my loot instead of the tiny plastic skull she had originally suggested.

My mother and I spent the next few days scouring local stores for traditional Ubangi clothing, but it came as little surprise that there weren't many places to find standard tribal wear in rural America, although cowboy boots and tube socks seemed more than plentiful.

So my mother scoured her closet, where she found—in the back, tags still on—her inspiration: a Wilma Flintstone–esque dress she had purchased but obviously never worn.

I watched my mother pull out that dress and stare admiringly at it, giggling, remembering something long ago, almost as if she had once expected to receive an invitation to a Kwanzaa party that never arrived.

The dress's pattern was more caveman than tribesman, but it featured a stretchy fabric that fit me surprisingly well, and it showed off my maturing curves. It also had an ample dart to hold my bosom.

My mother spent days perfecting my costume. She altered the dress, which was much too long, by shortening the hem, cutting it above the knee on a bias, and then removing the left shoulder strap before cutting the top at a diagonal so that just a hint of my large brown nipple showed.

Days later, my mother received a delivery and, much to my surprise, had somehow managed to locate, and I do not know to this day how or from where, a rubber Ubangi mask—a partial mask, to be accurate—that fit snugly over the top of my head, over my ears, and then around my jaw, encasing the bottom of my face. When I tried on the mask, it transformed my Anglo face into that of a Ubangi warrior. I now sported an Afro, a ridged forehead, an over-developed jaw, gigantic dangling earlobes, and a Frisbee-sized lower lip that looked as if it had been stretched with a dinner plate.

My mother gave me a pair of her old black sandals, to which she fastened dog biscuits on the tops to mimic bones. Another biscuit was intricately secured (read: glued) to my nostrils, giving me the look more of a girl with a deviated septum than that of a tribesman who was to be admired for his prowess in hunting and bedding women.

My face and body were shoe-polished black.

A rubber spear was secured to the end of our fireplace poker.

I wore my mother's wood-and-chain bracelets, as well as a necklace with yet another dog biscuit tied to it.

And I carried a pillowcase.

It was so . . . not right.

So . . . not politically correct.

"You look just like the photo in *National Geographic*!" my mother gasped when she was finished, holding me at arm's length in her bedroom. "Say *Oow-wa-boo-ga*! Say it!"

And then I caught the first full glimpse of myself: that initial moment when, as a child, you are supposed to be breathless with anticipation to see yourself as a creature or a hero, as somebody magical for one day, replaced by, well, horror.

I looked like I was ready to attend a Klan meeting.

I leaned closer into the mirror over my mother's vanity, a bright row of naked makeup lights illuminating my transformation, and, upon closer inspection, I instead decided I looked like a midget with a fetish for Afrocentric attire.

Think Billy Barty does Pam Grier.

When I scurried down our brown shag stairs to show my father, he popped open a beer, unwrapped a mini Hershey bar sitting in the giant bowl of candy we had waiting for trick-or-treaters, and shook his head.

"Honey, why don't you grab the camera?" my mother asked my father, following me around, picking my 'fro.

"Why don't we pass on pictures this year?" my dad said, returning to the local paper. "The boy will thank us one day."

That moment was, looking back, a noble gesture on my father's part, on par with dragging my lifeless body from a frozen pond or giving me one of his kidneys.

I went to the Halloween parade filled with a combination of horror and excitement, and was immediately bombarded with the types of questions that only kids can ask.

"Are you George—or Weezie—Jefferson?"

"Are you one of the Jackson Five?"

"Are you Dionne Warwick?"

I'm carrying a spear, have a lip the size of a toboggan, and have a bone implanted in my nose, I wanted to scream, but I knew they just saw chubby Wade in black body paint, a dress, and lots of jewelry. I was also showing a hint of tit. And carrying a pillowcase.

We, thankfully, didn't have any African-American kids in our school, or I would have gotten beat down.

I marched around the playground, where a neighbor's dog ate the bones off my sandals, and then around the gym, where each grade marched in front of the crowd, one class at a time.

When it was my class's turn, I stood at the back of the line and waited until the very last minute, stopping cold, separating myself from my costumed competitors, turning toward the faculty judges who were sitting at the top of the bleachers, and began to scream the lines my mother had helped me rehearse:

"Hello, Americans! Do not be frightened! I am a Ubangi tribesman. The Sudan is my homeland. My giant earlobes and lip are a symbol of beauty in my country. Do you have questions about me or my homeland?"

Imagine crickets chirping, followed by mass hysteria.

I sprinted to rejoin my class, humiliated, hiking up my dress to cover my exposed breast. While waiting for the winners to be announced, I mainlined Snickers to bury my pain, discovering it was difficult to eat anything—much less tiny chocolate bars—with a lip the size of a flying saucer.

I had already given up hope of winning anything, considering the reaction I had gotten from my peers, until I heard, "Ummm... the tribal bride...umm...tribesman...second place...nice job."

I gasped.

You could sense that the faculty judges were searching for words.

But you could also sense that they felt compelled to give me some sort of public acknowledgment for taking a risk, for trying to educate the masses. But mostly it was a sympathy vote, as my elders wisely realized I would probably be candyjacked and gang-raped later in the evening by a group of older boys who were confused but enticed by my costume.

I don't even remember what I won.

All I know is that it felt great to be a winner.

And I know my mom felt the same: She not only proved her mothering skills to our town, but also showcased her vast knowledge of foreign affairs and her quest for racial harmony.

Still, the next year, when my mom pulled out her *National Geographic* ready to top her previous year's costume, I told her thanks, but no thanks.

I was still being called Weezie by a few classmates.

I couldn't take that chance.

"You always need to take a chance in life," my mom told me, nodding her head sadly. "You have to think beyond the walls that confine you, Wade: Use all your imagination. That's why God gave it to you."

But I couldn't.

So I played it safe.

I went as a vampire.

And didn't win a thing.

For a very long time.

What a Drag!

Last Halloween, I found myself crammed into a claustrophobia-inducing changing room at Goodwill while Gary attempted to dress me in a ball gown.

"You...can't...fit...into...a...size four!"

"Yes...I...can!"

"Then I'm gonna have to break a rib!"

"Just do it already!"

We were screaming at each other while ignoring a snaking line of women who had not only been patiently waiting for us to finish but also weighing in on my $4.99 options every time the door swung open.

"You're a summer, baby," a black woman told me when Gary went to get more gowns off the rack. "Red makes you look drunk. No offense."

Her description was filled with irony, considering there was a homeless man at the register screaming, "Is there a Starbucks in here?"

It was Halloween in Saugatuck-Douglas, the little Michigan resort area—the Fire Island of the Midwest—that Gary and I now called home. And when summer passed and fall and winter came to call in our resort town, the locals clung to any celebration that helped get them through the dark days and lake-effect snow.

In fact, our little town and its artsy residents went all out on Halloween. Even though the downtown was just a few blocks long and only a few hundred people stayed for the winter, the parade lasted at least an hour and drew a monster crowd.

Halloween costumes *couldn't* be bought from a box: They had to be homemade here, one-of-a-kind stage creations, works of wonder, innovation, and creativity.

As a gay man here, you didn't have the option of going cheap on Halloween. The pressure was on.

Last year I had made the mistake of dressing as a baby for Halloween. I thought I looked adorable wearing my bonnet and a bib that read, MOMMY'S LITTLE CUTIE, and carrying a pacifier and a baby bottle capable of holding a half dozen Cape Cods. But the problem was my outfit was purchased from one of those Halloween shops that pop up in strip malls in early fall and then disappear on November 1.

Gary had dressed the previous year as Endora from *Bewitched*— and looked shockingly like Agnes Moorehead—but my cookie-cutter costume had sucked his magic dry and prompted every bald Britney and every angelic Angelina to term Gary "a very bad mother."

"How could you let your baby leave the house looking like that, Endora?" Amy Winehouse screamed at Gary. "You have powers. Use them!"

So this year, Gary did.

His bewitching idea? To have me dress—for the first time ever—as a woman. Not just any woman, mind you, but as my dream woman: Caitlin Upton, Miss Teen South Carolina, the YouTube sensation who responded the following way when asked, "Recent polls have shown a fifth of Americans can't locate the United States on a world map. Why do you think this is?"

I personally believe the U.S. Americans are unable to do so because, uh, some, uh...people out there in our nation don't have maps, and, uh, I believe that our education like such as South Africa and, uh, the Iraq everywhere like, such as, and...I believe that they should, our education over here in the U.S. should help the U.S., err, uh, should help South Africa and should help the Iraq and the Asian countries, so we will be able to build up our future for our...

The Miss Teen bell, blessedly, chimes here.

Now, I already looked a lot like Caitlin, even without makeup. I had her cheekbones and that rather bland blonde Southern look, thanks to my years growing up in the Ozarks. And I knew after a few drinks I could be even dumber.

But after two straight weeks of shopping with Gary for the right wig, the right dress, the right jewelry, the right heels, the right makeup, I was exhausted. I was ready to head to the Halloween shop, buy some vampire teeth, and call it a day, just like my old fraternity brothers did. I mean, they simply threw on a football jersey thirty minutes before a party and called themselves Tom Brady. I kinda missed those days.

But I still had to find my dream gown.

"Here, let's try this one on," Gary urged.

"It's a size seven!" I screamed. "I refuse solely on ethical grounds!"

"How about this one?" Gary said, holding up a skintight peach-colored gown. "It's a six."

"It's ugly!" I whined. "And I need some padding in the bra, and a little ruching in the waist would be nice."

I thought Gary would slap me, but instead he smiled.

"Look at you with your terminology, Rachel Zoe. I kinda like it. Okay, wait here!" he said, exiting the changing room suddenly, leaving me completely nude and standing in front of a group of women. "Just a few more, okay, ladies?" he said to a chorus of groans. And then, in less than a minute, he returned with a size-five ankle-length silk eggplant-colored gown with spaghetti straps, a padded bust with a row of sequins underneath, a gathered waist, and a flowy ruffle down the side.

"OMG!" I screamed. "Where'd you get that? I didn't see it before."

"A woman in line, who was shopping for her daughter's homecoming dance, gave it to me. She said it would look better on you anyway."

I slipped it on. Barely. It was tight. I couldn't breathe. The straps dug into my shoulder blades. It was perfect.

As I stood in front of the mirror, smiling through the pain and loss of blood to my extremities, I asked myself the question every American woman has asked herself at one point in her life while standing in front of a full-length mirror illuminated by fluorescent lighting: *What price beauty?*

And yet I proudly walked out of that dressing room and spun around to show the line of waiting women. They gasped. And then spontaneously burst into applause.

"Honey, it's perfect!" said a woman who looked as though she hadn't bathed since the bicentennial.

"You look like a dream! Are you getting married?" asked another as she slid a Twinkie into her mouth.

I turned back to look in the mirror.

I *was* beautiful.

I *was* in severe pain.

Especially after Gary brought me a strappy pair of three-inch silver heels.

Still, I knew I made the quintessential American dumb blonde, and this made me happier than receiving my master's degree had.

To showcase our outfits—and to celebrate Halloween and friends' birthdays—we threw a massive party. It started at seven, meaning Gary and I began getting ready at three. And between the shaving, the plucking, the powdering, the spraying, and the fluffing, we needed every minute of those four hours.

Gary walked out of the bathroom first in a cropped white wig, strand of pearls, pink sweater, retro skirt, and apron having turned back the calendar some fifty years to become June Cleaver.

"Ward, you were a little hard on the Beaver last night," Gary said, lifting up his skirt and apron to reveal his visual punch line for the night: He had shoved one of Marge's stuffed toys—a PetSmart beaver—under his pantyhose and between his legs.

"No wonder I'm gay. I always knew these things had teeth!" he said, fingering himself and pointing at the beaver's faux-fanged mouth.

And then June set about perfecting her daughter's pageant hair, culminating with the installation of a sequined crown atop my head and the placement of a Miss Teen South Carolina banner over my shoulders.

When he was finished, he stood back and nearly began to cry. "Now you can look!"

I turned to face the mirror.

I looked just like Caitlin Upton.

Okay, I had an Adam's apple and a little underarm hair, which I refused to shave, but I looked pretty, albeit a touch more like Linda Hamilton from *The Terminator* than a teen queen.

Gary was sniffling. "My God, you make a pretty woman. I'm kinda proud and kinda freaked out, all at the same time."

Still, I knew: This year I was finally ready for the gays.

In essence, our Halloween party—like every gay Halloween party—consisted of a throng of drunk men in drag. There was an army of Amy Winehouses, a pack of Palins, a Carrie Underwood, a Jessica Simpson, an Elvira, the Lennon Sisters, Dame Edna. And while the costumes were fabulous, the looks spot-on, I knew from the gay gasps and requests for photos that I had no competition this year.

That is, until I saw a woman I firmly believed had ovaries standing at the bar, sipping champagne from a fluted glass.

It was Sophia Loren.

Young Sophia.

Sultry Sophia.

I watched her turn slowly, giving the crowd a bitchy once-over, and then she proceeded to walk directly up to me. She lowered her giant Italian eyewear menacingly, and—in front of twenty or so partygoers—said in an Italian accent that was as thick as rigatoni, "Who are you supposed to be? Miss Teen ... *1985*?"

The crowd gasped, just as host Mario Lopez had done when the real Miss Teen South Carolina flubbed her question.

Oh, no, she di-unt! Not at my party!

Still, I knew that this was my moment.

My moment to not be a baby.

My moment to shine, to establish myself.

I remembered what my mom had told me all those years ago on Halloween: "You always need to take a chance in life."

I finally had.

"Just as I thought," Sophia suddenly said, sounding both sexy and disgusted, before I could even utter a word. "Too old to talk. Afraid her dentures will slide around in that old mouth."

The crowd roared.

Sophia started to turn, leaving me humiliated. Gary strode up, ready to save me, ready to flash his beaver to distract the crowd.

He began to lift his apron, but I shook my head no.

"Is that backless?" I asked Sophia as she walked away.

"But of course it is!" she said with a snarl. "Do you have cataracts, too, my darling?"

"I wish I did," I replied in my best Southern accent. "Then I wouldn't be able to see all those exposed fat rolls. Perhaps you should do a back row ever' now 'n' then, sweetcakes, to add a little definition to your lats. We Americans call it 'exercise.' Oooh, but I forgot that all y'all Europeans like to be a little meaty."

Sophia turned, spitting mad, but not before I reached out to pinch a layer of her exposed back fat and said, "Can y'all say, 'Pasta'?"

Sophia lifted a hand, ready to slap me or knock my crown off or destroy my makeup, but I had worked too damn hard to crack this Halloween glass ceiling, so I said, grabbing her hand in midair, "Listen, be-yatch, you know in your heart Audrey Hepburn deserved to win that Oscar for *Breakfast at Tiffany's*."

The crowd roared.

And then Gary showed them all his beaver.

But not before I had learned exactly—just like my mama and all those gals before me who had sacrificed their bodies for beauty—what it took in this world to be a strong, proud, pretty American woman.

That's No Way to Talk to a Viking

Gary works as an innkeeper at a bed and breakfast that is consistently ranked as one of the most romantic in the nation, the fact of which he never ceases to remind me.

"A couple celebrating their fiftieth anniversary renewed their vows at the inn today."

"A husband surprised his wife by leaving a trail of rose petals that led to a bottle of champagne and a candlelit dinner."

"A man pampered his partner with breakfast in bed followed by a massage."

I rolled my eyes at all of this because I knew the person doing the surprising clearly didn't do anything whatsoever, except use his opposable thumb to pick up a phone and dial Gary, who then made all these miracles occur just like a Keebler elf.

And then I made the mistake of saying this out loud.

"You don't have any clue what day this is, do you?" he said.

"Sure do," I replied. "Saturday."

"I'll see you tonight," Gary said, leaving to inn-keep for the day.

"Okay," I said, thankful he wasn't mad. "Have a good day."

Gary's job was hard on me because I was more of what I like to call a practical romantic, meaning I paid the electric bill and went to the grocery store, gestures I considered sweet and necessary, thoughtful yet functional.

I mean, you try having breakfast in bed with no food; and I bet it's no picnic to eat by candlelight simply because your power has been shut off due to late payment.

Still, I realize that I am not a classic romantic.

This third Saturday morning in October, I headed to pick up a caramel Silk latte from the local coffeehouse—part of my very important weekend routine—when a barista informed me that it was Swedish Day.

"Did you do something sweet for your man this morning?" asked the barista, who always kept me in the loop, especially before I am fully caffeinated.

"What are you talking about?" I asked, strumming my fingers on the counter. "And give me an extra shot."

"I bet Gary's working at the inn today, isn't he?" she said. "And I bet it's a full house."

"He is. It is. How'd you know?"

"It's Swedish Day. It's huge in the Great Lakes region."

"What on earth do I do for Swedish Day? Rent Ingmar Bergman movies?" I asked, sipping my latte. "Oooh, coffee's strong and sweet, just like me."

"Just be really romantic when he gets home," she said. "*Really* romantic, got it?"

I nodded, but left baffled.

I had never heard of Swedish Day.

Still, I lived on the coast of Michigan, which was made up of an odd amalgam of resort towns with weird histories and bizarre celebrations like the Blueberry Festival, the Goose Festival, the Mac-and-Cheese Festival. And I lived due south of a Dutch town called Holland, which was absolutely giddy about its ancestral namesake. Holland was a highly conservative little town, the polar opposite of our little resort towns, which worshipped all things Dutch: tulips, windmills, wooden shoes, and, of course, a very vengeful Lord. I figured that Swedish Day was just some sort of Dutchy Valentine's.

But what did one do for one's lover on Swedish Day?

I did a little online research but could find no "Swedish Day," so I studied a little about Sweden and then went shopping, hitting the "international aisle" of our local supermarket, which consisted mostly of refried beans and sauerkraut.

Still, I persevered, and then spent the afternoon cooking.

When Gary walked in after inn-sitting all day, I screamed, "*Valkommen!*"

He jumped.

And then screamed when he saw that I was wearing a Viking helmet.

I ushered Gary to a candlelit table, where a Swedish Day feast of herring, Swedish pancakes, and Swedish meatballs was waiting. Baking in the oven were pepparkakor, bona fide Swedish ginger cookies.

Gary stared at me, touching the end of my helmet's horns.

"They're sharp!" he said. "What on God's green earth is going on?"

"Happy Swedish Day! I bet you're surprised, but I wanted to go all out for you."

I tonged a couple of meatballs and then forked a few pancakes and placed them on his plate. And then I joined him, still wearing my Viking helmet. "I just wanted to do as much for you today as you did for everyone else."

"It's *Sweetest* Day! Sweet-est Day," Gary enunciated, slowly, "not Swedish Day. Sweetest Day is like a second Valentine's Day, except more for couples instead of young romantics. Husbands surprise their wives with flowers and then take them out for a romantic dinner. That type of thing."

I shoved a Swedish meatball—which I must say was delicious—into my mouth and immediately wanted to cry out of absolute humiliation, like when a kid wets his pants at school.

"Don't," Gary said, laughing. "It's okay. Really. I love that you tried. You really went for it. Made an effort. And that's all that matters to me."

He smiled, ate a meatball, and said, "You know, I can't say that I've ever had an authentic Swedish meal."

He then took a bite of his pancake and said, "Not bad."

Although Gary passed on the herring, he did lead me into the bedroom, where he told me to take off everything but my plastic Viking helmet.

NOVEMBER

~~~~~~

"Thanksgiving is an emotional holiday. People travel thousands of miles to be with people they only see once a year. And then discover once a year is way too often."

—JOHNNY CARSON

Turkey with the Torso

There was a homeless man I used to pass many fall Sundays in downtown St. Louis as I made my way to Rams home football games.

This particular homeless man was hard to ignore because he had no arms or legs but was, rather, simply a torso in a rusting wheelchair.

Make that a drunk torso in a rusting wheelchair.

The man was always drunk—*very* drunk—making every word he uttered sound exactly the same:

"Ouwannadoobledie?!"

It was a disturbing sound or word—I could never really discern the difference—made doubly so by the linguistic dilemma of whether he was asking a question or making a statement.

I must admit that my grammatical compass was off-kilter those Sundays as well, because I was usually drunk—*very* drunk—considering I had been tailgating since early in the morning.

My favorite phrase, usually screamed in a thunderous roar, was "GOOOOORRRAMMMMMSSSSHHHH!"

On our way to and from the game, one of my best friends would always toss a couple of dollars into the homeless man's cup as we passed.

He did it against my protests.

"He's just going to use it to drink," I would say.

"No shit!" my friend would reply. "Can you blame him? And you know he needs the cash. I mean, he's not faking it. Just look at him."

But I never did.

For some reason I couldn't.

Perhaps it was because, as I used to joke with my friend, the only things that seemed to separate me from the torso those drunken Sundays were a bar of Ivory, some two-hundred-dollar football tickets, and a pair of legs.

My joke wasn't as funny as much as it was sad, I knew, but I felt perhaps that something deeper was affecting me.

Perhaps, I thought, I was prejudiced.

Maybe that's why the image of this homeless torso stayed with me throughout autumn in the city. Despite the beauty of the trees exploding in color, of the appearance of Halloween decor, I often pictured the face of this homeless man on the jack-o'-lantern adorning our front porch, or his torso as the tippy scarecrow in our front yard.

Somehow I mustered the courage to share my story with Gary, a miracle of sorts, considering I prefer to hide unsettling things and let them build into life-scarring neuroses.

He looked at me and I could tell the wheels in his head were spinning, preventing him from saying what he really thought. Instead he just smiled, and said, "Thanks for telling me."

And then late one fall afternoon, as Gary and I were leaving the mall after shopping for Thanksgiving table runners and any leaf-bedecked tchotchke that could be tossed onto a buffet, Gary accidentally smacked a bum in the head with a Williams-Sonoma bag containing a ten-pound turkey platter he had just purchased.

This homeless man, begging for leftovers while seated over a grate outside California Pizza Kitchen, yelped when Gary strode out the mall doors and struck him, and then quite literally fell forward.

"Sir! My God, are you all right?" Gary yelled, stroking the man's face. "Wade, what should we do? Wade? Wade?"

By now I was standing some twenty feet off, having tiptoed away like Scooby-Doo used to do. I was not only embarrassed by the spectacle but also nauseous because the man smelled like piss, BO, vomit, and Boone's Farm.

"Get over here and help me!" Gary yelled. "Now!"

"Not my fault," I said. "And I haven't had a hep-B shot."

The man began to come to, slowly, moaning loudly.

Suddenly I grabbed the Williams-Sonoma bag out of Gary's hands, yanked him to his feet, and dragged him into the parking lot.

"What are you doing? We can't just leave him!"

"He's fine!" I yelled. "And he was drunk and lying over a grate *before* you whacked him with a turkey platter. Believe me, he's got bigger problems than a headache."

"My God, you're a *monster*!" Gary said.

I looked at him. He was staring at me, his mouth open.

He finally said out loud what he'd been holding inside, finally uttered the words even I was too frightened to formulate in my own mind.

I got in the car and gripped the wheel.

Then Gary slammed his door and I was entombed in silence.

For days.

Gary, in fact, did not speak to me for what seemed like an eternity, and when I would catch him looking at me, it was if he had finally come to realize that the love of his life was actually a vampire, a werewolf, or Mussolini.

I really could not have blamed him if he had wanted to leave me: How I had responded—or, rather, not responded—was cold, inhumane, heartless.

But hadn't we, I tried to reason with myself, *already* done our good deeds? I mean, we recycled, we were cordial to Republicans, we donated to the Humane Society.

Still, Gary's cone of silence forced me to think about my actions, or, should I say, inaction: Perhaps I responded the way I did simply because I grew up in rural America. I was not used to seeing homeless people.

Perhaps I felt that nothing I did—or anyone did—would truly ever make a difference in their lives; perhaps it was already too late.

Perhaps my nonresponse was the only way I could trudge through the inhumanity of life, shutting off my emotions like a bathroom faucet.

Or perhaps I truly felt the homeless deserved their fate.

Yes, perhaps, just perhaps, I was a monster.

Gary smashed our silence one night after work as I was trying to season and stir-fry cubes of tofu, which stubbornly refused to taste like anything but our kitchen sponge.

"I had an unusual lunch today," Gary said.

Whenever Gary said this, I braced myself: His "unusual lunches" have nearly led him into joining a cult, buying a log cabin in Wisconsin, becoming a gay porn star, and debiting a Viper.

"Uh-huh," I said, tossing a touch more hoisin sauce onto the tofu.

"We're going to volunteer at a homeless shelter on Thanksgiving."

And with that I spasmed, flicking a sizzling-hot piece of tofu into my cornea.

"Blind or not," Gary said unsympathetically, "you're still doing this."

I rued my Thanksgiving invitation with the homeless for weeks, already feeling ghost pains from my lost pumpkin pie, mom's turkey, stuffing, sweet potatoes, Macy's parade, and Cowboys and Lions football games.

"I already miss my green-bean casserole with Durkee's french-fried onions on top," I told Gary.

"At least you have legs," he said. "Oh, and a house."

What I didn't have, it seemed, was an option.

The morning of Thanksgiving, I found myself in the kitchen of a drafty inner-city homeless shelter, peeling potatoes on a concrete floor next to an elderly woman without teeth and a giant mountain of a man who at any minute could have picked me up and shoved my head into the cauldron of water boiling next to him.

I looked over at Gary, who was chopping apples and slopping pumpkin into bowls while dancing with a man whose entire arm was a tattoo of a snake.

The shelter was helmed by an energetic preacher who believed that a good dose of Jesus and a hot meal could work wonders on a man.

I was hoping that combo might just also do the trick for me today.

The goal of the shelter was to get a homeless person into a solid routine—bed by nine, up at six for breakfast, in line for a chance to work a temp job by seven—and then, slowly, one hour, one day, one week at a time, get him back into the routine of life.

I looked around.

Most of those surrounding me were men, most were black, but they varied greatly in age.

"Most are addicted to drugs or alcohol," the preacher told me. "But many just fell on hard times: Some lost a job, some lost a wife or child, some lost a limb or a friend in service to their country, and they just weren't able to recover.

"Like Joe here," the preacher said, nodding at the mountain of a man peeling potatoes next to me.

Joe looked over at us and smiled a smile that he seemed to force out from somewhere beneath impenetrable layers of sadness. "My family was killed on Christmas seven years ago," he said, his muscled jaw clenched and quivering. "My wife and my babies."

"My wife and my babies, my wife and my babies," he said again.

And again.

And again.

Until I had to excuse myself and run to the bathroom.

When I returned, I peeled some more potatoes, and then some onions, and then a few layers of my own hard outer shell, all while listening to Christian hymns in the kitchen, and I thought of my life this Thanksgiving morning—this day when Americans finally stop for a minute to gorge, spend time with family, and, supposedly, be thankful for their bountiful blessings.

I thought this Thanksgiving about just how close I came at one point in my life to being like Joe, being this close to not recovering from the death of my brother, from the sudden loss of too many family members, from not being the son I thought my parents deserved.

I had nearly committed suicide, but somehow I found my way back.

What separated me from Joe? Why had I been so fortunate?

Nearly a hundred of us—homeless men, homeless families, volunteers, children, mothers, black, white, young, old—shared Thanksgiving dinner that Thursday at noon, the city sidewalks quiet, the wind their only companion, the most profound moment coming when we all linked hands and prayed.

And I did pray that day. I didn't just tap my foot until I could dig into my parents' dinner. I prayed for Joe and these families and these men whom I ignored every day as I got on with my life, a life that was full and blessed.

I prayed that day to be a better person.

I was, for the first time in a long time, thankful.

After we finished dinner we played some games and then cleaned the dining hall and kitchen. Before we left, I asked the preacher if I could pack a plate to take to a friend.

"Of course," he said.

I told Gary of my plan as we drove farther into the city, toward the Rams dome, and he seemed genuinely touched, amazed at my transformation.

I found my torso near the same spot he occupied most Sundays. Today, however, the streets were empty—just like his cup—the Thanksgiving parade long over, no one shuffling to a football game, no one giving him a dollar or two.

Everyone was home, safe, warm.

"Happy Thanksgiving!" I said, placing a full turkey dinner on the wheelchair tray in front of the man.

The torso bent down, smelled the food, and then flipped it into the air with his forehead.

"Ouwannadoobledie?!" he screamed. Or asked. "Ouwannadoo-bledie?!"

I listened closely, trying to pick apart what he was trying to say, just like I do during the first ten minutes of every BBC drama or Emma Thompson movie.

Was it "I wanna drink?!" "I wanna die?!" or "I wanna kill you?!"

No matter. Each seemed chilling in its own right.

"Can I take you to a shelter?" I asked. "Can I help you?"

"Ouwannadoobledie?!" he screamed. Or asked. "Ouwanna-doobledie?!"

And then he flipped the pumpkin pie I had just set in front of him high into the air and onto the concrete.

I backed away, plucked his piece of pumpkin pie off the sidewalk, the only item still intact, still trapped in plastic wrap, and I took it home.

"What more could I do?" I asked Gary on the drive.

"I don't know," he said, rubbing my shoulder. "At least for once you tried. You cared."

I laid down on my favorite couch and ate the torso's pie while watching the second half of the Cowboys game. I was warm, safe, blessed, happy to be back in my home, happy that I had indeed tried.

But just as I was about to doze off in front of the roaring fire, very satisfied with myself, it was then I realized: I *was* a monster.

A true American monster.

Although I hadn't pillaged any cities or ransacked the Brooklyn Bridge, I felt I'd done something more heinous this Thanksgiving day: I had filled myself not only with pumpkin pie but also with the satisfaction that I had changed, although I hadn't really been transformed in any discernable way except to cease my fire-breathing ways for one day of the year, knowing the very next Sunday I would once again walk past a legion of homeless people like an upper-middle-class zombie with a two-hundred-dollar football ticket instead of a heart.

Where's My Marshmallows?

For years I traveled home every Thanksgiving a single man. I would arrive and be offered a seat at the foldout card table where the children sat while all the married couples ate at the dining-room table. That night I would be offered the couch in the den with the metal support bar that had the psychic ability to follow my spine all night, no matter which way I rolled.

Then I met Gary.

And I believed my dreams had finally been answered: I would be offered a seat at the big table and a bed with a mattress that wasn't made from glass shards.

I didn't realize I was instead doubling my pain, until we attempted to plan our first Thanksgiving with each other's parents, who quite simply refused to compromise their holidays in any way to accommodate our new status as a couple.

So I instituted the rules I learned from the children with whom I used to sit at my family's Thanksgiving card table—not the five-second rule for food on the floor or rock, paper, scissors for the last dinner roll. Rather, Gary and I flipped a coin to determine which set of parents would "win" us on Thanksgiving day.

"Heads!" Gary yelled as the quarter rotated in midair.

"Fuck!" I yelled when it came to a stop. "Fuck! Fuck! Fuck! Fuck!"

Thus we arrived at my parents' house in the Ozarks on Monday night for a pre-Thanksgiving Thanksgiving and were greeted by my mother, whose countenance seemed to say: "Just remember that a *Tuesday* Thanksgiving does not count as a real Thanksgiving. Just ask your mother how she'd like to celebrate Christmas in April."

Yes, my mother, it seemed, felt as if she had received the short end of the wishbone.

And I must admit that I felt the same way, really, though I dared not say it to Gary. But come on: Thanksgiving on a Tuesday? It was sacrilegious. I mean, if Thanksgiving were religious.

So I kept my mouth shut. Literally.

I opted not to warn Gary about my family's holiday eccentricities. He could figure them out on his own.

And he did.

By noon on Tuesday, my mother, already on her second pot of Folgers, began telling Gary an elaborate tale about how the Jews, rather than the Pilgrims, were the first to celebrate Thanksgiving.

Rather than contradict her, distract her, or try and explain my mother's fascination with Judaism to Gary, as I typically would have, I remained mute.

"I saw on TV that the french-fried onions that top our green-bean casseroles today were actually invented by the Durkeesteins, but they had to drop the 'stein' out of fear for their lives, kind of like Sacagawea, whose original name was Saca*jew*ea. So we are really celebrating a Jewish holiday, like Hanukkah."

Gary looked at me. I simply smiled.

He tried to turn his attention to the TV, but my father—who was already on his second glass of wine, which had taken twenty minutes to trickle out of the box—was screaming at the stock ticker on CNBC and the radar on the Weather Channel as if his yelling might alter the price of Procter & Gamble or blow that stubborn low-pressure system out of the Midwest.

I stood up, rather enjoying this chaos, and dribbled myself a glass of wine, realizing the day might fly faster if I were very drunk.

I turned to find Gary standing shell-shocked in the middle of my parents' kitchen, just out of view from them.

He looked drained, slap-happy, ashen.

"I'm sorry," I said, feeling immediately guilty. "She'll settle down once she switches from coffee to wine."

"That's not it," he said, and began pointing.

I followed his finger up to the top of our refrigerator, where our Thanksgiving turkey sat.

It had been sitting out, unthawed and fully stuffed, for five hours now.

"We're...going...to...die!" he mouthed slowly.

"It's fine," I whispered. "It's the way we always do it."

"Well, it's not the way sane people do it!" he whisper-yelled.

And then my dad busted Gary, following his finger point, and said, "Lookin' good, ain't it, boys?" He came over and touched its damp skin. "Not quite room temp, though."

When my father went to pee, Gary motioned for me to head upstairs, gesturing wildly, as if he had just found a bomb in the cargo hold of the plane and was trying not to tip off the hijackers.

"First of all," Gary said as soon as he got me to the upstairs guest room, had bolted the door, and moved the mannequin-sized spray of eucalyptus so we could sit on the bed, "has anyone here in the country ever heard that a *stuffed* turkey's not supposed to sit out at room temperature *all day*!" He said this panicked, in a half scream, half mumble, like the teen campers did in *Friday the 13th* before they were beheaded. "Second of all, I like my stuffing cooked in a separate tin, so it gets crisp on top. I'll gag if I have to eat soft stuffing. And third—yes, there's more—is anyone going to be sober enough to actually serve our dinner?"

Now, this ticked me off.

In fact, I was beginning to miss the way things used to be: sitting at the children's card table, sleeping on the uncomfortable couch, everything.

I mean, we arrived too early for me to see any of my family. *His* Thanksgiving was going to be on a *Thursday*. When people *had* Thanksgiving. People were still at work today. And talking about how great Thanksgiving *was going to be*.

And so I said, like a fifth grader, "I guarantee my parents' Thanksgiving dinner will kick your parents' dinner's ass."

Gary did not speak to me the rest of our first Thanksgiving together.

The man who had never taken a nap in his life, who thinks naps are only for the weak or those on life support, wound up fake sleeping on the couch upstairs all day—me telling my parents that "he's just exhausted from work"—before he appeared for dinner and sat silently through the entire meal.

The one and only noise he made was an audible gagging sound, strictly for my benefit, when he ate the soft stuffing.

But, damn, my dad's turkey was good.

I knew I was in for payback when, on the drive to Gary's parents' house, we stopped at a gas station that sat between a silo and a hay field, and Gary said his first words to me in hours: "My mom tends to overcook her turkey in order to ensure it's not contaminated. Oh, and all the grandkids are joining us."

We were the only SUV at the gas station. Everyone else was filling up their tractors. A windburned young farm boy who looked as if he was smuggling an anaconda in his jeans leered at me while I pumped gas, and I thought briefly about running away with him, sitting behind him on that tractor, holding on tightly to my man as he plowed a field even if it meant he had to hit me occasionally because he didn't understand what he was feeling. That would still be better than what I was about to endure.

Because I quickly learned that while my parents follow no set rules at the holidays—they improvise recipes, they wing the time to eat, they lounge around, they drink a bit too much—Gary's family has hard and strict codes that must be followed.

First, his mom cooked every single item ("No help needed!") following recipes that had been handwritten on hundreds of index cards, passed along from grandmothers and great-grandmothers. Every ingredient was measured, even though every dish had been made hundreds of times before and really required only three ingredients: sugar, Velveeta, or Jell-O.

Second, dinner was always at noon, meaning Gary's mom started cooking at three A.M.

The food also adhered to strict rules: Everything was prepared to meet the complete and utter satisfaction of the grandkids, all other guests be damned. ("The grandkids like this," or "The grandkids won't eat this, you'll see," Gary's mom started telling me five minutes after we had arrived, as though I was being prepared for the fact that they were conjoined twins who could eat with only one shared mouth.)

Which is the reason why, although Gary's mother is the single best baker in the world—I mean, she makes Mrs. Fields and Mrs. Smith seem like lunchroom cooks—the rest of the dinner was prepared with little seasoning, so that no one could possibly be offended, and why the turkey ended up cooking, I would guess, for nine hours. When it came out of the oven, it simply vaporized.

Still, there had always been one Thanksgiving constant in my life, one tradition that pulled me through all those years at the children's table, that made Thanksgiving Thanksgiving: Marshmallows were always melted on top of the sweet potatoes.

Until today.

When I saw the casserole dish go into the oven, I softly asked Gary, "Umm, isn't she forgetting to melt those mini-marshmallows on top of the sweet potatoes?"

Gary's mother heard me, stopping in midmotion, a look of absolute panic on her face, as if she had just discovered that Lancome was no longer giving out a free gift with purchase. She looked at Gary, who looked at me, who looked back at his mother, who looked at her son again, her thoughts now clearly channeled into his body.

"The grandkids don't like marshmallows," he whispered, as though he were trying to talk me off a ledge.

Gary's brother's family had just arrived, and Gary's mom was throwing everything into the oven to rewarm it. There was no time for an incident.

I wanted to go ballistic. I wanted to run through the floor-to-ceiling dining-room windows I knew were hidden behind the floor-to-ceiling blackout drapes. Maybe then I'd know if it was sunny or raining today. But instead I gritted my teeth and smiled and walked grimly into the living room where Gary's dad and the boys were watching sports. At least I could watch some traditional NFL football—the Lions and Packers, or Cowboys and Redskins.

"*You* like sports?" one of the grandkids asked incredulously.

He's had "the talk," I realized.

"Sure do."

"Wow!" he said, staring at me all wild-eyed, like Pam Anderson was his prom date.

I sat down on the couch next to Gary's brother and immediately fell into the middle of the collapsing twenty-year-old sofa, my head coming to rest on the shoulder of his brother as if he'd taken me to a drive-in on our first date and I was gently nuzzling him.

"Sorry."

I tried to straighten my spine enough to sit upright, and then tried to adjust my eyes enough to make out the picture on the TV his parents bought when Eisenhower was president. After a few seconds of hard staring, I realized they were not watching football at all: They were watching a Class 1A Illinois basketball game between Podunk High and Hooterville RVIII, watching guys who were five two playing center for high schools of two hundred kids and asking, very seriously, out loud, "Think these guys have a shot at the pros?"

I dribble better than they do, I wanted to yell. *And I look better in a tank top.*

I grunted my way off the couch and went directly to the guest bathroom, where I did the only thing I could: barred myself in until I could regain my sanity.

All righty, mister, pull yourself together, I thought, sitting on the toilet in a bathroom that looked like the middle of a birch forest in Wisconsin: pinecone wallpaper and carved wood toilet-paper holders and baskets filled with twigs.

I sat and stewed.

I wanted my marshmallows, dammit.

I wanted my Thanksgiving to be the way it used to be.

Upset, I started to analyze the situation, never a good idea when you're bitter: I knew for a fact that the grandkids were not allergic to sugar, since they'd had sixteen snickerdoodles and three fruit punches in the fifteen minutes they'd been here and were now just manically punching each other in the back.

I was near my breaking point, close to opening the bathroom door and screaming, "The turkey's been in the oven for about nine hours. It's done, okay? Those redneck oompa-loompas will never play pro ball, and there is no liquor anywhere in the entire house, so I'm close to drinking the rubbing alcohol out of this bathroom cabinet just to get a buzz. Give me something today, anything—just the tiny, stinkin' marshmallows please!"

And then out of nowhere it hit me: I and both of our families were freaking out because we were all afraid of a little holiday change.

There was a knock on the door.

I put my head to the crack in the frame and heard Gary's voice, speaking very calmly, like presidents do when they announce we're going to war. "She's adding the marshmallows," he said. "And please don't kill yourself in the bathroom. It won't do any good. My mother will just decorate around your bloodstain with a few well-placed pinecone accessories."

I laughed. I needed to laugh.

A few minutes later I emerged, and we were all finally seated at the table as a family. I felt good. This was all going to be okay.

And then, out of nowhere, the bomb dropped.

"What's on the sweet potatoes?" a grandkid asked.

No one said a word.

"What *is* this?" the other one asked, picking up the ladle and then slapping it back down.

"Marshmallows," I said.

"Gross!" they screamed at the same time. "That's so gay!"

Time stopped, the earth slowed considerably, and the table turned silent. It was then that I actually saw the soul of Gary's mom fleeing her body. Thanksgiving was officially ruined. I would never be asked back. Gary and I would now forever eat Swanson's TV dinners alone at home on Thanksgiving, both of us crying in the dark and pretending that the apple brown Betty really wasn't so bad, despite the fact that the corn had baked into one side of it.

But in the blink of an eye a holiday miracle occurred.

Someone farted—so loudly, in fact, that all of our water glasses as well as the cornucopia platter holding the turkey actually vibrated.

Everyone started laughing, and, just like that, Thanksgiving was saved.

And Gary and I started a brand-new Thanksgiving tradition: We began to embrace one another's families. And they began to embrace us, no matter the day or the holiday.

And those marshmallows?

Well, they never tasted more goldeny delicious.

There's an Elephant in the Room

One of the worst days of my parents' marriage came mere weeks into it, before I was even born, over a November pot-roast dinner when my mother admitted, as she scooped mashed potatoes for my father, that she had just voted for JFK.

For my father, this was a more horrifying revelation than if my mother had yanked up her apron to reveal, say, a kangaroo pouch or a foot-long penis.

My father simply eased his chair back, according to family lore, left the table, and "went for a drive."

My father is a lifelong Republican.

I come from a family of lifelong Republicans.

The elephant is as much a part of our DNA as astigmatism and a wicked arch.

Like singles today who seek others with similar interests—SWM seeks SWF, NS, loves dogs and kids, not into water sports—my father intentionally sought out someone who shared his political interests as a way to keep the GOP family spawn swimming conservatively upstream.

My father returned home that election night to massive defeat both on the home front and the national scene, but he coped by turning my mother into a stereotype: She had voted for JFK because she was a young woman, immature, pliable, and Kennedy was rugged, attractive, manly. My mother had been deceived by the media, by TV, by looks over substance, but this was an aberration.

Unfortunately for my father, my mother has always been a free thinker, and I believe something altered our family genes that November Election Night when my mother voted for Kennedy's rugged good looks over Nixon's sweat-drenched bod because—like an experiment gone bad—I was later produced, like the Fly, and I turned out to be, horror of horrors, not only a Democrat but also a boy who liked meat other than pot roast.

"I voted for JFK because I will always believe in hope, in dreams, in miracles," my mother told me when I was still too young to understand what she was saying.

Still, I was able to understand from an early age that I took after my mother both politically and sexually, and network TV—the "great evil," as my dad often called it—was my initial gauge.

My mother and I not only used to get inexplicably turned on watching Hal Linden and Kevin Dobson play Simon Says during *Battle of the Network Stars,* but we also used to become inexplicably incensed listening to my father curse Walter Cronkite and his "liberal tendencies," decades before that phrase became a heralded conservative battle cry.

"Why don't you just switch the channel?" my mom would say to my father when he watched the *CBS Evening News.* "Watch someone else."

"I need to keep an eye on Cronkite," he would say, before adding, "and Nixon doesn't take any fucking prisoners."

He would then sometimes shake his head in admiration.

"That doesn't even make sense," my mom would answer, turning to head into the kitchen.

My dad viewed politics as he did any sport, be it football or boxing: He expected it to be ruthless and dirty, bloody and unpredictable. In fact, he screamed at the TV more watching the nightly news than he did watching Friday-night boxing or Sunday football.

In addition to the favorite phrases my dad used to yell at my brother and me, such as "Get your ass out of bed!" and "Clean your plate!" and "What're you doing in that bathroom?" my father also had a stockpile of catchphrases he loved to bombard newscasters and Democratic politicians with such as "term limits," "welfare state," and "pull yourself up by your own bootstraps."

I understood where my father was coming from, though. My family was self-made. We were, as cliché as it may sound, pull-ourselves-up-by-our-own-bootstraps-type folks. My grandfathers labored in mines and rock fields and sold vacuums; my grandmothers sewed. They worked like no one else I've ever known just so they could have the American dream: a home, a car, a better life for their children.

And the lifetime of dirt they collected under their nails meant their families wouldn't have to scratch and claw as hard just to make it through every single day. My mother and father were the first in their families to graduate college.

Ultimately, the older I got, I ended up following my father's advice and turning away from my mother's: To win in politics and life, I thought, you not only had to fight the odds and be determined, but more than anything else you had to be ruthless.

As a result, this is the philosophy I brought to school. Determined not only to make my father proud but also to conquer the popular crowd, I ran for political office.

When I stumped for student council, I ran against a girl who was undoubtedly smarter and significantly better qualified, as well as prettier and more popular.

She deserved to win.

The posters of my contestant showed her looking like a supermodel in her cheerleading uniform. Mine said simply, WIN WITH WADE. Her campaign manager, a fellow cheerleader, was obviously more savvy and astute; she was more in tune with what the electorate wanted than was my campaign manager, a girl who played piccolo and dreamed of being a mechanical engineer.

But the best, most qualified candidates, I had learned, didn't always come out on top.

"Nixon doesn't take any fucking prisoners," my father told me as my election neared.

So I began by defacing a few of my competitor's posters, drawing mustaches on her face and hair across the chest of her cheerleading uniform with a black El Marko.

On some of her posters, I penciled this important question across her chest: "Do you want a boob representing you?"

I spread rumors that she was failing algebra and I started handling my own media outreach, which included hanging some rather disturbing but attention-grabbing posters that featured baby seals being beaten, with the following slogan: WADE WILL CLUB THE COMPETITION!

When it came time for my final skit in front of the student body, I pulled a few of the most popular kids from every grade and had them do asinine things, promising them everything from more pizza parties to soda in the lunchroom.

And it worked.

I won.

That night my mom strolled into my bedroom before dinner. I expected her to congratulate me on my upset win. Instead she told me that she knew what I had done to win.

Down to defacing the posters.

"Ethics," she told me, "is what you do when no one is looking or telling you how to act."

I took this to heart the next fall when I ran for class office. I spoke about improving the school lunches and doing away with study hall so we could add much-needed advanced classes. Not exactly the issues rural high school kids care much about. As a result, I lost to a hot guy who made his final speech while cloaked in a mesh football-practice half jersey. He asked the class, while pointing at me with a flexed arm, "Come on, who would you rather have representing you? Me or him?"

I mean, I was ready to blow him after his five-second speech.

Fast-forward a few decades to 2000, the train wreck that was Bush vs. Gore.

Ethics.

The best candidates didn't always win.

Politics, as my dad had taught me, were brutal and ruthless indeed.

That election (and the 2004 election) became watershed moments in my life. I felt, as a gay man, ostracized from my own nation, hated, bullied, just like Gary among those who used to spit on him in school.

I also knew I had once won using the same tactics.

During these eight years, my family stopped debating politics for the first time in our lives. Even through the good and bad, the natural ebb and flow, the checks and balances of our political system, no matter how bitterly my father and I had debated over candidates and issues, we always did so with a sense of love and respect, almost like two tiger cubs playing.

But during these Bush years, when I would visit or we would chat on the phone, we focused solely on the weather or sports.

My father, I knew, firmly believed in the president and his views on morality and "family values."

And this hurt me, hurt me so deeply as to leave a stinging void in my chest every time I would visit or hang up the phone.

And then in the fall of 2008, when I was visiting, my mom fixed the ultimate meal of irony: pot roast and mashed potatoes.

It was a tense visit. Gary had been campaigning tirelessly for Obama. Both of us once again felt that this was not simply an election but a referendum on our lives. Electing Obama could change our nation forever. It would provide hope to any person who ever felt ostracized, different. Yet I knew my father had long admired McCain, his tenacity and fight, his heroism.

The only sounds that night at dinner were nervous knives cutting too deeply, scratching the plates, a spine-tingling scream none of us could voice.

"Dad, this has been a nasty election. Too nasty, don't you think?" I asked, trying to bridge our gap.

"Damn right!" my dad bellowed. "And it needs to get nastier. McCain and Palin need to take those liberals to the ropes!"

I had felt the same thing at one time when Obama fell behind in the polls, screaming at the TV for him to get nasty, to get dirty, to not simply deface some posters and air some negative commercials but literally to gut his competition.

"You have to vote for Obama," I said suddenly, without warning, staring directly at my father. "Missouri is a battleground state. You have to do it for me. For your son."

Knives screamed.

"Dad?"

"How about this weather?" my dad said, ignoring the Republican elephant in the room. "It's been so rainy."

I fought back tears and gummed some potatoes.

I did not talk with my parents until November 5, the day after Obama had clinched the presidency. My mom called, and it was a gentle conversation as we tiptoed through the thorns, both of us knowing what was to come in future years: the strain, the silence, the occasional yet unspoken tension at family dinners.

But our talk was heartfelt and necessary.

And then, in a whisper, she confided in me that she had voted for Obama. "It seemed the only ethical thing to do. As a woman, to walk into a booth in rural Missouri and..."

Here she stopped, not crying exactly, but weeping, bawling, her words coming out like ghosts that were being exorcised.

"...be able to vote for a black man in my lifetime...it means so much."

She took a deep breath and calmed herself.

"You know, I always wanted to be a doctor, and it just wasn't what women did when I was growing up," my mother, the nurse, told me. "And you...to have lived a lie for so long because you didn't feel worthy, to not be able to marry the one you love. I know so many others have suffered so much more, but each of us had a dream... and then each of us had to put that dream away...this election is the first step in changing that cycle."

"What about Dad, Mom?"

"Your father will always be your father, Wade. But..."

And here she stopped.

"...just know he loves you, despite how he will always vote."

In my heart I still wanted—needed—to believe that when Election Day arrived, my father stepped into that voting booth and decided to do the only thing he could: vote for his son.

But ethics, I know, as my mom first taught me, is what you do when no one is looking, and such lessons are hard to learn, especially when there is always an elephant with you in the booth, occluding your vision.

DECEMBER

"When we recall Christmas past, we usually find that the simplest things—not the great occasions—give off the greatest glow of happiness."

—BOB HOPE

Blue Christmas

If Martha Stewart were to have full-body electrolysis, breast decon-struction, a penis implant, and, well, basically just go whole hog and transgender into a man, she would be Gary.

Gary *is* home.

He is coasters, and table runners, and twig lamps.

He is right scent, right season.

He is place settings, and teacups, and dish towels that cost forty dollars apiece but can never be used.

And Gary *is* holiday.

He is bedecked Fraser firs and red-twig dogwood centerpieces, he is mistletoe and twinkle lights. He has the perfect recipe for a Thanksgiving sweet-potato casserole or a Father's Day breakfast-sausage bake.

In his wallet.

In his previous life, Gary was responsible for bedecking the city of St. Louis in all its holiday splendor. He was Simon Doonan for an entire town, not just a window. He raised forty-foot firs and trimmed them in more shiny shimmer than Liberace's panties. He hung forests of poinsettias from the ceilings of malls, making holi-day shoppers both spend more and believe they had just witnessed the arrival of the baby Jesus. He would've flocked the Gateway Arch if he could've gotten approval from the airport.

And when Gary was finished with the city, he focused on our home, decorating it like the White House *and then* tossing a holiday party.

Every year around Halloween, Gary began thinking seriously about the theme for our holiday bash. I could tell because his face would always grow serious and tight, like Martha's does when she ties a duck with rosemary-infused twine or is firing a kiln to make her own dishes.

All of our parties, no matter how intimate, had themes, like Winter Wonderland or Gingerbread Castle. We had never been Velveeta-on-Ritz–type hosts, even for unannounced drop-bys. We held a Frost & Berries holiday party, meaning everything—food, decor, the table, drinks—had to be frosty and berrylicious. We served frosty cranberry punch out of a frosty antique cut-glass bowl. We had tuxedoed waiters with frosty hair. We transformed pine roping into an old-fashioned garland by stringing it with popcorn, cranberries, and twinkling frosted lights. But the pièce de résistance was a flocked, berry-bedecked Christmas tree that Gary hung upside down over the dining-room table à la *The Poseidon Adventure.* People actually gasped.

Even our Super Bowl parties had themes, much to the chagrin of my old fraternity brothers. "What does 'Cheer Squad 2006' have to do with the big game?" they would ask. But it gave Gary endless opportunities to decorate our mantel and big-screen with pom-poms, serve popcorn out of megaphones, and choreograph his own halftime show.

One evening just before Halloween, as I watched Gary line our porch with pumpkin lights and scatter our yard with hay as if we lived on a farm and needed to feed the horses, his face grew serious and tight and he looked up in the witch's hat he was wearing and said, "I've got it! Let's go simple. Let's go retro. Let's do a Blue Christmas, just like Elvira."

"Elvis," I said to him. "You're mixing your holiday metaphors."

"Our theme is simplicity. Simple, simple, nostalgically retro simple!"

Simple to you is like casual Friday to Karl Lagerfeld, I said to myself.

"What? Did you say something?" he asked, before yelling "Boo!" so loudly at a neighbor that I could swear she started to reach in her purse for pepper spray.

Having a *simple* dinner party to Gary meant loads of cash and lots of time. It meant filling McCoy pottery with cranberries, and vases with lake stones and floating votives. *Simple* meant creating a canopy of pine boughs and bittersweet over the dining-room table.

Just something *simple* meant spending four hundred dollars on new place settings and glasses because the dishes we had "weren't simple enough."

And as simple luck would have it, we, of course, didn't have anything amongst our forty red-and-green holiday storage containers that was "blue" enough for our Blue Christmas.

"I want ice blue, frost blue," Gary told me in Target, "not the tacky royal blue that straight people love. I want everything to look dipped in ice, like a winter sky at night."

Speak-y English, I wanted to say.

But I quickly got the point five hundred dollars later.

"I desperately need some ice-blue tapered candles," Gary then said.

And I desperately needed something, too, I thought: I desperately needed a turkey baster inserted into my pee hole to dwarf the pain I was experiencing.

Another three hundred dollars later—after buying candles and faux ice blocks and icy blue penguins and ornaments we wouldn't even use—I cracked standing in Michael's while looking at luminaries.

"How can a quarter ounce of paper," I asked, my voice rising with each syllable, "cost four dollars?"

"Well, each luminary has this adorable cutout of a northern star..." Gary began.

"That's a rhetorical question!" I yelled.

"What's wrong?" Gary asked. "Don't you want to throw a holiday party?"

I did. But I also wanted to retire before I was 112. And we hadn't even hired the caterer or bartenders.

And, to be honest, I always felt stupid and worthless when it came to tossing our holiday parties. I was never really allowed to do anything except pay for it.

That's when it hit me.

"Hey, why don't you let me handle the food? I can do it," I begged like a child. "You want simple. I can do simple, I swear. I can do retro."

"Don't go..." Gary stopped himself before saying the word *cheap.* He couldn't right now. I controlled the funds. And I looked insane. "Okay."

I spent weeks agonizing over the food, finally deciding on a menu I knew I could do well: garlic-rubbed standing rib roast, maple-coffee-glazed pork tenderloin, and baked apple turnovers, among many other things. I would hit only the best produce markets, the best butchers.

But as I began to price the menu on my own, the Rouse genes took over, the ones my grandmother passed on to me, the ones that forced me to buy the bruised peaches in the sale bin.

So when I walked into the grocery with my list in hand, I reasoned that my original menu was simply too grand for all this exceedingly well-planned simplicity.

Standing in the produce aisle, an idea so grand in its simplicity and yet so perfect for our theme knocked me over the head.

"Stuffed peppers!" I thought. "They're simple. They're retro. They're fun. I can use red and green—it's not blue, but they'd be oh-so-old-fashioned Christmasy."

When I returned home and told Gary of my new menu, he, honest to God, twitched, just like Wile E. Coyote does when an anvil falls on his head. But Gary wasn't in a position to fight me—literally, or he would have—considering he was hanging off a ladder in mid-air attempting to dangle blue spruce limbs from our chandeliers and ceilings in order to create an in-the-middle-of-the-winter-woods effect.

And yet, though he was suspended and had wire in his mouth, he managed to give me his patented "Don't fuck this up!" look.

Gary tweaked and tucked and terraced the next few weeks, up until the very last moments before our Blue Christmas guests arrived, leaving me free to run with my retro menu that included fondue and fun fifties finger foods. I was thrilled with the menu, excited, finally, by my lone contribution to one of my partner's perfect parties. Instead of simply dressing up, looking pretty, and then falling into the tree because the only thing I'd been entrusted to do was pretest all the holiday drinks, I was actually supplying one of the most important elements for any party.

I was laughing and dancing and replenishing food in a drunken Blue Hawaiian–cocktailed haze when I noticed that two of our guests—no matter how hard they tried, no matter how they balanced their plates, no matter what they used—couldn't cut through their green peppers.

Houston, I thought, we have a problem.

And we did. I realized, too late, I had never actually cooked stuffed green peppers in my life. Especially for fifty. This was my mother's recipe. They all were. And she had made them all sound so easy; but then again, I realized too late, she was a nurse. She made catheterization sound easy.

I looked at the fondue. It was clotted and cold. I looked at the pigs in the blanket. They resembled uncut cocks.

No one was eating.

Everyone was whispering.

I was drunk.

"Eat up!" I screamed at the crowd, shoving raw hunks of meat and bread and cheese into my mouth. "It's *soooo* good!"

In a stupor, I handed out even sharper knives, never a smart idea being drunk and handling cutlery, and then to prove my point I used one to try and saw a pepper open. I grunted and, finally, succeeded, only to watch a wall of water cascade from the middle. The rice was undercooked, the meat raw, the peppers like concrete.

My dinner was a disaster. More likely, spoiled.

And, to the horror of Gary, I started eating it like a junkyard dog.

I'd spent eight hours—and roughly forty-two dollars—making this food.

It wouldn't go to waste.

And I wouldn't be humiliated.

"It's okay, Wade," one of my friends finally yelled. "Really, it is."

And then she shared with the crowd the time her award-winning soufflé fell when everyone clapped at its arrival. And then someone else told of how they forgot to turn on the oven at Thanksgiving. And someone else tried to cheer me up by recalling how he had used cumin instead of cinnamon in a dessert, causing all his guests to aspirate their coffee.

While everyone laughed and shared, I realized we all occasionally wilt under the pressure to be perfect. Life is so *not* perfect. That's why we have friends. That's why we love to be entertained. So we can just be for a little while.

I looked around. I wanted to share this newfound wisdom with Gary.

He, however, was already on the phone. Ordering two hundred dollars' worth of Chinese food to be delivered by the angry tranny. He was none too amused that his Blue Christmas had turned into Chinese New Year.

After everyone left I lay in a chair, staring up at our tree and our blue-spruce-forest ceiling, icy blue lights whirring in front of my drunken eyes, Elvis continuing to croon "Blue Christmas."

As I began to pass out, Gary tossed a blanket over my body, pulled a holiday stocking cap over my head, and said, "We won't be going *simple* anymore, will we, Mr. Peppers?"

He then kneeled down and kissed me on the cheek, an icy cold smooch that fit in perfectly with the party's theme, a kiss to let me know—silently—that my hands were tied. Forever.

And then I puked peppers.

But just like Martha, Gary had already planned for that.

A blue ice bucket to catch my hurl was already waiting on the floor next to me, along with a frosted blue dish towel with dancing penguins to dab my mouth.

High-Whisk Communication

I can track the spiritual decline of Christmas—make that the moral decay of our entire country—not to technology's dark hold on our children, or even gay marriage, but to something much more sinister: the Christmas form letter.

The Christmas letter is the most vile of holiday traditions, started by and now embraced by people the world over.

It has become our generation's fruitcake.

In gay terms, the Christmas letter is the equivalent of getting a braided belt for the holidays, or seeing a bride walk down the aisle with a spiral perm.

It's difficult to quantify the horror. Or the reasoning.

For those of you who don't know, the Christmas letter is that annual form letter that families send in the middle of an unsigned holiday card from the dollar store.

The letter not only combines poor writing and eye-glazing dullness, but it is also a completely self-absorbed and self-indulgent endeavor, wrapped in a hypocritical shell of compassion.

Most galling to me is the fact that there is nothing personal in this seemingly personalized Christmas letter, not even a signature. (I mean, is it too much to sign a name?) The letter is Xeroxed—sending the exact same message to hundreds of different people—while the card is too flimsy to display, and the photo of a vacant-looking family sitting in front of a fake fireplace at the Sears Portrait Studio is downright disturbing.

Why must you all wear matching red sweaters and smiles that say, "The electroshock therapy is going quite well, thank you"? The worst parts of the photo are (1) I can actually see the faux fireplace's extension cord winding its way off to the side, and (2) Why are you so tan? I know it's because you took this right after you got back from vacation in the Wisconsin Dells. You told me about it in your letter.

I came to peace with the Christmas-letter perpetrators, much as I came to peace with the fact that George Bush would remain our president, by coming to grips with a few important facts: First, I realized what a blessing it must be in life to be so cluelessly egotistical and self-obsessed; second, I came to understand that the facts being presented are flawed from the get-go; third, I was no longer duped by the supposedly exciting news being presented, just because multiple exclamation points had been added to the ends of incomplete sentences; and, last and most important, I came to know that I would never really be close to those who offended me.

In reality, most of the Christmas letters I received were from "acquaintances," people I heard from once every year, former schoolmates or work colleagues who happened upon my address and thought I might be interested in the tortuous minutiae of their lives.

But then something changed: I opened our mail one early-December day to discover no fewer than a half dozen Christmas letters...all from good friends.

I was especially surprised to receive an eerie form letter from a woman whom I'd always deemed a true friend, a funny, smart, creative, hip woman with whom I'd stayed in touch closely, even after the start of her own medical practice, the birth of her children, the building of a new house. I did anything I could to help her out when she needed it, no matter how busy I was at the time.

Her letter was so crass, so impersonal, so devoid of human emotion, that it shook me to the core of my soul. So in order to cope, I did what I would normally do: I wrote about it. To be specific, I wrote my own letter, which I share with you now:

Dear Friends:

What a year! Can you believe it's already Christmas? Can you believe that Junior is five (5!) and baby Hortense is two (2!)! The last 12 months have been a blur. In January, we hosted a Super Bowl party for six. It was the largest party we've ever had in our new ranch house. Everyone just loved our home. Susie said the open concept "was to die for," and she just LOVED the garden watering-can wallpaper border I stenciled in the kitchen! I was worried the taupe color I'd painted every wall in the house was too intense, but almost everyone complimented me on my adventurous color palette. Gary sure wasn't happy the Patriots won again (I think he lost A LOT of money, at least $20!), but his Stouffer's bread pizzas were a HIT! (Everyone thought they were homemade!)

On Valentine's Day, Gary surprised me with a red rose and takeout from Applebee's. (He knows how much I love the riblet platter!) Junior made me a cardboard heart in preschool, which I still have hanging on our new STAINLESS fridge! We discovered that Hortense loves riblets, too (You should have just seen her face!!!)! Red means Valentine's, though!

March brought some very EXCITING news for Gary. He was promoted to junior assistant director to the associate vice president for marketing, who is a DIRECT report to the company's junior VP for branding. WOW!!!! He is thrilled, but it's meant a lot of long hours and more travel. But he just LOVES going to Evansville and Paducah. (I think he just loves room service! He doesn't get that at home! Ha Ha!)

April brought an exhausting search for a new nanny and housekeeper. Our previous nanny informed us she was going back to school this summer (thanks for the notice!) to get her master's in special education. Her announcement caused me much reflection; I so miss teaching nursery school at our parish. It was SO fulfilling, but I know home is where I am supposed to be. God has told me that. But then I learned that our housekeeper was moving back home (Spain or Turkey or Bosnia or something. She's always tan!). Thankfully, my parents and Gary's parents were able to watch the kids more, but that just left me three days a week to run errands and have lunch with friends. (Thank you ALL for letting me talk "adult" a few times a week!!!)

To get ready for summer, we both started an intense exercise regimen. Two nights a week, we took Junior and Hortense for walks around the neighborhood (Guess who got to push the stroller?), and then we both ran at the Y on Saturdays (I never trusted their "daycare"—SO many dirty germs!), but Gary's tendons got inflamed and I got shin splints, SO we just decided to eat better. We started Atkins (you all know how much Gary LOVES his bacon and eggs—lol!) but we both LOVE pasta and ice cream SO much. Life's too short anyway, right? Who has time to exercise ALL the time? Not us—we've got our hands full with two kids.

In June, I got what I really wanted for my birthday—A NEW MINIVAN! We'd been looking for months, but one afternoon Gary just drove up in a green Voyager. It has eighteen (18!) cup holders and third-row seating (it's been IDEAL for Junior's soccer practices). I couldn't be happier, and it's SO sporty. I definitely feel VERY "city mom" driving it.

We went to Cancún for vacation in July. It was SO hot and

SO rainy! Who knew it ever rained there (NOT me!), but there was this awesome Applebee's right in the hotel lobby, and it served the same stuff as in the States (Can you believe it?). Oh, I learned the Mexican word for milk is "leche" and bathroom is "baño" (WEIRD, huh?). Gary got SO burned the only sunny day; he was miserable the rest of the trip.

Well, Junior finally started kindergarten! It doesn't seem possible, right? I cried all morning, but my sisters Becky and Lisa took me out to lunch at this great new restaurant called "The Cheesecake Factory." It was the BEST food I've ever had, and the portions were SO big I had enough for lunch the next day. Junior just loves Catholic school, btw.

September through December was filled with school activities—I help chair our book fairs and fish fries and run car pool for soccer games. Hortense is SO proud of her big brother. The only bad news (besides that horrible presidential election!) was that my mom had to have her corns removed a few weeks ago (OUCH!!!). But she's on the mend. I'm taking her out for a little "pick-me-up" lunch at Applebee's (SO good!).

God bless you and yours. And Happy New Year!

(P.S. This letter will self-destruct in 60 seconds. Ha Ha!)

Love,

Wade, Gary, Junior, and Hortense

When I was finished, I showed Gary my letter and told him that we needed to pose for a photo with our dogs—all of us wearing red sweaters—in front of the fireplace. He didn't laugh.

"You can't send this out, Wade. Everyone will get offended. People will hate your guts," he said. "Just ignore it. Sane people know half the stuff in those letters is just bullshit anyway."

So, against my better judgment, I stashed my letter, trying to put the incident behind me.

And then one Saturday evening just after Christmas, I ran into my good friend who'd sent the letter that sent me into orbit.

I was standing in line at Williams-Sonoma, waiting to return a very nice whisk I'd received as a Christmas present from my mother. Since I couldn't wear a whisk, I was returning it for cash so I could buy the Kenneth Cole belt I had asked for instead.

Whisk, belt...whisk, belt. I was still baffled at the grave difficulty my mother had obviously encountered in trying to decode my gift list.

Which had been typed.

"I got your letter," I said to my friend when I saw her come into the store, her kids in tow. I was chuckling softly, rolling my eyes in that "Why the hell would you, of all people, do something like that?" sort of way. I thought she, of all people, would understand, would provide a funny, satisfying explanation.

"We're just so crunched for time lately," she said very seriously, glancing down at her children. "Family, obligations, work."

Then she said it.

"And, well, ummm...I don't know if you would understand."

I wanted to cram my whisk down her throat.

In fact, I wanted to use it to beat her face repeatedly, instead of the egg whites for which it was intended.

And what exactly wouldn't I understand? I wanted to ask. I mean, I know every meaningless detail of your life.

Let's see: You just hired a new au pair who looks like Uma Thurman. You just redecorated your kitchen using a French Provençal theme. Your kids are taking Spanish. Your husband was just promoted to head of marketing for Hardee's. You told me all of this in your letter, remember? This is so difficult? It's too much for me to comprehend?

I stood there with my whisk, smugly self-satisfied knowing that I had never sent out a holiday letter about my family's banal existence like she just had, sharing endless but meaningless details about their lives.

Why couldn't she just write about her family in a book, like I did?

Who had she become?

And then her daughter, a baby Britney, and her son, a mini Joe Montana, started to cry, started to point at each other and say, "Oopsy, Mommy, oopsy! We're wet!"

My friend looked down and screamed, "You're not wet! You are *not* wet!"

"We're not, Mommy?" baby Britney asked, her little pink pants turning a soggy red.

I wanted to laugh.

More specifically, I wanted to tell her kids, "You're okay. It's all okay. I peed a little bit on myself last week when I drank three bottles of water and couldn't make it home in time from the gym."

I wanted to tell my friend, "And btw, I know you despise your mother-in-law's 'Christmas morning hash'—despite what you said in your letter—because you told me last year when you were drunk."

Instead I said nothing.

My friend said it all.

She stormed out of Williams-Sonoma, her perfect French Provençal house of cards having tumbled down. She had left this fun little bed-wetting tidbit out of her holiday letter, of course, in order to present only the glossy perfection of her life.

But she couldn't hide from the one big fact that unites us all: We're human. We all occasionally wet ourselves. No one is really better than anyone else. We're just all trying to make it through the year as best we can. We screw up sometimes. We succeed sometimes. We laugh. We cry. We go on.

Those are the things we should really share with each other this holiday season, right, if we dare send a letter? We should share the truth. We should share the insanity.

And so I listened to this inner voice.

I turned and followed my former friend out of the store, proudly keeping my mother's whisk.

My Holiday Miracle

This is my mother's dream: She is standing at the Wailing Wall in Jerusalem. A leper approaches her, and she takes him in her arms. A bucket appears by her side, and she begins to wash the leper's feet. He sobs. And then she kisses the wall and sees Jesus.

My mother tells me this dream a few days before Christmas as she is hooked up to an IV, getting a mother lode of chemo. She is wearing an ash-blonde wig, cut in an updated pageboy that—and I hate to admit this—looks better than her real hair ever did.

"Although this is the first time I've shared it with you, I've had this dream my whole life, Wade," she tells me with extreme conviction. "Ever since I was a young nurse. I feel I must go, before...you know..."

And then her voice cracks.

I don't know what to say. I do not want to upset her. My mother, you see, has lung cancer, and I have come home to play the part of a caring, gentle, nurturing son. It is a role that does not come easily much of the time, I am sorry to say.

I want this to be a perfect Christmas—one free of drama, scenes—considering, let's just be honest, it may be our last together. But that is a lot to ask our family.

I stare at one of the stained-glass windows the oncology ward has used to brighten this sterile white space. It is of a dove with an olive branch flying over a rainbow. The window is ringed with twinkling holiday lights, and a little side table holds a twinkling tree, both cords simply left to hang, joining the hundreds of other cords snaking to monitors and machines.

I think of Gary, who would have a conniption trying to hide all these cords. "You should never see a cord at the holidays! A tree should look magically lit, as if it were just sitting in a snow-covered forest. A home should look like a gingerbread cottage!"

I see no magic today.

My mother looks up at her IV drip and then back at me: "Will you help me get to Jerusalem, Wade? Before my cancer kills me?"

I stare at her, open-mouthed.

And then I turn my attention to the holiday decor the hospital has hung to try and divert patients and visitors from the harsh reality of what they are confronting. I stare at the trees and the lights and all of the cardboard cutouts of Santa and Rudolph and presents, while mothers, fathers, grandparents, and children of all shapes, sizes, colors, ages sit expressionless, IV drips attached to their arms.

Happy holidays!

There once was a time when there was no cancer, when these folks were just like me, and time was an endless commodity to be spent thoughtlessly, like pennies.

I smile at an elderly woman, her daughter clutching her hand. Both can barely muster the energy to nod.

I wonder if my mother and I will be here on Mother's Day, or the Fourth of July or Valentine's or Easter, if I will once again look to cardboard bottle rockets and American flags and hearts and Cupid and bunnies and colored eggs to keep me from doing the one thing I want to do: cry.

If I look at my mother right now, I *will* start crying, and possibly never stop. I do not want my mother to sense my fear, my terror, my pain, though I'm sure it is written all over my face.

It is strange to speak so calmly of this thing that will kill my mother. And there is no doubt: It will kill her. She has the worst kind: small-cell lung cancer. Approximate time to live: one to two years.

We all think cancer will never touch us, any of us, and yet it always does. It always seeps into those we love when we aren't looking. And yet we talk about it in measured meters, as if the cancer were a cold-blooded murderer we already know is going to get away scot-free.

All we are asking for is a little time before he strikes.

Time that my mother needs, it seems, to go to Jerusalem.

I gather myself internally and say the only thing that pops into my mind.

"We're gentiles, mother. And it's Christmas. Aren't you mixing religious metaphors at a very sensitive time of the year? Can't we just go to Naples, Florida, if you're seeking a little adventure?"

She laughs, but she has that determined look in her eyes, the one that I have known my entire life. She is a force of nature, my mother, when she wants to be.

"Tell me what you know about the Kotel," my mother says to me.

I stare at her. I feel like a kid who didn't study for a test when a teacher busts him in front of the whole class. I don't know what a Kotel is, although I'm inclined to say it's some sort of Jewish Mexican dip that you mix with Velveeta.

"The Kotel is the Wailing Wall, Wade."

And then, like lightning, it hits me: The only thing I know about the Wailing Wall is that I once truly believed it was called the "Whaling Mall," a sort of outlet shopping center for maritime enthusiasts with stores that sold ship's wheels and captain's hats and Moby-Dick paraphernalia.

That's how Jewish I am. I didn't even know anyone Jewish grow-ing up, except Joan Rivers. I mean, I was raised in the Ozarks.

"The Wailing Wall is the most significant site in the world for Jews," my mom tells me. "It is the last remnant of their temple, and Jews from around the world gather there to pray. People write notes to God and place them between the ancient stones of the wall. I feel I need to do that before I die."

"I'm still not following, Mom," I say to her.

"I need to understand how the most persecuted of people, the most persecuted of religions, can still have such resounding faith. I do not question my own faith, but I have been punished enough in my life—we have both been punished enough in our lives—that we need to seek to understand why we believe."

With that, my mom pulls out her Bible and begins to read.

"Shouldn't you be reading the Torah?" I ask sarcastically, not knowing how to respond. She gives me a sad look, so I open *my* Bible, the latest copy of *InStyle*, and stare at a photo of Debra Mess-ing, who looks amazing.

When my mother is not looking, I glance back up at her.

We could not be two more different people, my mother and I.

And yet we could not be more the same.

We have been tested by tragedy. She has lost a son, I have lost a brother. She has lost her parents, I have lost my grandparents. She has lost a sister. I have lost an aunt.

And for a while we nearly lost each other.

Mother.

Son.

Now friends.

I stare as my mother reads her Bible. She has become flushed, hot, and has removed her wig now, leaving just intermittent patches of sad, wispy hair, like on those abused Barbies you see in antique malls. The twinkling lights around the stained-glass window bounce off my mother's shiny head, giving her the look of a painted, pop-art saint.

She catches me staring, smiles, and whispers, "I love you, sweetie."

How can she have such faith, I wonder. And how can I have so little right now?

What I would really like to do, if you want to hear the unabashed truth, is tear the Bible out of her hands and throw it through the stained-glass window and scream, "Screw this! Somebody get angry! Somebody tell me how this could happen! On Christmas!" Maybe then that would lend me some clarity, help me understand how God could do something so awful to all these people sitting in here, to my mom, a woman who has never done a bad thing in her life except care for the dying and sick.

As a former hospice nurse, my mother healed those who were in pain physically and spiritually.

Now she must heal herself?

I do not believe in God.

My mother closes her eyes and mouths a prayer.

And then suddenly I start crying, and I cannot stop myself, the tears just won't stop, and I am sobbing, drooling, gasping, hunched over, bawling, babbling, "I love you, Mommy, I'm so scared, Mommy," until she is forced to get out of her chair, dragging her IV along, and come to me, to take me into her arms.

She is hugging me now, telling me it's going to be okay, even though we both know it's not.

This is supposed to be my role. I am supposed to be the caretaker now. But she is the strong one. She has always been the strong one. I am the comic relief. I am the wuss.

As my mother gently rocks me, like she did forty-three years ago when I was a baby, I realize I must do this one thing for her—after everything she has done for me, done for everyone else. I have no other choice but to fulfill her final prayer and get her to Jerusalem.

But she is not well enough to travel. I cannot get her there right now. And I don't know, to be honest, if I ever will.

I drive my mother home after her treatment and, after she naps, we turn on *Wheel of Fortune* and add the final touches to the Christmas tree.

Ever since I can remember, my father, like a true, logical engineer, has always believed in a one-color Christmas, preferring that everything—garland, ornaments, outdoor lights, candles, tree skirt—be monochromatic. We always had to choose as children: all red, all green, or all blue. My dad was partial to all blue, so every few years our house was basked in an eerie shade of Dodger blue, making our Christmas pictures look as if someone had spilled Nyquil over them, our faces glowing like Ozarkian Smurfs.

This year the tree is all red.

I have spent decades in this room decorating and lighting this tree, wrapping gifts with my mother, sipping hot chocolate, watching *Wheel of Fortune*.

Ever since I can remember, we have watched *Wheel of Fortune*, and now, here, sitting in my childhood home, in the living room next to my mother, I finally realize how much we have all aged: me, her, my father, Pat, Vanna.

I sit on the couch and stare at the wheel spinning, my life a blur.

The years have all passed so quickly, like flipping though the pages in a photo album.

"Let's mix it up this year," my mother suddenly whispers, shaking me from my thoughts while my father watches the wheel and screams wrong answers. My mom puts away the solid red tree topper and reaches deep into a plastic bin for a showy angel whose wings light up. "Here," she says, holding it out to me. "You place the angel, my angel."

When I am done, we sit on the couch and stare at the tree, just as we did when we were young and there was no cancer.

Suddenly I stand and return with a ripped piece of notebook paper and a pen.

"Write your prayer," I tell my mother.

"What?"

"Write your prayer. What would you ask God if you were at the Wailing Wall?"

She looks at me as though I have lost my mind, but jots her prayer and then folds the paper neatly in two.

I take her hand and lead her outside in front of our house, which is built largely of mammoth Arkansas stones. Over decades, the mortar has chipped away, leaving holes.

"It may not be the Wailing Wall, Mom, but it is your home. I'll try and get you to Jerusalem one day, but for now let this be your holy place."

My mother hugs me and then gets on her knees, in the dark and cold, and begins to pray, before placing her note in the exterior stone wall of our house.

The moon is bright. It illuminates the snowflake pattern on the crocheted cap she is wearing to keep her head warm.

When she is done, she stands and we head back inside. We make hot chocolate, sit in front of the fire, stare at the tree, and watch *Wheel of Fortune*.

"What did you pray for in your note?"

My mother laughs heartily. "I knew you'd ask. You've always been inquisitive."

"Is that a nice way to say nosy?"

"Yes."

"Tell me," I say, a bit too desperately.

"I thanked God for a blessed life. I asked Him to take care of my son after I was gone, and I asked that He give you strength and faith, because you will need it."

My mother, just as I thought, did not whine, or cry, or ask why.

She thanked God for a blessed life. And asked him to protect the weak.

I am forty-three years old.

I no longer believe in Santa Claus, or that life is anything but a bruising experience, but I have now come to realize that as an adult I *must* believe, as a child does, in something magical, be it faith, hope, God, Rudolph, the Easter Bunny, or the Wailing Wall.

Because that is the only thing that keeps me upright, going, keenly aware of the fact that perhaps, just perhaps, I have right in front of me the best holiday gift I will ever receive: Christmas with my mother.

Vanna turns a lit letter, and my mother grabs my hand.

The phrase is "Jewish Delicatessen."

I guess it with only a few letters in place.

Acknowledgments

To "TEAM WADE!," which includes my fabulous agent Wendy Sherman; my talented, tireless editor Julia Pastore; my steadfast publishers Shaye Areheart and Maya Mavjee; my creative publicity team of Dyanna Messina, Campbell Wharton, Rachel Rokicki, Sandi Mendelson & Co.; my marketing magician Kira Walton; my fabulous cover designer Kyle Kolker; Carol Fitzgerald and her wonderful Web team at the Book Report; my friends and family; my main mutts Marge and Mabel; to all the incredible bookstores, sellers, and staffers whose support has meant the world; to libraries for promoting reading and keeping authors' work alive forever; and to Team Wade lead cheerleader Gary Edwards, whose spirit fingers and halftime performances keep me sprinting for the end zone. I am designing us all uniforms (with a logo and mascot of either a latte, laptop, stylish waders, or my face...I haven't decided) to wear for our inaugural appearance on *Oprah*.

ABOUT THE AUTHOR

Wade Rouse is the critically acclaimed author of the memoirs *America's Boy, Confessions of a Prep School Mommy Handler*, and *At Least in the City Someone Would Hear Me Scream,* and editor of the humorous dog anthology *I'm Not the Biggest Bitch in This Relationship!* He is a humor columnist for *Metrosource* magazine. Wade lives outside Saugatuck, Michigan, with his partner, Gary, and their mutts, Marge and Mabel. For more information, visit www.waderouse.com. Wade Rouse is available for select readings and lectures. To inquire about a possible appearance, please contact the Random House Speakers Bureau at rhspeakers@randomhouse.com.